BIOGRAPHICAL RESEARCH METHODS

Sara Miller McCune founded SAGE Publishing in 1965 to support the dissemination of usable knowledge and educate a global community. SAGE publishes more than 1000 journals and over 800 new books each year, spanning a wide range of subject areas. Our growing selection of library products includes archives, data, case studies and video. SAGE remains majority owned by our founder and after her lifetime will become owned by a charitable trust that secures the company's continued independence.

Los Angeles | London | New Delhi | Singapore | Washington DC | Melbourne

BIOGRAPHICAL RESEARCH METHODS

MARTA J. EICHSTELLER
HOWARD H. DAVIS

$SAGE

Los Angeles | London | New Delhi
Singapore | Washington DC | Melbourne

SAGE

Los Angeles | London | New Delhi
Singapore | Washington DC | Melbourne

SAGE Publications Ltd
1 Oliver's Yard
55 City Road
London EC1Y 1SP

SAGE Publications Inc.
2455 Teller Road
Thousand Oaks, California 91320

SAGE Publications India Pvt Ltd
B 1/I 1 Mohan Cooperative Industrial Area
Mathura Road
New Delhi 110 044

SAGE Publications Asia-Pacific Pte Ltd
3 Church Street
#10-04 Samsung Hub
Singapore 049483

Editor: Umeeka Raichura
Senior Assistant Editor: Hannah Cavender-Deere
Production Editor: Prachi Arora
Copyeditor: Sharon Cawood
Proofreader: Thomas Bedford
Marketing Manager: Ben Sherwood
Cover design: Shaun Mercier
Typeset by: C&M Digitals (P) Ltd, Chennai, India

Library of Congress Control Number: 2021948538

British Library Cataloguing in Publication data

A catalogue record for this book is available from the British Library

ISBN 978-1-5297-3085-2
ISBN 978-1-5297-3086-9 (pbk)
eISBN 978-1-5297-8867-9

From Marta
To My Dad
From Howard
To Susan

TABLE OF CONTENTS

ABOUT THE AUTHORS

Marta J. Eichsteller is Assistant Professor of Sociology at University College Dublin. Her research and writing projects focus on the qualitative and cross-generational aspects of social inequalities from local, national and global perspectives. She has worked on projects on local civil society participation in Poland and the UK, European identifications, and sustained escapes from poverty in the context of international development across Africa and South East Asia. She is particularly interested in the biographical aspects of social change and their implications for social inquiry.

Howard H. Davis is Emeritus Professor of Social Theory and Institutions at Bangor University, Wales, and a former co-director of the Wales Institute for Social & Economic Research & Data (WISERD). His research and writing have focused on social theories of culture; cultural formations and transitions in post-Soviet societies; and social identities at local, national and international levels. He has been responsible for a wide range of research projects on culture, language and identities, including several based on biographical methods.

ACKNOWLEDGEMENTS

The idea for this book was formed during one of the biographical methods work-shops during the Euroidentities project. While sitting in a stuffy room, full of students and professors fuelled on coffee and cake, we observed and participated in conversations and arguments on the nature of biographical narratives and their immense value for social sciences. We are enormously grateful for those colleagues and friends who created such an inclusive and academically fertile environment that set us on this journey.

We are grateful to those at Sage Publications who helped us with this project and guided us through the process.

We would like to thank Graham Day for his help and valuable comments.

We also gratefully acknowledge the thoughtful and encouraging contributions made by several anonymous reviewers.

1

DISCOVERING BIOGRAPHICAL NARRATIVE RESEARCH

Objectives

By the end of this chapter, you will be able to:

- Recognise the potential as well as the challenges of biographical narrative research methods
- Identify some major misconceptions about the character of the research process and research designs involving biographical research methods
- Understand the process of becoming a biographical researcher through the development of skills, innovation and creativity.

The unexamined life is not worth living. (Socrates)

The investigation of human life, its sequence in time and embeddedness in place, lies at the core of biographical narrative methods: life understood not simply as a biological existence or psychological awareness of self, but as a social construct. Influenced by external forces, such as historical events, oppressive regimes and institutional opportunities, and steered by the individual will to survive and thrive, biographies provide unique accounts of social life. These accounts, seen as a product and part of social structures, give us an insight into the inner world of making meanings, forging identities and reproducing knowledge processes that lies at the foundation of most, if not all, research questions in the social sciences. Biographies, however, do not give us a clean and self-explanatory type of data that can fit neatly into standardised scientific, theoretically derived frameworks. Biographies are creative, complex and often unstructured. For social science researchers, biographical narratives have a far-reaching potential, but they also pose some significant methodological challenges. For those willing to try, we hope that this book will be a guide through the diverse field of research methods which make use of biographical narratives.

To begin with, let us introduce ourselves. Importantly, as researchers in the social sciences, primarily in sociology, we are naturally shaped by our own biographical experiences – both by the social structures we inhabit and our unique experiences in professional and personal settings. As the authors of this book, we aim to combine and share what we have learned about biographical research on our respective intellectual and professional journeys, which reflect generation, culture, gender and many other differences.

Two generations of biographical researchers
Howard's story

My professional training in the UK involved learning about both quantitative and qualitative methods at a time when the distinction between the two was strongly marked by disputes over their contrasting claims to be discovering truths about society. A commitment to either positivist ('scientific') or interpretivist ('humanistic') ways of knowing defined one's identity as a researcher and there was little discussion about combining different types of data or methods of analysis. I embarked on research in the field of economic sociology and followed the general preoccupation with structural questions about social class, and relations of production and social movements, becoming well acquainted with French as well as British sociology in the process. The contingencies of a professional career meant I had a change of direction towards a new focus on media and culture. This included the experience of research as a team member working with colleagues from several disciplines and methodological backgrounds. The practical emphasis on joint problem solving and combining the strengths of different team members laid the foundations for a more pragmatic attitude towards questions of method. I did not use biographical research at this stage, but my work on the themes of media and culture highlighted the fact that social communication involves complex interactions between the institutional processes that generate cultural output, the characteristics of that cultural content, and the acts of interpretation that give it meaning. The work of cultural intermediaries like writers, producers and performers begs the question: how much is their social influence 'personal' and how is it related to their biographical experiences?

In another change of direction, my interest in the state socialist regimes of Eastern Europe and the Soviet Union found expression in a series of projects on the post-Soviet transition after 1989. This was the time when Russian, French and British sociologists were pioneering methods of biographical narrative interviewing designed to capture the experiences of those generations who had lived through those regimes and their turbulent changes without the means to tell their stories. Thus, I became familiar with one of the most influential late 20th-century developments in oral history and biographical method. I began to include a biographical element in some of my own research interviews. Real immersion in biographical methods came with being part of the Euroidentities project (described later in this book). It combined workshop training in biographical narrative interviewing, strongly influenced by colleagues from Germany and Poland, coordinated data collection by seven European partner teams, and joint data analysis. I was privileged to be part of an international network of partners (including co-author Marta, then a researcher and doctoral candidate) who were pioneering a new, large-scale, comparative approach to narrative interviewing.

Most of my career has been a blend of research, teaching, supervision and academic management. Providing research training for postgraduates has been a particular interest, and my experiences in trying to produce an integrated syllabus in methods for students from a range of social science disciplines is part of the inspiration for this book. The presentation is informed too by the experience of designing and delivering specialist training courses for researchers and doctoral students. I have also learned much from supervising PhD students, several of whom have used biographical methods, in fields such as migration and language learning. In sum, what do my experiences bring to this topic of biographical research? First, they encourage a positive orientation to biographical narrative data within the context of methods more generally, not just biographical research as an exclusive speciality. That is why we spend a considerable amount of time on combined or mixed methods later in the book. Second, I have learned at first hand from most of the national traditions of biographical research in Europe and beyond. While there are important differences in philosophy, style and execution between these traditions, they speak to each other in a similar language and make progress in dialogue. Third, I have found that there is no substitute for practical learning. The purpose of this book is to provide the understanding and resources which make that possible.

Marta's story

I had a very privileged introduction to the biographical research field. After my master's degree in Sociology, I was looking for a job in academic research and came across a research officer position in the Euroidentities project that aimed to investigate the evolution of European identification through the use of biographical narrative methods. The project consortium involved seven European teams. My research training involved some qualitative methods, and I was interested in the research topic but initially felt sceptical about the chosen methods. Being involved in a collaborative international research project was an extraordinary learning opportunity. Throughout a series of workshops, I had a chance to work with the experts in the field and see their way of engaging in all aspects of the research process – from data gathering and data management to analysis and writing up. From the student perspective and then as a colleague, I was involved both in productive discussions and methodological disputes about what biographical methods are and what they can contribute to our understanding of European identities. During three fascinating years of learning on the job, I came across multiple methodological approaches, often rooted in different academic disciplines, including sociolinguistics, sociology, cultural anthropology and psychology. These differences were additionally intensified by the varying linguistic and national traditions of 'doing' biographical research. Examining this complexity and diversity became my personal research project and formed the leading theme of my PhD thesis.

Alongside my work as a research officer, I started my PhD project using data from the Euroidentities project but with a shift of focus towards cosmopolitanism. I set up a research design that applied three distinct analytical biographical methods to the same data to investigate and compare the differences in procedures and findings. I will share some of my findings and observations with you throughout this book. Working on my PhD brought a different focus from my Euroidentities project work. I had to engage with the philosophy of science and mixed method literature and search for more innovative ways of tackling qualitative data, such as QCA. At the same time, together with Howard, I began to teach a postgraduate course on Biographical Methods in Practice, which became a template for this book. Subsequently, we also worked together on several other qualitative research projects.

As my academic career progressed, I was approached by a think-tank working in the field of development studies to work as a consultant on a project involving a biographical data component using Q-square methodology. This was an entirely different challenge involving quantitative and qualitative coding of life history interview data presented in tandem with panel survey reports. Projects like this are very intensive, very demanding and require a negotiation of findings between qualitative and quantitative evidence. In the mixed method context, being a qualitative

researcher means that you need to know your value in relation to the other methods used, and you must be able to position your findings with what may seem
contradictory evidence from other methods. In this book, we hope to convey the
necessary skills as well as the confidence to use them in academic studies and
research in other professional fields.

Finding your feet in biographical research methods

Building on our experiences in the field of biographical narrative research, as well
as methods teaching and training, we have identified several common difficulties
and misconceptions about biographical narrative methods that make it challenging
for students and new researchers to master this particular research approach. First,
biographical narrative methods refer to a very diverse field. This diversity starts at
the level of basic concepts, reflected in the variety of labels that include oral history,
life stories, life history, life-course research, life narratives, autobiographical narratives and many others, and continues through the theoretical and philosophical
academic disciplines embedded in national and linguistic traditions that create a
somewhat complicated picture. For those utterly new to the field, this may seem
overwhelming. For those entering the field from the point of view of a specific
perspective, for example, or following a particular school of doing biographical
research, you may find this diversity frustrating. It is not a neat picture. There are
overlaps and convergence points, but there are also conflicts and methodological
stand-offs. We have designed this book to be your guide to this exciting and
dynamic field, and hope to give you the confidence to participate in and contribute
to ongoing debate.

The second challenge for students of biographical narrative methods is the often
limited understanding of what biographical data are and can be used for. When
thinking about biography, we may imagine a book written about someone's life
story, or some briefer descriptive information, like a website or social media 'bio' on
someone's achievements in life. This form of text is intuitively associated with who
the individual is. For the social sciences, however, biographies are about the individual within society. The process of data gathering, the analysis and the findings
of biographical narrative research are designed to answer research questions about
how society has shaped the choices, opportunities, trajectories, perceptions and
identities of individuals up to the point they believe they have reached. Within that
understanding of what biographical narrative method can be used for, we can see a
broad variety of topics and interests that those methods can be applied to.
Throughout this book, we use multiple examples from a diverse range of academic

disciplines, from criminology to natural sciences, medicine and cultural anthropology, to illustrate the research interests and applications that benefit from the unique perspective that biographical narrative methods allow.

The third challenge in learning and mastering biographical narrative methodologies stems from a limited understanding of the nature of the research process. The design of methods courses often gives the impression that a project starts with a research question and ends with well-described findings. However, a neatly defined project will constantly evolve alongside every new literature search, your growing methodological expertise and practical contingencies, such as budget considerations or a change in circumstances, including unforeseen events like a global pandemic. It will also be required to contribute to the broader discussion within your field on the topic and the methodology. In research training, we often focus on what we consider interesting about our research project's findings and conclusions, but what makes your project valuable and scientific is an explanation of how your project changes the things we know or do not know about your chosen field of research. In our study illustrations, we outline three elements to each study. We show you specific *methods and design* to demonstrate the diversity of samples, designs and approaches that aim to investigate specific research questions. Then we show you *study findings* that are the outcome of the investigation, and the *generalisations* that authors of the study make while linking their observations to broader debates within their respective fields of study. This way of thinking about your research project will be an essential part of the research process: whether a dissertation, thesis, report or academic article.

The final challenge of biographical narrative research training lies in the relatively broad skill set required to engage with different types of biographical narrative analysis. While in quantitative methods training, it is pretty clear that you need to be able to run a specific type of software and interpret specific types of findings, biographical narrative methodologies, depending on their disciplinary traditions and established way of doing things, may send a contradictory message. On the one hand, within some biographical research schools, there is a strong interpretative tradition that insists on intimate work between the researcher and the text. On the other, there are 'objective hermeneutic' traditions that insist that interpretations of biographies should be done in a group setting. Some schools will insist that data should be coded in one of the available qualitative data-management packages, such as NVivo or Atlas.ti; others would argue that this will disconnect the data and undermine their biographical coherence. It is not unusual to see a student starting a project with the eagerness to learn how to do qualitative coding of the data, only to get discouraged halfway through and go back to paper-based analysis. It is also common to find that excellent data sets that could be used for other publications are set aside because the paper-based analysis was not robust enough in the first place.

Our approach is that qualitative researchers need to constantly develop their analytical skill set and adjust to the ever-changing circumstances of research. All the analytical toolkits presented throughout this book have their unique strengths and limitations. The skilful researcher needs to be able to identify, choose, learn and apply them to their best advantage.

How to use this book

We have structured this book as a form of systematic response to these challenges, so that it can be used as a reference text to address particular issues or as a step-by-step course to build up a researcher's skills and methodological imagination. The book is divided into three main sections that correspond to the three main parts of the learning process. Students can use this book as a comprehensive course and guide to their individual research projects; and teachers and researchers can use it as a reference book for a specific biographical research technique, research design or project implementation issue. In more detail, each part of the book explores the aspects of biographical research methods and research project execution and design shown in Figure 1.1.

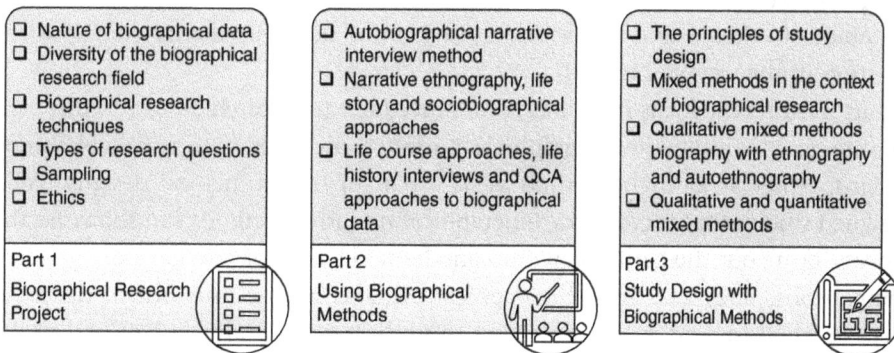

❑ Nature of biographical data ❑ Diversity of the biographical research field ❑ Biographical research techniques ❑ Types of research questions ❑ Sampling ❑ Ethics	❑ Autobiographical narrative interview method ❑ Narrative ethnography, life story and sociobiographical approaches ❑ Life course approaches, life history interviews and QCA approaches to biographical data	❑ The principles of study design ❑ Mixed methods in the context of biographical research ❑ Qualitative mixed methods biography with ethnography and autoethnography ❑ Qualitative and quantitative mixed methods
Part 1 Biographical Research Project	Part 2 Using Biographical Methods	Part 3 Study Design with Biographical Methods

Figure 1.1   How to use this book

Part I is an introduction to biographical narrative methods. In this part, we outline the main approaches that use elements of biographical research methodologies. We highlight the diversity of underlying assumptions and theoretical frames of reference used by different academic disciplines within different national traditions. In this part of the book, we explain that biographical narratives are a unique type of data used to investigate complex social relations, but that they need to be decoded for scientific inquiry. Step by step, we walk through the essential elements of biographical narratives to unravel their analytical potential, such as how the narrator decides on which stories are worth telling, how we deal with issues of truthfulness, how people assemble a coherent story, and how we can use this knowledge to design research tools that will allow us to collect the best type of data. We consider how deep we would like narrators to go with their narration, and the ethical implications of that. Part I of this book will help you to plan how to use biographical narrative methods in a research project and to identify the skills that you need to learn to succeed in your research.

Part II is more about the practical approaches to biographical narrative methods. It focuses on building your analytical toolkit and understanding the relations between biographical data, whether in their unstructured, semi-structured or structured form, including their connection to various forms of analysis. This part outlines three key analytical methods: autobiographical narrative interview method, narrative ethnography, and qualitative comparative analysis (QCA). Each analytical method is set up to illustrate the theoretical foundations it is built on, the analytical steps and procedures involved, and the types of generalisations that can be drawn from this form of analysis. For each method, we provide several illustrations from published research projects to showcase the diversity and applications of biographical narrative research. Each analytical method can be separately studied and applied. However, this section of the book is designed to expand analytical skills beyond any single tradition of biographical narrative research, and to foster the ability to design and apply the research tools that will answer your research question in the way you intend.

Part III shifts the focus from analytical procedures to research design. In this part, we aim to accommodate biographical narrative methods within suitable study designs, either as a single method or as a part of mixed method designs. Well-designed studies that incorporate biographical narrative methods can showcase the process, bring out the contrasts within and between cases or provide cross-national comparisons. They can bring biographical evidence to the forefront of the argument or use it instead as an illustration to support other findings. This part of the book shows how research designs have evolved from single method and qualitative mixed methods to quantitative and qualitative mixed method designs. We provide ample illustration to show the rich diversity of research designs that use biographical research methods across academic disciplines. Each section of the book can be read as a stand-alone chapter, but together they are designed to expand the methodological imagination and foster creativity in future methodological innovations.

2

THEORETICAL APPROACHES TO BIOGRAPHICAL NARRATIVES

Objectives

By the end of this chapter, you will be able to:

- Differentiate between types of biographical research
- Understand the origins and assumptions of different approaches
- Define key terms such as 'biography', 'autobiography', 'narrative' and 'life story'
- Follow the procedures associated with alternative biographical perspectives.

I don't ask people about [Soviet] socialism, I want to know about love, jealousy, childhood, old age. Music, dances, hairdos. The myriad sundry details of a vanished way of life. It's the only way to chase the catastrophe into the contours of the ordinary and try to tell a story. Make some small discovery. It never ceases to amaze me how interesting everyday life really is. There is an endless number of human truths. (Alexievich, 2016: 7)

This chapter sets out the key features of biographical narrative research as they have developed in the context of various academic and national traditions. It outlines the basic assumptions authors make about the meaning of biographical data and explains how this has led to a number of variants of biographical research. Different orientations to biographical data have their own distinct procedures and ways of doing analysis. Within this chapter, we highlight the value of biography for social research. At the same time, we aim to be realistic about the complexities involved in taking personal stories, biographical and autobiographical narratives as evidence for interpreting society and social questions. Informed choices about research design need to be based on a good understanding of theory as well as research techniques.

What is biography?

In a literal sense, biography means an account of someone's life. It may be authored by the subject of the biography, written by someone else, or the result of a collaboration. Whether it is an autobiography or a biography, there is an important distinction to be made between the 'life' and the 'writing'. On the one hand, there is the person, understood in terms of their physical body, and the sequence and sum of their life experiences. On the other, there is the story and how it is told. This conceptual contrast between the person as the source of biographical data and the telling of their life begs fundamental questions about our understanding of persons, about the 'knowability' of a person, and the meaning of their experiences. These are matters of philosophy and social theory which cannot be ignored in biographical research.

The self (myself, herself) is the category we typically use as a shorthand to describe the persons we think of as 'me' and 'them'. While this self appears to refer to the core of our material and conscious being, it takes very little reflection to see that this sense of self is malleable, changes over time and is not just about the self as an isolated individual. It embodies the concrete experiences we have had in the past, live in the present and anticipate in the future. For many decades, social theories have criticised essentialist notions of the self and have offered various alternative conceptions of the self as a form of subjectivity which is dynamic, pliable and closely connected with social-historical reality. In this view, the self is a structure of internal and external relationships through which one constructs self-understanding and negotiates an image of oneself with others – an identity, or identities in the plural.

This means that the evidence of a person's biography is the product of a reflexive process and collaboration between that person and their interlocutors. The 'facts' and events in a person's life can be known and corroborated by external means (birth and death records, school reports, curricula vitae, and so on). They can stand outside the influence of any particular interpretation, but they alone are insufficient to provide a story. To describe experiences and to interpret them is a subjective undertaking, requiring language and communication. Biographies are not objective statements; they are expressed in and through acts of narration that occur at specific moments in time and place, such as an interview or a conversation. Their meanings are only fixed in the process of telling the life story. The question of subjectivity is inescapable because, as every historical biographer knows, the influences that inform the life story are laden with cultural baggage and shot through with the personal biases that can only produce a 'version' of the story.

In social research, the relationality of biographical data is important for two reasons. First, the data are produced through an interactive process between the researcher and their respondent or (interview) 'partner'. This applies whether the style of the interview is autobiographical or a life story narrative. Interaction requires the narrator to address an audience and therefore present their story in a way that is adjusted to the listener. While this is essentially no different from what happens in a conversation, the research setting is likely to prompt certain responses, such as a wish to account for crises, successes and failures, social influences, or relationships. Second, research is conducted for public purposes, so the relationship will usually support an account which tries to figure out connections between the self – 'the personal troubles of milieu' – and society – 'the public issues of social structure' (Wright Mills, 1959).

Another question which is vital to biography, as well as a core concept in social theory, is 'agency'. It refers to the capacity of individuals to act independently and to influence their circumstances, or not. Lack of agency is experienced as limitations on a person's freedom to decide or act. Biographers typically seek to explain how a person directs their actions according to some strategy or plan. The more prominent they are, the more their actions are likely to be attributed to their own impulses and decisions. 'Mover and shaker', 'heroine' or 'go-getter' describe people who overcome obstacles to success. Yet even the most decisive among leaders or creative talents are shaped by their circumstances and social context. A starting point for biographical research is a view of the person as an agent with the capacity to act physically, mentally and socially out of self-interest or altruism. But this must be combined with the expectation that self-agency will be challenged and sometimes derailed by pressures from the social environment.

Influential aspects of the social environment include interpersonal relationships (especially in childhood and youth but throughout the life course too), social institutions and cultural systems. Institutions are relatively stable patterns of social organisation which sustain and reproduce societal structures. For individuals, they are simultaneously the opportunity and means to solve problems of existence, while, at the same time, presenting obstacles to change and progress. A person's working career can be used to illustrate this dual aspect of employment institutions as a source of opportunities and constraints that exist concurrently. Cultural systems are also large-scale, enduring structures which shape social practices, thinking and behaviour. Therefore, when we think about life stories and biographies, we are thinking about forms of narrative that make sense of an individual's experiences in this wider context and give meaning to them.

These, then, are some of the theoretical considerations for biographical research. The raw material of biography does not communicate without interpretation. We approach it with key concepts in mind: the self, relationality, agency, institutions and culture. These ideas are broad but relevant to all aspects of biographical data. To develop a good understanding of the research process as a form of theoretical practice, it helps to learn from the pioneers of a number of different styles of research. The following sections will therefore explore in detail a selection of studies which have helped to shape the field, paying close attention to the nature of biographical evidence, the forms of biographical data, the sources of meaning and the criteria for explanation.

Biographical evidence

One of the cornerstones of biographical research is a study of Polish migration to the USA just after the First World War (Thomas and Znaniecki, 1919, 1958). It stands out as a major innovation in social research methods as well as a contribution to understanding the experience of transnational migration. This five-volume classic sought to explain the social disruptions which occurred in the relations between individuals and their surrounding society, first in rural Poland and then in working-class America. The work opens with a chapter called 'Methodological Note', which is actually a pioneering discussion of fundamental theory and method. It seeks to reconcile the 'objective' elements of social life with the 'subjective' characteristics of the members of the social group (1958: 20), assuming them to be correlated through values, attitudes and rules of behaviour. In contrast to the then prevailing studies of migration using attitude surveys, the research uses letters, documents and personal stories combined to display the concrete evidence of participants' lives. The records occur naturally in the form of family correspondence, for example, while a whole volume is devoted to the written autobiography of just one immigrant – Władek Wisznienski – which is presented as a first-person narrative with annotations and critical commentary. Władek was not a well-educated man but he responded with relish to the invitation to write his story, which reads as a comprehensive narrative of his origins, migration journey and adjustment to life in America. The authors' commentary explains the difficulty of selecting 'representative' cases but argues that this can be done rationally according to a 'theory of human individuals as social personalities' (1958: 9), which is to say inhabitants of social worlds which can be characterised as 'ideal types'. Władek is contentiously described as belonging to a bohemian, 'culturally passive' type or category (one of three personality types – Philistine, Bohemian and Creative), because he illustrates the tendency for an individual's life to become disorganised under rapid transition. But one strength of this life story approach is that there is sufficient evidence provided for critics to develop other interpretations. The authors make a strong claim about theory and method:

> Life-records of concrete personalities have a marked superiority over any other kind of materials. We are safe in saying that personal life-records, as complete as possible, constitute the perfect type of sociological material, and that if social science has to use other materials at all it is only because of the practical difficulty of obtaining at the moment a sufficient number of such records to cover the totality of sociological problems, and of the enormous amount of work demanded for an adequate analysis of all the personal materials necessary to characterize the life of a social group. (Thomas and Znaniecki, 1919: 6–7)

The scale and depth of the Polish peasant study is impressive and is a reminder that biographical research does not have to rely exclusively on interviews. Thomas and Znaniecki's research approaches the documents of life as evidence of the construction of a self which is relational, socially embedded, and dependent on context in space and time. Narrative in this view is not evidence of something else (the person's experience). As Stanley points out, 'their analysis is concerned with stories, primarily the written stories in Polish peasant letters and Władek's life history, because they are (part of) social life, not a proxy for or a commentary about it' (Stanley, 2010: 148). The personal is evidence of the social but not separate from it.

Chicago School

Thomas and Znaniecki's research at the University of Chicago was a forerunner of what became known as the 'Chicago School' of sociology (Bulmer, 1984). This tradition was informed by the theory of symbolic interactionism, a term coined by Herbert Blumer in 1937, using ideas from pragmatism and the philosophy of George Herbert Mead (1934). As the name implies, symbolic interactionism was concerned with meanings in everyday social interaction, and the potential of shifting, unstable situations to generate social worlds – for example, the worlds of family, delinquency or race. In terms of methods, researchers became less inclined to use personal documents, and research evidence was drawn increasingly from direct observation, intensive ethnographic fieldwork, and social mapping. The lines of investigation were diverse, although there was a common interest in the experiences of groups outside mainstream society, including delinquents, the homeless and migrant workers. The concept of a 'case study' was used to describe the relationship between detailed empirical evidence and the generalisation to wider settings. In the first of a series of Chicago studies of urban life, Anderson (1923) collected more than 60 life histories of 'hobos' to understand how they live, but 'to emphasize not so much the particular and local as the generic and universal aspects of the city and its life' (p. ix). Shaw's *Jack Roller* (1996 [1930]) reconstructs the life history of Stanley, a young man who steals valuables from those who get visibly drunk. The story is based on interviews and Stanley's written record, which is treated as a case study which can be used to develop generalisations about the biographical origins of delinquency. 'The case is published', says Shaw, 'to illustrate the value of the "own story" in the study and treatment of the delinquent child', not as an end in itself. He asserts that cases are valuable evidence because they depict a total situation and combine the factors, processes and sequence of events in which behaviour occurs. Of course, Stanley's biography was shaped by Shaw's presentation, and it would be naïve to assume that he is just 'telling it like it is' (Gelsthorpe, 2007). This issue will be taken up in the sections below. The Chicago School authors were pioneers in eliciting data using ethnography and life history, but they were theoretically committed to explaining the organisation and disorganisation of urban life, using generalised explanations from a wide variety of data sources. While they were certainly intrepid explorers of personal meanings and subjectivity, they were not opposed to using statistical and documentary material.

By the 1940s, life history and biographical research had become more marginal within the social sciences. It was the time when quantitative empirical research and quasi-experimental approaches were developing apace and becoming institutionalised at Columbia University and elsewhere (Lazarsfeld and Rosenberg, 1955). In this context, life histories were seen as being too descriptive, idiosyncratic and unscientific. However, the commitments of the Chicago School did not die. They were echoed in the generation of scholars who emerged in the 1950s and 1960s (Hughes, Becker, Goffman, Strauss and Gusfield, among others) who are sometimes described as the Second Chicago School (Fine, 1995). Before considering how their work has influenced biographical research, we will consider what was occurring in the European context in terms of life history research and attitudes to biographical evidence.

As European theories and research mingled with influences from the USA, the social sciences became more fragmented. The rise of positivist, 'scientific' and statistical methods existed alongside, but often in conflict with, humanistic commitments in social history, anthropology and sociology. It is sometimes thought that the life history approach was totally eclipsed in the post-Second World War period, but it is more likely that such activity being pursued in Poland and Italy, for example, was not known outside those countries. While there was no equivalent to the Chicago School in Europe, there was a parallel interest in small-scale communities, cohesion and social change. In the UK, for example, this was displayed in 'community studies' (Day, 2006), which used participant observation, ethnography and sometimes descriptive surveys to characterise both urban and rural population groupings as bounded places of belonging. There was a strong interest in the details of local residents' lives as data for family and economic relations, social class, religion and politics. However, biographies were not used in themselves as evidence and it was not till after much critical commentary that communities came to be acknowledged as sites that are symbolically constructed through the interaction of individuals within the broader social fabric (Cohen, 1985). Other writers who were interested in capturing forgotten, excluded or dying cultures drew on life stories as a primary source of information and experience (e.g. Evans, 1956; Blythe, 1969). Elsewhere, anthropologists were using biographical accounts – notably Oscar Lewis, who used the new technology of tape recording to capture the autobiographical narratives of the poor Sanchez family in Mexico City (Lewis, 1961). In these stories, he sees family networks, interpersonal relations, time orientations, value systems, and patterns of economic survival that contribute to a sense of community, as well as the condition he describes as a 'culture of poverty'. In many of these contributions, there is a motif of 'giving people a voice' but what this meant was not always spelled out. Another example was the Mass Observation project in the UK which collected diaries and stories from volunteer writers between 1937 and 1949, and again after 1981 (Sheridan, 1996). Authors who maintained the theoretical interest in everyday life and the individual as a biographical entity in this period included C. Wright Mills (1959), who spotlighted the intersections of biography and history in society, and the value of a 'sociological imagination'. These ideas were essential to the challenges that were developing to macro-theories and to what Wright Mills called 'abstracted empiricism'. But it was not until the 1980s that there were clear signs of a resurgence in life writing and life stories in social science research.

Harrison (2008: xxiii–xxv) attributes the rise in interest to three main factors: the growth of oral history within the discipline of social history; the influence of second-wave feminism; and anti-discrimination struggles which sought to give expression to oppressed people in their challenge to power. These are closely inter-related but deserve some separate discussion because of their different foundations in research practice and philosophy.

Oral history

Oral history is the recording of people's memories, experiences and opinions. While it is focused on the individual, it is not primarily an attempt to reconstruct the life story as a sequential narrative, nor to verify the key events in a person's life. It aims to capture the subjectivity and salient experiences of people who are otherwise likely to be hidden from the historical record for reasons of age, sexuality, health, political views and outsider status. It has been a distinctive way of eliciting bio-graphical evidence on topics such as childhood, gender, occupations, ethnicity and community life. Paul Thompson, a leading social history practitioner, published *The Voice of the Past* (1978) and extended the reach of oral history into new areas and new disciplines, using extended interviews to generate core data. He explains how it originated as a blend of semi-structured and open-ended interviewing: 'You are always prepared to drop your questions, just listen, and in the early stages of the interview, you try never to interrupt, you try to get the person flowing, and only then you introduce your questions' (Thompson, 2004: 83). Oral history making has been successfully promoted as a popular, not purely professional, activity, for exam-ple through the member organisations of the International Oral History Association, and for this reason it may appear partisan, unrepresentative and lacking credibility. But there have been serious attempts to put it on a theoretical footing. First, the oral history record does not exist in isolation: it is only interpretable as 'part of a collec-tive tradition which preserves the memory of the group's history beyond the range of the lives of individual members' (Portelli, 1981: 102). Like earlier life story approaches, the attitude to the evidence is deeply subjective but not exclusively personal. It understands that meaning is relational and dynamic. Second, the inter-view is a dialogic event with its own features, including an open, egalitarian attitude to speaking and listening. Oral sources have their own credibility which comes from the language, emotion and specificity of their accounts. Third, oral history has engaged with the issue of generalisation, whether from quite opportunistic small samples, theoretical samples, quota samples or case histories. The following exemplary studies illustrate how the oral history tradition developed and dealt with these questions.

The French sociologist Daniel Bertaux made a pioneering contribution to research using life stories (*récits de vie*) in an effort to understand production relations within the occupational world of artisanal bakeries (Bertaux and Bertaux-Wiame, 1981). A sample of a hundred stories revealed the relations between master bakers, apprentices and family members in the present and the past, and the value of their common-sense knowledge. This 'ethnosocial' approach prioritises 'direct witness' to past events and is compelling when the informants share the same culture and continue to be immersed in the same social world – the bakery. The authors explain that their approach is less concerned with procedures of interviewing and analysis, and more interested in deciphering the relationship between the microcosm of the life story and the logic which governs the milieu or social world as a whole. The assumption is that the data give a good indication of 'how it was' for the participants, notwithstanding problems of memory or the impact of the researcher. Like Bertaux (1981), Thompson pushed the boundaries of oral history in his studies of the social worlds of fishing, city banking, stepfamilies and other groups, while working with colleagues across disciplines and exploring ways of sampling, analysing and generalising from life story interviews. In the same period, Ken Plummer (1983) was championing the use of life stories and other personal documents in the tradition of the Chicago School. His 'telling sexual stories' research (Plummer, 2002) was an important contribution to the understanding of gay coming out and survivors of abuse. He also articulated the key principle that changing social conditions make the telling of different stories possible at different times.

The demise of the Soviet Union opened up exciting opportunities for researchers to directly investigate the experiences of people who had lived through the state socialist regime after 1917. Among the many scholars who conducted oral histories were Bertaux, Thompson and Rotkirch, working alongside the Russians represented in the volume *On Living through Soviet Russia* (2004). The period between 1917 and the late 1980s had been relatively closed to social scientists and there were important questions about the USSR which did not have satisfactory answers. Did Soviet people internalise the state ideology? How free was everyday life? What were the experiences of different genders? How did values change from one generation to the next? In the years of *glasnost* and the 1990s, the conditions were ripe for elites and ordinary people to tell their stories without fear of reprisal. For some, it was cathartic and a way to expose a repressed history; for others, a chance to fill in gaps and bring coherence to their family history. This rich seam has continued to be mined by researchers and writers (e.g. Alexievich, 2016) and now includes the experience of the post-socialist transition more widely (Khanenko-Friesen and Grinchenko, 2015). In terms of method, this strand of oral history has led to important discussions about the reliability of memory and the role of oral history in supporting new versions of national ideology. It has provoked less debate about the data as such, or forms of interviewing. In an overview of oral history and theory, Abrams (2010) emphasises that the oral history interview is a communicative event involving constructions of the self and identity, not just a window on the past. It allows for several models of interpretation. It may be used to recover voices and place them on the historical record, 'the reminiscence and community' model. It may be used as evidence to illustrate or support an argument. And it may be used as a source to apply a particular analytical model (Abrams, 2010: 15). Oral history, like life story research, has generally emphasised the first two of these types of interpretation. To explore the third, it is helpful to consider how feminist authors have developed their analytical practices.

Feminism

In the political and cultural movement which became known as second-wave feminism, researchers set out to illuminate the forms of discrimination that women experience in all walks of life. Studies were distinguished by the commitment to give voice to women who were previously neglected in social science: for example, housewives (Oakley, 1974), daughters (Rowbotham and McCrindle, 1977) and female workers (Pollert, 1981). Interviews were conducted with emancipatory intent and were designed to minimise the power differential between the interviewer and the interviewee. As the volume of studies grew, researchers paid more attention to the theoretical underpinnings of their work. Reflections on life story and oral history methods were caught up in the wider discussion of gendered power relationships, researcher standpoint and feminist theories of knowledge. The key assumptions in these theories are that knowledge is socially situated (hence shaped by social position and gender), and that research should consciously align itself with the experiences of those who are subordinate or marginal to the mainstream. To correct the bias of existing disciplines, feminists argued that researchers should account for the relations of their own production (be open about their own autobiography) and adopt styles of writing which locate themselves in the activities of their research. According to these criteria, life stories are sympathetic to feminist research because they are sensitive to the way the story is produced through interaction, and help to liberate previously unheard voices. The evidence can contribute to a form of objective knowledge supported by reflection and self-critique from the standpoint of women (Harding, 2004).

These debates about theory were by no means limited to the sphere of life stories and biography. More recently, they have developed through engagement with post-structuralist and postmodern notions of knowledge and meaning, and their critiques of reason and narrative knowledge. While these ideas need not detain us here because they extend far beyond the research process as such, they have informed one concept which is important for life story research, namely intersectionality (Collins and Bilge, 2016). This is the idea that forms of inequality and oppression, such as race, gender and class, are linked and exacerbate each other. In a life story, intersectionality is likely to be reflected in the overlapping scripts that a person relies on for their sense of self and identity. It is a useful way to think of the structural and symbolic objects which are the context for the life story. It directs attention to those aspects of biographical evidence which stem from the resources available to the narrator in the wider culture.

In this section, we have seen that biographical evidence has a long history and many uses in the context of life stories, life history and oral history. Research in this tradition displays some regular features: it places a high value on subjectivity, it shows awareness of the social interaction that generates the data, and it recognises that the data are the starting point for inferences about the wider social context. However, the development of biographical research has highlighted several issues which call for further scrutiny. They are: the characteristics of the data that are produced; the sources of meaning that narrators and researchers call upon; and the units of analysis and interpretation. We next turn to consider the essential properties of a biographical account.

Data structures – stories as told

Documents of life (stories, life histories, biographies, autobiographies) are more than statements about experience which provide resources for social research. As we have seen above, they do represent 'the life' of the informant to the extent that they describe and mirror the characteristics of the person's life in a more or less truthful way. The informant allows us to enter their 'social world', so to speak. Yet the diversity of stories alerts us to an important distinction: the difference between the life as lived and experienced, and the life as told. There is one person, one life, but many ways of telling the story, depending on the point in time, the perceived purpose of the telling, and the type of social interaction within which it occurs. This distinction has become vital to several branches of biographical research which examine the biographical narrative as an object of investigation in its own right. Many of these ideas are informed by social theories of language, linguistics and communication.

Life course and process structures

In studies of language and interaction, a fundamental assumption is that reality is constituted through concrete exchanges using language. Stories we tell make sense of our lives and try to reconcile who we are and what we might become, in the contexts of family, community, gender, work, class, ethnicity and culture. The sense making is visible in the structure and process as well as the content of the story. Even extempore autobiographical storytelling follows rules of communicative practice which include ways of presenting the self and others, social categorisation, social inclusion and exclusion, formulaic speech, and so on. In a study in Germany about life under National Socialism, Kohli (1981) emphasises that autobiographical texts have structural properties which reflect the difficulties of talking about the historical events and experiences of that period: the 'silences, justifications and lies'. In the version of autobiographical narrative interviewing developed by Fritz Schütze, a German sociologist who adopted and disseminated a symbolic interaction approach, combined with ethnomethodology (Garfinkel, 1967) and sociology of knowledge (Hamilton, 1974), the two dimensions of structure are:

- process structures of the life course: biographical action schemes, institutional action schemes, trajectories of suffering, processes of biographical transformation
- constraints of narrative production: the requirement for the narrator to be specific about the details of their biography, as well as comprehensive.

Schütze's important contribution, including the concept of process structure, is explained more fully in Chapter 4, where we show how the principles apply to the analysis of autobiographical narrative data. Essentially, Schütze sees the interview as an organised interaction, with opening and closing practices, sequences of description and argumentation, modalities of exchange which convey emotion and engagement, and a communicative style which stems from the particular milieu of the informant. The style of interviewing is based on extended, open-ended and uninterrupted narration of the life story, followed up by questions and answers that stem from the narrative itself. The origins and development of this tradition are explained more fully in an overview of the 'German School' by Apitzsch and Inowlocki (2000).

If the narrative is more than an accumulation of facts and experiences, how is it used for generalisation in this approach? The approach is inductive, which involves moving from observations to empirical generalisations and from those to a theory which interconnects the themes. The process involves four analytical stages. First, the interview narrative, treated as a single case, is examined to identify the chronology and process structures of the life course and the categories (e.g. relationships, milieux, identities) the narrator uses to describe their social world. This closely resembles the 'initial coding' procedure in grounded theory (Charmaz, 2006: 47–53) which is widely used in qualitative data analysis. It aims to derive categories or themes which will not need to be revised even when further data are added, and which generate stable meanings. However, the formal structural approach is more concerned with text structures and linguistic forms than a typical constructivist approach. The second stage focuses on other social mechanisms that are not directly revealed in stage one – for example, the influence of collective memory or national culture, and the degree of abstractness in the storytelling. The third stage is to make a comparison between cases, to observe similarities and to draw out contrasts between them. This helps to establish the range of variation and the scope of the mechanisms that play a role. Finally, the generalisations are combined to form answers to research questions. A compelling answer will require the researcher to constantly compare the formal structure of the biographical text with the content (what is said). Abstract categories like 'European mental space', which was used in the Euroidentities project (Miller and Day, 2012) to account for the meanings of Europe in everyday lives, need to be confronted constantly with new pieces of data until a state of 'saturation' is reached (Glaser and Strauss, 1967: 61–62), that is when new data do not provide additional insights.

Biographical narrative interpretative method

A variant of a formal structural approach is the biographical narrative interpretative method (BNIM), developed by Tom Wengraf and Prue Chamberlayne (Wengraf, 2001, 2010) and building on work by Rosenthal (1998). It combines the interview method of Fritz Schütze with other elements, making a sharp distinction between the data of the biography (the 'lived life' or life history) and the narrative (the 'told story'). Wengraf explains that they are analysed separately, before the two analyses are brought together:

- The *lived life* is composed of the uncontroversial hard biographical data that can be abstracted from the interview material and any other helpful source. This can be seen as a long chronological sequence of the 'objective' historical facts about the person's life, the life-events as they happened, independently of whether or how they are referred to in the interview.
- The *told story* is the way that the person presents him- or herself – both in their initial narrative and in their answers to specific questions – by selecting certain events in their life (and omitting others) and by handling them in a certain way (and not in another). (Wengraf, 2000: 145)

The assumption is that the two dimensions influence each other in a dialectical fashion. Comparing the *lived* and *told* life is the key to understanding how a person subjectively forms their identity, acts and interprets their actions in context. The comparison will highlight themes which are omitted, glossed over, treated gingerly, thrown away as asides, or explained at length. For example, someone who has experienced a divorce may acknowledge it as an important experience with lasting consequences in their life, or they may not include any details of it in their narrative. BNIM assumes that a divorce is a fact in the person's life that fits into a chronological sequence of personal relationships. The way it fits into the narrative (or not) is a matter for investigation and generalisation about the relationship between the 'inner' and the 'outer' worlds of the person.

The procedures of BNIM begin with the narrative interview, generated by a version of the question 'Can you please tell me your life story?' This initial narrative is facilitated by the interviewer, but with the minimum of interruption. It is expected to produce an elaborated version of the life story controlled by the interviewee, including events and experiences which are personally important. The narrative will eventually be drawn to a close by the interviewee. The second step is for the interviewer to ask questions which relate directly to the narrative, echoing the topics and themes used by the narrator. They might start with the phrase 'you said that...'. The reason is to supplement the narrative with clarifications, additional details, and to fill in apparent gaps. Both steps closely resemble the Schützean type of autobiographical narrative interview. A third step is to ask questions about themes that the interviewee has not addressed, but which relate to the interests and theories of the interviewer. They will also be designed to elicit narrative, for example by prompting: 'perhaps you could say something about your time in ...'. These questions may have a thematic emphasis. The interview data thus contain life-course information, accounts of experience, and themes that the informant chose to elaborate on. BNIM lends itself to research questions which pose psycho-social and well as sociological questions.

The analysis proceeds on twin tracks: reconstructing the objective life events; followed by an analysis of the telling of these in the interview. Thinking in a deliberate way about the social-historical context creates awareness of how the subjectivity of the narrative is situated in time and geographical and social space. In track one, the researcher does not simply generate a chronology; the biographical data are used to generate an understanding of how somebody who lived their life in a particular setting might be expected to tell their story of that life. Track two involves an analytical description of the telling of the story, using methods of text sorting which distinguish between narration, argumentation and evaluation.

The aim is to characterise the way in which the biographical topics are addressed, so the text-sorts do not correspond exactly to units of the verbatim transcript. This stage is enhanced in BNIM by a panel process involving several researchers who share their interpretations of the data.

The next stage brings together the two tracks in order to develop explanatory hypotheses that explain the connections between them. The case presentation which results will take account of both the inner-world and outer-world dynamics of the story, and the contingencies involved. Individual cases may be compared and contrasted to develop more far-reaching explanations, typologies and theories. Wengraf has regularly published instruction manuals and updates to explain the principles of the approach, and how it works in practice (e.g. Wengraf, 2010). BNIM has been applied to a wide range of research questions as diverse as Chamberlayne and King's (2000) cultures of care project, the EU's Social Strategies in Risk Societies (SOSTRIS) investigation of social exclusion and risk, multi-generational studies of the families of victims of the Nazis and of Nazi perpetrators (Rosenthal, 1998), and a psycho-societal evaluation of a community development setting (Froggett et al., 2005).

In this section, we have shown examples of biographical interpretation which see an important analytical distinction between the life story and the telling of the life story. This has led various authors to systematise the approach to interviewing and analysis of the interview text, drawing on a range of insights from theories of language, narrative and interaction. The strong focus on the meanings of the interview transcript, as revealed by process structures and mechanisms, leaves open further questions about the context and framing of biographical renderings of experience. This is our next theme.

Key terms

Life story

A narrative version of a life, produced in a social interaction, to make sense of experiences in the past. It will be fluid, interpreted and reinterpreted over time, depending on the type of interaction. The created and constructive elements of the life story distinguish it from the life history.

Life history

Chronological reconstruction of a life story, typically from a personal account (written or oral), with additional material from diaries, letters, media sources or official records. It will usually contain life stages such as childhood, education, marriage and career. It implies a notion of 'validation' or a cross-checking of sources.

(Continued)

Oral history

The use of oral sources in history. Like life stories, oral histories focus on the reconstruction of lives through the reporting of first-hand experiences. In oral history, the narrator has a prominent role in providing the evidence but less control over how it is contextualised.

Biography

A structured account of a life given by another, consisting of linked episodes and details.

Autobiography

The writing of one's own history; a structured account of one's own life; a self-portrait in the form of a narrative or memoir.

Autoethnography

Research and writing that seek to describe and systematically analyse one's personal experiences in order to understand them in relation to their context or specific themes. It combines characteristics of autobiography and ethnography.

Narrative

An ordered account or story that conveys experiences, events, values and explanations according to a set of cultural conventions. In biographical research, it is orientated towards sequential organisation and connectedness over time.

Stories in context

In the approach known as narrative ethnography, a key concern is how the individual's unique experiences and changing perspectives are mediated by the context. The context includes the immediate setting of the interview itself but also the wider social context (social inequalities, current events, media tropes, and other aspects over which the individual has no control). This is mediated through the interaction between the interviewer and the interviewee at the time of the interview. The approach was developed by the American scholars Jaber Gubrium and James Holstein (1995) in response to ethnographers who were increasingly treating their participants as active interpreters of their social worlds, not only informants who provided descriptions. They say:

> we must emphasize that lives are not constructed arbitrarily in a contextual
> vacuum. Whether it is the personal past, the present, the future, a
> combination of them, or the life course as a whole, participants work at

characterizing their lives in relation to the interpretive horizons of social settings, using available interpretive resources. (Gubrium and Holstein, 1995: 46–47)

An example from their own research would be a resident in a nursing home who provides a life story and in doing so, gives an indication of the home's quality and the conditions of living in residential care, in relation to that resident's life as a whole. The individual can be considered an ethnographer of their own life. The interview will contain references to the institutional context, such as policies for resident safety, costs of care or quality of staff. This is the process of biographical work, which is the construction of interpretations from categories of local, organisational structures and extended social worlds, as well as immediate experiences. As an approach, narrative ethnography is orientated towards the external organisation of life stories as well as the properties of the text – how stories are produced, where certain stories are likely to be encountered, how they circulate and whose interests they represent. This is how it differs from the approaches we have discussed previously.

The analytical procedures of narrative ethnography reflect this understanding (Gubrium and Holstein, 2009). We will elaborate on them fully in Chapter 5, with examples. Research questions in this approach are concerned with the everyday work that people do to assemble stories and the contingencies that storytellers face. The vocabulary of methods includes the concepts of 'narrative reality', 'narrative environment' and 'narrative adequacy'. First, the object of analysis is the situated practice of storytelling, as well as the substance of the story. The story may be generated by an interview but an extended autobiographical narrative is not essential. Narrative reality is performative, and the data may come from ethnographic interviews or from any setting in which stories are told (e.g. a personal conversation or a courtroom). While other approaches acknowledge that a life story is an interactional accomplishment (typically involving an interviewer and a narrator), narrative ethnography elevates this to a fundamental precept. The second key concept, narrative environment, refers to the contexts in which the work of story construction and storytelling gets done. They are 'critical for understanding what is at stake for storytellers and listeners in presenting accounts or responding to them in distinctive ways' (Gubrium and Holstein, 2009: xvii–xviii). Environments include close relationships, local culture (in small groups, communities), jobs, organisations, and less fathomable environments such as gender, class and ethnicity. For example, family background and social class often provide the impetus for everyday life stories and meanings. Environments are not simply external circumstances which condition a narrative; they are also the pretext for activating narrative interpretations. This brings us to the notion of adequacy. Standard criteria for a 'good story' might include truthfulness, detail or lack of digression, but in narrative ethnography the quality of the story relates to situated background knowledge. Gubrium and Holstein recommend that researchers 'look for the ways in which storytellers and listeners interactionally construct the adequacy of the storyteller' in the circumstances of the telling (2009: 213).

The Euroidentities project (Miller and Day, 2012) helps to illustrate the possibilities of the narrative ethnography approach, using data from a large international set of autobiographical narrative interviews (see also Study 3 in Chapter 7 for a full description of this project). The research question was: how has European identity been evolving over time? Analysis across countries highlighted the different national environments for talking about the 'idea of Europe'. Language, for example, is a common theme across the interviews. Language speaking is a universal aspect of human experience, but it is an important source of variation in transnational mobility, its opportunities and barriers. Narratives of mobility become more intelligible when languages are interpreted as a form of narrative environment (Davis et al., 2017). Europe itself appears as an environment: it features in many German narratives as an antidote for war and as a guardian of peace, whereas narratives from the UK speak of 'the continent', a destination 'out there' commonly associated with holidays abroad or migration. Interviews with Polish expatriates refer to opportunity structures in Europe for work and education. Since the UK Brexit referendum in 2016, the sense of belonging to the EU and Europe has become an inescapable part of the UK narrative environment for international comparisons. Language and national identity are therefore more than topics for narration and argumentation; they are sets of resources which vary between different national groups and which the latter use to make sense of their experiences.

Units of analysis and interpretation

The core unit of biographical research is the individual story, usually rendered as a recording, transcript or text. While this sounds straightforward enough, it raises questions about boundaries and what is included or excluded. Our description of biographical research indicates that the boundaries between the person, their story, their commentary and the researcher's interpretation are relatively fluid. The elements of structure (process structures, plots, themes and so on) are treated differently in the various analytical traditions, which leaves room for discretion for the researcher who is getting to grips with biography. We will consider in a later section the design and sampling choices that researchers need to make (Chapter 7). For the moment, let us imagine the unit of biographical analysis as made up of concentric rings, with the person, defined by their experiences, embodied in time and space, at the centre (see Figure 2.1). This person generates their story or stories, the second ring, where the researcher finds multiple features that make the story intelligible to others. The third ring is the narrative context or environment which is needed to interpret the story as a social phenomenon. The unit of analysis is therefore a composite of these elements.

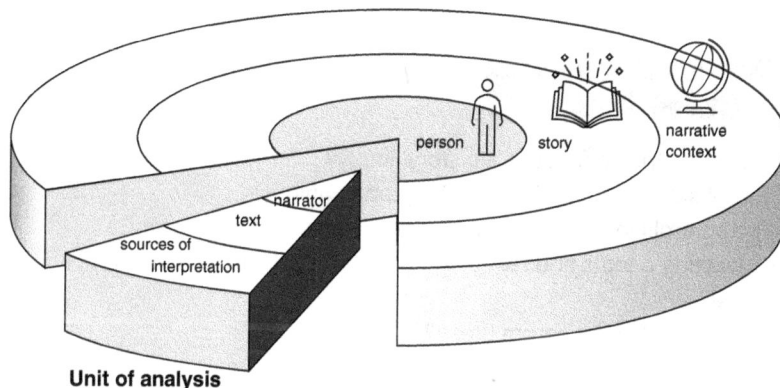

Figure 2.1 Constituents of biographical research

An individual life – a sample of one – can be the subject of research simply because it represents challenges overcome, unique achievements, cross-cultural encounters, moments of peril or finding safety. Some autoethnographers adopt this approach. But it is more common for cases to be selected according to thematic interests and to be motivated by research questions from an existing field of study. The many examples in this book show how a wide variety of important themes are addressed through biographical research on multiple cases.

Summary

It is almost inevitable that, as biographical research has grown in popularity, and has spread throughout the global research community, its manifestations have become more diverse and complex. In this chapter, we have traced its origins and presented in outline a number of approaches to research using biographical data. While there is significant diversity in their underlying assumptions and theoretical frames of reference, they unite around the commitment to evidence from life stories as recounted by the people who live them. There is also a less frequently declared theoretical presumption: that in modern society the self is malleable and biographical work is the necessary means for an individual to develop and assert their personhood. The approaches reflect different national traditions in philosophy and research strategy and are overlapping, convergent and divergent. We have not had space to explain in detail how they may be combined, yet this is not at all uncommon. The resounding message is that the interpretation of biographical sources cannot simply be derived from the record or transcript. The 'text' does not speak for itself. To paraphrase Karl Marx: people make their own stories, but not in circumstances of their own choosing.

Questions to consider

1. What does the concept of 'life story' imply?
2. In what sense is an individual's biography unique?
3. Who controls the content of a biography or an autobiography?
4. In selecting a topic and research question, what alternatives might I decide to take?
5. How should I choose from these?

3

INTERVIEW PROCESS AND ETHICS

Objectives

By the end of this chapter, you will be able to:

- Understand the potential and limitations of biographical research stemming from the subjectivity of data
- Understand the link between a research question, research design and type of data
- Identify the size of a study and sampling logic
- Address ethical issues in biographical research
- Understand the interview situation and setting
- Identify the main interview considerations, such as its length, transcription, translation and organisation
- Understand the organisation of the interview and the skills required.

> Social science cannot remain on the surface of social becoming, where
> certain schools wish to have it float, but must reach the actual human
> experiences and attitudes which constitute the full, live and active social
> reality beneath the formal organisation of social institutions. ('The Polish
> Peasant in Europe and America', Thomas and Znaniecki, 1958, Vol. II: 1834)

Biographical research provides empirical data that offer a unique glimpse into the
social world, as a person's biography forms an important source of knowledge about
individuals as well as their society. However, a biography is a type of social data that
requires understanding and an analytical approach capable of decoding the symbolic meanings and embodied attachments. Just as a photograph can be used as a
source of empirical data, a biography is like a snapshot of the individual in time. To
fully understand its meaning, the researcher needs to understand both the character
of biographical data and how they should be used as empirical material in scientific
investigation.

Decoding biography for scientific investigation

While a number of academic disciplines use some form of biographical and narrative data, life stories or autobiographical narratives constitute a specific type of
material (as explained in Chapter 2). According to Atkinson (1998: 8), a life story:

> is the story a person chooses to tell about the life he or she has lived, told
> as completely and honestly as possible, what is remembered of it, and
> what the teller wants others to know of it ... A life story is a fairly complete
> narrating of one's entire experience of life as a whole, highlighting the most
> important aspects.

The concept of telling one's life story often seems a natural act of narration within
a society in which stories form an integral part of conveying knowledge and communication; there is a sense that knowing someone, especially intimately, is the
same as knowing someone's story or stories. The fact is, however, that not many
people have the chance to tell the entire story of their life in the form of one coherent narrative. Even in the case of written autobiographies, time requirements and
the absence of an active, present listener change the way in which a life story is told.

Life stories are a unique type of data and should be seen for what they are: a personal account. During the interview, the interviewee uses their power to share
important events with the interviewer, to omit those they do not wish to share, to
interpret the events and build a narrative account that justifies their actions and decisions. A biography is a subjective type of data and should therefore not be treated as

a direct source of knowledge about someone's life. To decode biographical data for social research, we need to highlight several key aspects of the biographical process that shape and influence life story accounts and how we analyse them.

Stories worth telling

The life story in itself is the subjective account. It is assembled to document the biographical process of the construction of self as well as the mechanisms of sustaining these perceptions over time. According to Linde (1993), the selection of events included in the biographical narrative has two important features. First, the events are chosen to present the narrator as a worthy person, someone who deserves to be listened to. The life story is then geared up to demonstrate the individual's social world and present their current position in a positive light. Second, the events included in the narration need to be identified as worth reporting. Events considered 'normal' and 'usual' will entwine with milestones such as parenthood, divorce, career advancement, illness, religious conversion or transnational experiences, to become the essence of what constitutes the narrator's identity. This is an important twist on the maxim that history is written by the winners; the life story is written from the point of view of the winner.

Issues of truth

The focus on the worthiness of the story brings up the important aspect of a life story's truthfulness. If the individual presents a subjective interpretation of self, anchored in the idea of self-worth, we cannot expect that the account will be entirely complete and true (see Chapter 2). People carry experiences they are not proud of that are likely to be omitted, interpretations that are tainted by outside influences, and finally memories that, with time, can be influenced or forgotten. Most of those shortcomings are not intentional; they are a natural feature and a code of storytelling. In biographical research, it is better practice to strive for honesty rather than complete truthfulness, and to accept that a biography is about the individual's journey in the world.

The art of storytelling – three constraints to narration

To tell a life story is a complex cognitive process, which does not operate at random but requires narrators to carefully 'assemble their stories, artfully picking and choosing from what is experientially available to articulate inner lives and social worlds … they strategically construct their accounts, organizing experience in the process' (Gubrium and Holstein, 2009: 30–31). In the process of storytelling, the narrator unconsciously follows the cultural and social conventions of telling their life story, thus engaging in a complex emotional and cognitive process of bio-graphical work (Kohli, 2005). There are three basic cultural conventions, often referred to as narrative laws (Apitzsch and Siouti, 2007) or constraints (Schütze, 2008). Every storyteller unconsciously fulfils these social demands and shapes their life story into a form which is familiar to the listener (present or imagined):

1. The first autobiographical demand put upon the narrator is **the need to condense** the life story into one textual form (Schütze, 2008). A life story is a unique narrative unit bound to the present circumstances of the narrator, as the life story is anchored in the current state of the narrator's consciousness. The narrator is required to choose the most relevant events that have shaped the overall biographical process. The narrator reflects back on a sequence of events that have led them to the current place and time. This reflective process is strongly embedded in the interview situation itself. In contrast to writing down one's story, the narrator needs to tell the story to the other party in the interaction – to the listener. The life story is enclosed within the temporal frame of the interview and needs to follow the rules of social interaction. Those constraints impose on the narrator the need to 'condense' the story, to choose the most relevant and the most significant events which have led the narrator to the present situation. The process of condensing the life story assumes that the narrative connections between the agent and the social structure can be accounted for. The convention of coherence (Linde, 1993) is one of the most powerful mechanisms which ensures that the events relevant for the story as well as justifications follow, if not true events, at least genuine interpretations of them.

2. The second narrative constraint deals with the narrator's **need to elaborate** on the experiences and events in detail so as to be able to justify them and connect them together within one logical process. An intentional omission of relevant events immediately results in discrepancies within the logical order, which the narrator is forced to 'correct' as the story continues. Such additional stories, introduced in order to regain narrative coherence, take on the form of 'background constructions' (Schütze, 2008) and often indicate a life story episode which, in the narrator's own perception, is problematic, shameful or emotionally painful. Elaborating on specific events creates narrative units, seen as particular episodes or turning points. These particular chapters of the story are not entirely independent and should be analysed in relation to the overall sequence of the life story.

3. The final constraint of the biography imposes on the narrator an **obligation to finish their story** and to tie together all loose threads (Schütze, 2008). Usually, life story narrations begin with a biographical introduction, the preamble. This is the moment when the narrator searches for the beginning of their biographical experience, as well as the overall underlying patterns highlighting their current biographical situation. In a similar manner, the biographical conclusion, the coda, brings the narrator to the present, encourages evaluating the overall story and dares the narrator to look towards future possibilities. Between the biographical preamble and the coda, all the narrative, argumentative and descriptive elements of the life story need to be tied together into a logical and coherent structure. Those elements of the narrative that are left open and unfinished create a sense of dissonance and thus cause a feeling of incoherence, which the narrator feels obliged to address in order to make a final point.

What stories say about the individual and what they tell us about society

The life story is not a simple sequential reporting of events. It is a narrative account crafted to follow cultural norms. In many respects, a biography is like a Facebook wall: only a selected type of information makes its way into it and some of the information is less likely to be truthful. What then is the reason for looking into individual biographies? Well, understanding what you see and what it represents is a good start. According to attribution theory, we are all naïve psychologists who observe the world and add meaning to our and other people's actions. We tend to see other people's circumstances and actions as linked to aspects of their personalities: when judging them as unsuccessful, for instance if a person is not being promoted at work, we think the reason is that they are not smart. But where there is success, we tend to attribute it to external factors, such as luck. In contrast, we tend to see our own misfortunes as an outcome of social circumstances. If we don't get a job promotion, it is because of a conflict with our boss. But we attribute success to our hard work – for example, when we succeeded in running a marathon it was because we trained well. This shift in perspective and attribution of life events towards external social factors provides social researchers with invaluable insights into patterns of meaning making as well as the impact of social macro-structures on an individual's life. Biographical research taps into the individual cognitive processes that expose individual agency (the capacity to act independently and control outcomes) in the process of constant negotiation between individual will and the broader constraints of social structures.

Research question and research design

Understanding the constraints of biographical data brings the discussion on biographical methods to the issue of the research question and research design. The use of biographies in scientific inquiry requires that we understand what type of research questions can be answered with the help of biographical research. The unique strength of biographical research lies in its dynamic relationship between the individual and the social. Some disciplines may be more interested in individual processes, while others study structural adjustments, but biographies capture the dynamic relation between these two aspects over time. In the social sciences, a good research question should therefore address this dynamic relationship. There are three broad types of dynamic that are most suitable for biographical research and, depending on the specific academic discipline, they can be used to formulate a suitable research question:

1. The interplay between agency and structure – this is well-suited to biographical research. Life stories are accounts of an individual who executes their own biographical actions in ways that are framed by relevant social structures, which create opportunities or limitations for those specific actions. In this context, biographical research can tap into the areas of conflict between an individual and society, for example in studies of racial, class or gender injustice. It can also investigate the process of identity formation and belonging, for example in studying the formations of groups, communities and social movements.

2. The interplay between biographical and historical time – studying the interplay between the 'big' society-level stories and 'small' individual stories is a very exciting part of the biographical research agenda. Biographies include historical events as well as their individual interpretations, and are thus well suited to research questions that aim to tackle issues of collective memories and social forms of remembering. Biographical research is also applicable in investigating 'biographical work' that involves processes of sense making directed towards specific historical events and ideological shifts, such as migration, activism or war experiences, including the processes of legitimacy.

3. Trajectories of individual and social change – finally, biographical research is well-positioned to investigate research questions associated with sequences of individual and social change. Embedded in the concept of biographical trajectories, biographical data can be used to address issues associated with growth and decline in various aspects of life, including economic wellbeing, health and illness, and issues of social status or political power. Biographical research can focus on the personal narratives of growth, such as overcoming

a challenge or embracing fatherhood, as well as social narratives of change, including the emergence of precarious working conditions or issues of conflict reconciliation.

Understanding the types of questions that can be answered with the use of biographical methods is the first step in a successful research project. The next step involves a set of decisions that ensure the research design is best suited to answer the research question.

Designing your research

A decision on the research question is the first step in the process of designing your study. From this step onwards, think about what you need to answer your question, where to find your data, how to capture them and how you plan to process them. The decisions you make at the outset of your study will have significant consequences for the rest of your study, and the more informed your decisions are, the better. The greatest regret expressed by students in our biographical research training was: 'I wish I'd known this before I gathered my data.' To avoid disappointment later on, you should ask yourself what type of data you need to answer your research question.

Understanding the depth of biographical data

The modern world delivers numerous sources of narrative biographical material: various genres of literature, personal documents such as diaries, letters or blogs, and a range of forms of information-based, policy, academic and cultural materials are all widely accessible due to the exceptional growth of social media and digital archives. Those **naturally occurring data**, including biographical elements, can be used for scientific investigation and are often used within historical, literary and cultural studies, conversation and discourse analysis (Alleyne, 2015). Within the social sciences, however, more methodologically systematic and uniform data are desirable. A set of life stories, gathered with the use of uniform tools, in which the story is delivered, ideally in one attempt and in a situation that does not interfere in the storytelling, constitutes a methodologically strong data set that can be used in a variety of research designs. In this context, biographical narratives can be gathered by interview where 'the informant or respondent is treated as a repository of answers or stories about their inner life and social world. The interview is seen as a means of tapping into that repository' (Gubrium and Holstein, 2009: 37). Yet, biographical interviews can take very different forms, ranging from a relatively free-flowing narration to highly structured interviews (Roulston, 2011). This is particularly important, because the choice of interview technique will determine what type of analysis can be undertaken, thus directly affecting your ability to answer your research question.

Different types of biographical interviews are designed to achieve different biographical depth, where depth refers to the amount of detail and discursive richness of the information provided. The biographical depth depends on the researcher's ability – and often confidence – to relinquish control over the biographical story to the narrator. Some biographical interview techniques let the narrator tell their story in an unstructured way, giving the narrator the power to tell their life story in whichever way they find most relevant, including their selection of events, justifications and overall structure (see Chapter 4). Other types of biographical interviews assume more control over the process and impose a researcher's framework on the narration, directing the interview. This control can be relatively light-touch, when the researcher imposes some type of timeline on the narration or focuses it on specific life events (see Chapter 5), or quite significant, when the life story is told by answering direct questions (see Chapter 6).

Table 3.1 Research design implications, depending on depth of biographical data

Type of data	Unstructured	Semi-structured	Structured
Example	Autobiographical narrative interview (see Chapter 4)	Biographical narrative interview (see Chapter 5)	Structured life history interview (see Chapter 6)
Type of research question	Broad questions addressing the 'how' of the biographical process	Focused on addressing specific elements of the biography	Hypothesis addressing the relation between defined outcome and number of conditions
Sampling	Limited number of cases (between 1 and 10 per researcher)	Theoretical sampling to capture the variety (6–40 cases per researcher)	Purposive sampling, quota sampling (<50 per researcher)
Resources	Transcription of few very long interviews Time-consuming analysis of each case	Transcription of the interviews (or summaries) Qualitative data analysis software (Atlas.ti, NVivo, etc.)	Transcription of large data set Qualitative data analysis software (Atlas.ti, NVivo, etc.)
Analysis	Focus on content and narrative structure of each case	Focus on content of the narrative case and cross-case contrast	Focus on the configurations of conditions and cross-case comparison

The decision on the depth of the interview will directly impact your analytical options. The more control you impose during the interview, the more limited your choice and analytical robustness will be. This relation is embedded in the unstructured versus structured type of data. If the researcher asks about an event that they think is important, the narrator will almost always answer. In this situation, however, the researcher cannot assign any 'importance value' to the event, merely occurrence. When the narrator mentions the same event in a free-flowing narration and without any prompt, this can be used as an indicator of its vital importance. Subsequently, unstructured data offer more analytical choices and the more specific questions can be asked following the narrative part of the interview.

Choice of depth and decisions made on the level of control when designing your biographical interview tool constitute a balancing act. Beside questions about the accuracy and validity of data, and ethical decisions about the individual's voice and power, the researcher also needs to address more pragmatic aspects of the research design, most notably sampling as well as resources (including time) that can be used for the research project (see Table 3.1). The depth of the interview will have a significant impact on those resources.

Practical aspects of biographical research design
Selection of biographical interviews

Following the decision on your research question and assessment of the necessary depth of the data, your next step requires a decision on the selection and number of cases (see also Baker and Edwards, 2012). Biographical research belongs firmly in the domain of qualitative research methodology and follows a non-probabilistic way of obtaining subjects for the study. This sampling logic restricts the ability to generalise findings across the wider population but permits 'generalisation about the nature of the process' (Gobo, 2008b: 405). Depending on the research question and design decision regarding the type of biographical data, there are two sampling strategies that you can use in your study (see Table 3.2).

Table 3.2 Sampling strategies in biographical research

Sampling strategy	Description
Key informant interview	This approach samples individuals, who have relevant biographical experience
Theoretical sampling	This approach samples concepts that we wish to explore with biographical methods

The **key informant sampling** strategy implies a limited selection of narrators whose stories feature an important biographical experience that forms part of the research question. For example, in a study on conflict reconciliation, key informants would have biographical experience with conflict as well as reconciliation efforts. Analysis of such cases would focus on the individual process of sense making in the situation of conflict as well as the biographical work on reconciling internal and external tensions. This type of analysis would benefit from unstructured types of data, a free narration flow and a limited number of cases. The classic study of Schütze (1992) on the pressure and guilt of young German soldiers after the Second World War involves a biographical interview with just one informant (see Chapter 4).

Theoretical sampling, on the other hand, focuses on exploring a variety of biographical patterns. According to Strauss and Corbin (1990: 176), theoretical sampling aims to capture the type of experiences that 'are repetitively present or notably absent when comparing instances, and are of sufficient importance to be given a status of categories'. In a research project on transnational educational biographical experiences, the categories would be related to the aim of transnational mobility, such as language studies, Erasmus exchanges and undertaking a degree abroad. Those three categories of international students would have different expectations, mobility experiences and plans for the future. The categories that emerge from the theoretical sampling carry a 'theoretical relevance to the evolving theory' (1990: 176) and focus on the contrast between the cases. In a research design that employs a theoretical sampling strategy, one should aim for maximum representation of this variety, termed *theoretical saturation,* in order to identify as many categories as possible. The number of cases in this design needs to be negotiated with the depth of the interview. More structured data would allow for more cases, but with the risk that lack of depth could affect the contrast and variety between those cases.

Tip from the field

Be prepared to justify who you interview and why

The sampling of biographical cases is an important part of the study design, and this particular methodological aspect is often scrutinised as an indicator of research quality. Because samples in biographical studies are relatively small, your justifications for selection are particularly important in academic publications and dissertations.

There are also a number of sampling strategies that aim to increase the representativeness of qualitative findings. According to Gobo (2008b: 406), 'in order to obtain representativeness, the sampling plan needs to exist in dialogue with field incidents, contingencies and discoveries'. This dialogue with other findings is especially strong in mixed method approaches, for example where a representative survey sample is used with a select smaller sample of qualitative interviews aimed at illustrating all the possible situations (purposive sampling), or sub-set characteristics such as gender balance or ethnicity (quota sampling).

Transcription and translation

Biographical narrative interviews form a type of rich data where the details and the language are part of the analysis. In order to capture those features, it is normal practice to record biographical narratives (see also the ethics section on informed consent, below). At the stage of analysis, recordings are a difficult medium to work with. One of the most neglected considerations in qualitative research, especially in biographical methodologies, is the issue of transcribing recordings. The field of ethnomethodology and conversation analysis is a major exception, where very detailed transcription conventions apply to talk-in-interaction (ten Have, 2007). In an attempt to save time and avoid this time-consuming exercise, it can be tempting to opt out of full transcription and decide on making notes. In biographical research, this type of shortcut does not pay off. In the case of unstructured data, the analysis of sequences and processes requires a detailed transcript, and even the analysis of a larger number of highly structured interviews requires good quality transcripts. (We have provided advice and guidelines for transcript preparation in Appendix 1.)

The quality of transcripts depends on the depth to which researchers are planning to approach the biographical narration. According to Gubrium and Holstein (2009: 34), a transcript 'must be fine-tuned to capture sufficient conversational detail to support the form of narrative analysis under consideration'. In the autobiographical narrative interview method that uses unstructured biographical data, the transcription needs to indicate hesitations, word repetitions, reactions such as laughing breaks, and a general description of the interview situation. The amount of detail in the transcription increases even further when the researcher plans to investigate the interview interaction itself or the type of discourse. For the types of analysis that focus on the content, a simplified word-by-word transcript is usually sufficient.

—Tip from the field—

Choose your transcription strategy early

Depending on the research project resources, it is common practice to use a transcription service, but students often depend on their own typing and translation skills in the preparation of transcriptions. It is a time-consuming and quite frustrating process and for that reason it should be factored into the initial research design. Before you start, you should answer the following questions:

- How many interviews can I transcribe?
- How much funding do I have in my budget to pay for transcription (if any)?
- How can I translate transcripts (if you work in more than one language)?

There are also voice-recognition software packages and applications, such as Otter.ai and Dragon, that can help in transcription. Some are open source, while others require a small subscription. Their accuracy depends on the quality of recordings and may not pick up nuances, accents and dialect forms. However, this type of software is a valuable resource. You will still need to check your transcripts against the original recordings and format them to the required guidelines, for example including hesitation markers and time breaks. But if time is an issue, software can speed up the process.

As more students and international collaboration studies use English as a working language, the issue of translation has become one of the key technical issues for researchers. As with transcriptions, there are a number of shortcuts, such as translation of extracts and interview notes, that are often employed to reduce the costs and time. These shortcuts only create a temporary solution and become problematic in the long term. The process of academic review (for dissertations and for publications) often requires re-analysis of the empirical material. Those revisions are often required a long time after the manuscript has been prepared. Going back and re-translating different elements is very time-consuming and often makes the necessary adjustments more work-intensive. Translating all the empirical material into the project's working language should therefore be standard. For students, this will enable more thorough analysis and supervision; for joint research projects, it will facilitate more in-depth collaboration and review by team members.

The practical aspects around translation are very individual. For example, Riemann (2003) discusses in detail the translation issues involved in an interview conducted in German with a Turkish migrant, subsequently translated into English for international dissemination. Our preference is to translate simultaneously while transcribing, but some students decide to transcribe their interviews in the original language and then translate them. Having two transcripts in different languages makes it possible to engage in two different linguistic environments. If you would like to discuss your data in a different national context, it helps to have appropriate material. Depending on the resources, there is also the option of paid translations, but those depend on the language and scope of the interview transcripts.

Ethics

Research ethics is one of the more dynamic debates in the broad field of social sciences. Ethical paradigms are constantly shifting and, depending on the academic discipline, methodology and interests, ethical guidelines and requirements are negotiable. According to Ryen (2008: 218), 'ethical challenges are expected to be handled in accordance with the official ethical codes and regulatory institutions'. The process of ethics approval lies currently with a research institution's regulations (universities and research boards), but practices can be called into question at any stage of the research process, from submitting the research proposal to publishing the findings. For that reason, it is important to seek out your institutional guidelines as soon as possible and, when necessary, gain additional clarification from national research committees and associations related to your academic discipline.

Ethics considerations should relate to the purpose of the research. The collection of the data should always be justified. The 'gold standard' of ethical research involving human subjects comes originally from medical studies and is based on three fundamental ethical principles: informed consent, the distinction between private and public, and an assurance of anonymity and confidentiality. These principles present a set of challenges for many social science disciplines, as some research, for example covert observations, does not meet these standards. It is then up to the ethics board to weigh the merits of the study, all possible safeguards and the researcher's personal reputation against those three principles.

Biographical research methodology adheres well to the principle of informed consent. The most common practice is to prepare and use two documents – an information sheet and a consent form:

- **Information sheet** – this gives the narrator key information about the project and the person conducting the research. It should include your institutional affiliation and contact details. If you work as a team, you should list all the people involved in the fieldwork, and if you are a student, you should also name your project supervisor. A version of this document should be made available to the narrator before the study. In a situation where research participants cannot read or understand the information, there are other solutions. A recording of the researcher explaining the research with the participant's clear indication of understanding should be sufficient.

- **Consent form** – a document that outlines the participant's agreement to take part in the research. It should clearly state how data will be used (academic publications, expositions) and recorded (voice recording, video recording, pictures). Given the growing importance of data protection regulations, such as the EU General Data Protection Regulation (GDPR), it may also be a requirement to state how long the data will be stored for and with whom it may be shared. The consent form should include a statement on understanding the information provided about the research (contained in the information sheet) and the participant's ability to withdraw their consent at any stage of the process. The document should be signed by both participant and researcher. There are, however, situations where a signature is difficult to obtain. In some situations, cultural norms, appropriateness and the relative status of the interviewer may affect the ability to obtain a signature. In these cases, it should be sufficient to record verbal consent.

The second principle of distinction between the private and public is more problematic. In medical studies, this distinction translates into the findings' aggregate nature. While private information, such as that a given person has diabetes, cannot be used, the aggregate information of how many people in the UK have diabetes is public information and can be used in research. Biographical research, along with other qualitative methods, has to tread a more indistinct line between private and public. Participation in research is voluntary and it is thus the participant's choice to make elements of their private life story public by telling them to the interviewer. However, problems and complications can appear in cases where the participant cannot make that voluntary choice, for example because of their diminished capacity or young age, as well as in situations where the information made public involves other people's private information. In this case, you will need additional clarification from your ethics board.

Finally, an assurance of anonymity and confidentiality should be part of the information sheet and consent form. This principle places the responsibility on the researcher to assure the safety of the material gathered during the research study and to protect the identity of participants. Secure data storage should be part of the ethics review, and most research institutions have encrypted 'server' space for data, but special care must be taken when sharing data with partners and using any third-party services, for instance for transcription and translation. This rule applies not only during the research project, but also after the project has ended when the data are archived and available for secondary analysis. This element is often overlooked in the fever of active research projects. As most research is publicly funded, the data gathered should not go to waste. In the UK, for example, most public funders require that data are archived. It is the researcher's responsibility to ensure that this process does not violate the confidentiality principle.

Most biographical data should be anonymised, which obviously includes the names of people and places. The procedures of anonymisation should be transparent. The researcher should keep a detailed log of name changes, to assure that in the future people with relevant access clearance can track back any relevant information. This process requires good data management and should follow the guidelines of the institution responsible for data archives. It is also common practice to embargo access to the data for some time, for example 10 years, as a way of ensuring the confidentiality principle.

To summarise, biographical data set archive standards consist of:

- fully transcribed and translated interviews with anonymised content
- a confidential log file listing the changes you have made to the transcripts in the process of anonymisation (including page numbers)
- a consent form for each transcript in your set
- a confidential log of all interviews with all key interview information (including date of the interview, interviewer's name and interviewee's details, such as name, age, gender, contact details).

Adherence to ethical guidelines and the rulings of ethical boards have become an essential stage in the research process for students, researchers and academics alike. However, with shifting interdisciplinary ethical standards and the profoundly disruptive effect of technologies, some ethical concerns transcend the standard guidelines of research practice and touch upon broader cultural issues that are associated with the power relations within society. This dimension of ethics discussion centres on the core principles of the value of research as a contribution to knowledge, the integrity of the research process, and respect for research participants in all circumstances. It is built on recognising the power relations within your field of study, awareness of those power relations while you are in direct contact with participants during your fieldwork, and understanding what implications your findings may carry for those people who trusted you with the information. These aspects of professional ethical codes are built on reflexivity, the ability to reflect on your role in the research process and handle the consequences of your actions for the people you research.

Biographical research in the field

Organising the project – individual and collaborative research projects

Biographical research methods are relatively versatile. Biographical data can be used in a variety of academic disciplines and can provide relevant empirical material to answer a large number of research questions. Biographical research methods can be applied within various research environments, including student projects, research projects and collaborative research. The scope of work will determine the research design and the level of control over the methodological approach:

- Student projects are small by their very nature. The sample and resources are limited, and they tend to be exploratory in nature. The key difficulty of this type of project organisation lies in the fact that the student is often alone during the process of gathering the data and primary analysis. Input from a supervisor is crucial for the development of the research practice as well as for organising findings.
- Small and collaborative research projects have a more supportive structure. Their multi-level system, with one or more primary investigators (PIs) and the input of research fellows (RFs) and research assistants (RAs), changes the dynamics of gathering and analysing data. The resources allow for bigger samples and more elaborate discussion, and there is also more scope for teaching and learning. These research teams can, however, be hierarchical, and entry-point positions for assistants will not leave much room for them to control the direction of research and its outcomes.

This distinction between types of research experience has a significant impact on how we teach and learn methodology. Student projects work for some but require supervisor guidance, whereas a research project offers practical skills but can be limiting in terms of individual growth. The best way to learn is probably to engage in both – to explore your own interests but also to observe the research practice of more experienced researchers.

Study 1

Biographical Study of African Women in Higher Education Abroad – A case study of African women in the UK (da Conceição Manjate, MA thesis, Bangor University, 2020)

Neila's MA fieldwork included nine biographical narrative interviews with African women studying at Bangor University at the MA and PhD levels. The study aimed to uncover the barriers African women have to overcome to access higher education.

The results of this research revealed that patriarchal structures embodied in African societies lead to experiences both in the private and public spheres that represent barriers to higher education. They involve the conflict between parents' verbal encouragement to education and assertiveness versus unequal gender relations between parents and among siblings; role strain; social practices and beliefs that encourage the prioritisation of early marriage instead of education; gender stereotypes and sexual violence against women at school. It was evident that barriers to education that do not stem from economic and demographic issues are often neglected, perpetuating the low access of African women to higher education. Socio-cultural beliefs and practices constitute some of the main hidden barriers to higher education in Africa. It is time to acknowledge that, to change this *status quo*, a positive social environment needs to be created, not hostile to women's higher achievements in education, and leading to more female role models, ultimately resulting in sustainable development.

Study 2: PhD Project

'Not from a Book': The acquisition of knowledge and its use in practice by social workers, with particular regard to alcohol, by Wulf Livingston, Bangor University (2013)

This doctoral research project investigated the relationship between alcohol and social work, and the professions' response to the increasing prevalence of alcohol in practitioners' workloads, leading to calls for more effective intervention responses. The problem is often reflected in the demand for social workers to receive more education about alcohol. This study instead highlights how they acquire knowledge and understanding of alcohol and its use in practice. Knowledge frameworks are likely to include both codified and non-codified elements. The study adopted a mixed method qualitative design which employed a self-administered questionnaire, extended biographical narrative interviews and case study vignettes with 15 social workers. The interviews elicited rich material on personal and professional experiences over the life course and how they interacted.

Four distinct themes developed from the analysis of the data. The first relates to the knowledge that social workers acquire from their own everyday experiences of drinking. The second draws on key work-based experiences of alcohol and how they complicate frameworks of understanding. The third is about the relationship between formal and informal knowledge acquisition that is displayed within the data. The final theme explores how spaces for extended dialogue, both within the workplace and research, can contribute to a greater understanding of the social work–alcohol relationship and the implications for social work education, policy, practice and research.

Organisation of the biographical narrative interview and the interviewer's skill set

The biographical narrative interview is underpinned by the intricate power dynamic between the narrator and the interviewer. Narrating your life story is a unique experience for the narrator, who is asked to assemble a continuous and coherent (Linde, 1993) life story that is embedded in (often difficult) formative experiences. More so than in ordinary interviews, the social interaction between interviewer and interviewee impacts on the quality and character of the life story. According to Gubrium and Holstein (2009: 39), 'in everyday life, the "same" account changes in meaning and in its consequences, depending on speakers' and listeners' purposes and the circumstances'. The role of the interviewer in the biographical narrative interview should be to foster and encourage this process of narration, but, more often than not, the interviewer exerts their control over the situation and interrupts the narrative process of narration. This is often done unconsciously – the interviewer is losing patience, wants to reciprocate by sharing some of their own experience, or simply help when the narrator is struggling. Good biographical research training and reflexive practice, which often come when you read your own interview transcript alone, with your supervisor or an expert, are the main pathways to developing your own interviewer skill set. Some general guidelines to the interview process are outlined below:

1. First contact and interview setting – depending on your sampling technique, finding the right narrators is an important skill. If your project is based on key informants, you may already have the right person in mind, or you may ask the person you know about for a recommendation. Known as snowballing, this technique is common and can be used in smaller research projects. Bigger samples are drawn more systematically from lists of people displaying certain characteristics, such as a list of alumni engaged in an international exchange from a university, or a sample of a national panel study. In most cases, initial contact is made via phone, an introduction letter or e-mail. This introduction should provide some information about the project as well as a possible time and place for the interview.

When organising the interview, you should be particularly mindful of the following:

*   **Space** – the location of the interview will affect the narration process. People will not feel comfortable sharing their story in a busy place, with many people around (which may also affect your recording's audio quality), but they may also be intimidated if you invite them to your office at the university, where you clearly have greater symbolic power. The most comfortable place for a biographical narrative interview would be the

interviewee's residence, but this may come with its own distractions, such as children running around and other adults interfering. Calm and cosy public spaces may be a good solution for people who feel uncomfortable about inviting you to their home, and they also increase your safety as the interviewer. As a researcher, you need to factor in all these aspects and choose the most appropriate space for your interview.

- **Time** – the length of the biographical interview will depend on its form and the skill of the interviewer. The longest interview we've come across was 5 hours long with a 70-page transcript. As most of the interviews will take 1–2 hours, you may want to make sure that there are no urgent upcoming deadlines that might rush the narrator. It is better to have more time outside the interview, for your introduction and post-interview chat, than to have an unfinished narration due to time constraints.

- **Online interviews** are a relatively new development in biographical research. Due to the cost of travel and time restrictions, online interviews appear to be highly efficient. They solve the issue of location, with both parties in their own space, but they do affect the time management of the interview, the type of rapport you are able to build with limited contact, and the ability to observe the participant's behaviour in the environment as well as their body language. A face-to-face interview is therefore still the quality gold standard for biographical interviews, but online interviewing is growing in popularity.

The first part of the interview is often informal, but in interpreting the interview later it can be important to keep a note on the circumstances of the interview. The note may look like this:

> I heard about Gosia from a mutual friend at university. I contacted her via e-mail in Polish and she responded to me in English. When we first met, she explained that her Polish was rather limited and she preferred to give her interview in English. That was due to the fact that she moved away from Poland when she was young, and she and her mother had been living in Germany. The interview took place at university, in the student canteen. It was holiday season and we were there alone. As a psychology student she was very interested in the technique of biographical narrative interviewing.

2. Starting the interview and asking the first question – the start of the interview includes introductions and a project explanation. It is during this part that the information sheet and consent form are exchanged (unless there was an earlier opportunity to complete this stage). The interviewer should be able to

answer any key questions and assure the research participant of their rights to confidentiality and anonymity.

This moment forms an important part of rapport building as it establishes the power dynamic within the interaction. It is in this situation that the interviewer sets the rules for the narration:

- If the aim of the interview is to **obtain an unstructured**, free-flow narration, you need to establish the narrator as a 'hero in their own life story'. This can be done by highlighting the 'worth' of this particular individual's story for the study and the significance of the narrator's individual perspective. The narrator needs to own the power over their narrative, and the role of the interviewer is to nurture that confidence by limiting their own interference in the process.
- If the aim of the interview is to **elicit the narrative, but with the specific direction** in mind, the interviewer needs to learn how to gently direct the flow of narration to the subject, using non-verbal cues if possible. Usually, asking a direct question will overpower the narrator.
- If the aim of the narration is **to find specific answers to a question**, the interview will take the form of a conversation, where two parties are in an exchange of power. The interviewer claims the right to ask questions and for the participant to answer them. This power exchange depends on personalities, but the successful interview will depend on the balance between the two.

The type of biographical research questions and interview structure depends on the theoretical and methodological choices of the study (Chapters 4, 5 and 6 will expand on these choices). But there are some key characteristics of a good interview technique that should be a part of the interviewer's skill set:

- **Active listening** is the ability to listen with attention and interest and to encourage the flow of narration with short verbal and non-verbal cues, such as eye contact, nodding and phrases such as 'I see' or 'Really?'. Active listening is not an easy skill and requires practice. Inexperienced interviewers often get impatient or lose their focus during an interview and miss important elements of the life story.
- **Fostering narration rather than argumentation** – a biographical interview is based on the mode of narration, with the interviewee outlining their actions across time. The narrative answers the question of 'how' things happened. During the biographical interview, there will also be some elements of argumentation, where the narrator feels the need

to justify their actions, and this is a valuable part of the interview. But when argumentation takes over, the interview becomes an opinion rather than a story. This can happen when the interviewer asks 'why' questions, indicating to the narrator that additional justifications are needed.

- **Identifying the significant biographical themes** – during the narrative part of the interview, it is important to keep the flow of narration, but in the background the interviewer should identify significant biographical themes and those elements of the story which seem to be missing. Those should be noted and explored after the narrative part of the life story has ended.

3. Finishing the interview and asking further questions – the biographical narrative interview comes to its natural end when the narrator does not have anything else to add, but, depending on the particular interview technique (see Chapters 4, 5 and 6), after the natural finish to the narrative there is scope to ask more specific questions. These can build on the interviewer's observations as well as themes relevant to the specific research question. This period of the interview is quite productive. After a spell of narration, the interview situation has usually reached a level of ease and relaxed comportment. It is important to use it to the best advantage.

The end of the interview should come with an expression of gratitude and assurance of the interviewee's rights. Some of the narrators may ask to see a transcript and those wishes should be noted and granted. The narrator may also request some changes to the transcript and those should also be fulfilled.

Summary

In this chapter, we discussed the nature of biographical research and its potential and limitations in scientific investigation. Biographical narratives are a subjective type of data that follow sets of cultural rules that need to be decoded for scientific inquiry. Those rules include the narrative point of view, the cultural constraints on the storytelling process and the understanding of the relation between the subjective and objective truth. Cultural codes focus the types of research questions that can be answered, with the use of biographical research methods on issues such as the interplay between agency and structure, historical and biographical time, and broader social change. We explored two main implications for biographical research design and methods, including the understanding of biographical depth as well as practical concerns such as access to a sample, and the availability of time and other resources that determine the size and scope of a research project. We discussed ethi-cal concerns and ethics best practice principles for biographical narrative interviews. Then we outlined the researcher and narrator relationships in the field, such as the organisation of research projects, including both student projects as well as small and collaborative research projects. The final part of the chapter explored the bio-graphical interviewer's skill set, outlining the personal competences that enhance the biographical narrative interview.

Questions to consider

1. How do we address the question of truthfulness in biographical research?
2. What are the methodological implications of naturally occurring biographical data and those generated by a biographical/life story interview?
3. What types of research questions can be answered with biographical research methods?
4. What practical implications should be considered in the design of biographical research projects?
5. Why is it important to understand the relation between the depth of the biographical narrative data and analytical frameworks?

4

AUTOBIOGRAPHICAL NARRATIVE INTERVIEW METHOD

Objectives

By the end of this chapter, you will be able to:

- Recognise the potential of unstructured biographical narrative data
- Be familiar with the theoretical background of Schütze's autobiographical narrative interview method
- Be familiar with the data gathering and data analysis procedures associated with the autobiographical narrative interview method
- Identify the types of communicative pattern: narration, description and argumentation
- Understand the relevance of biographical event sequence
- Identify relevant process structures: trajectories and action schemes
- Understand how to make generalisations using autobiographical narrative interview data.

Biographical narrative research can take very different forms. Depending on the analytical choices and research design, it can be calibrated to answer different types of research questions. The main distinction is based on the depth of biographical material, which includes the narrator's level of control over the narration process and the analytical approach chosen to take advantage of this type of biographical data. This chapter outlines the approach to unstructured biographical narrative data and demonstrates the methodological procedures associated with the autobiographical narrative interview method. Developed by the German scholar Fritz Schütze, this method is designed to capture and analyse biographical narratives to answer research questions that explore the relevance of 'how biographies are told, and why they are told in this way'. This type of investigation focuses on the narrative process structures of the account and its narrative sequences in a way that explores an individual's perceptions of the social positions of individual agents within broader social structures. This chapter outlines the method's background, the type of interview method that elicits unstructured biographical narratives, and the analytical procedures as well as examples of the method's application and generalisations.

Method background – exploring the grammar of a life story

The foundations for the autobiographical narrative interview method were laid by Fritz Schütze and are anchored in several theoretical traditions, including the phenomenology of Alfred Schütz (1972) and the symbolic interactionism of Anselm Strauss (1995). The method is 'a process-analytical procedure which provides an idea of the genesis of the course of social events and records social reality from the perspective of acting and suffering subjects' (Schütze, 1983, cited in Apitzsch and Siouti, 2007: 7). The autobiographical interview is a multi-layered account of social reality seen from the individual's perspective. According to Kallmeyer and Schütze (1976), the autobiographical narrative linguistically structures the life story with the use of three communication schemes: argumentation, description and narration. Among these three, the narration provides an insight into the areas of social actions, argumentation is used as a tool for evaluation and justification, and description allows the interviewee to place their story within a specific set of circumstances. In the autobiographical narrative interview method, we encourage narration rather than argumentation or a description of events to gain an insight into the process of negotiation between an individual agent and the social structures, and to understand the wider context of social change. This technique is used to reconstruct the process of creation, reproduction and transformation of psychological and social phenomena, to understand the course of biographical action as well as to retrospectively interpret the biographical events (Rosenthal, 2008: 50).

Schütze's methodology is unique and, over the last few decades, it has been used in several academic fields and been further developed by a number of bio-graphical researchers in Germany (such as Gabriela Rosenthal, Ursula Apitzsch and Lena Inowlocki) and Poland (Kaja Kazmierska, Marek Czyzewski and Irena Szlachcicowa). More loosely associated with this tradition are researchers from France (Catherine Delcroix and Daniel Bertaux) and the UK (including Tom Wengraf and Prue Chamberlayne). Currently, a new generation of biographical research is emerging, bringing innovative developments in research application into different academic and non-academic fields and expanding on methodologies, including more elaborate mixed method designs and use of technology.

Autobiographical narrative interview method and data collection

The autobiographical narrative interview method collects the whole life story, narrated from the perspective of the individual narrator with minimal interfer-ence from the interviewer. The interview aims to elicit the narrative, to make the narrator tell their story. This is not as simple as it seems. The contemporary text-based culture is mostly equipped to use argumentation rather than narration. People are used to being asked about specific opinions and attitudes, so often feel a little lost when asked to tell their story, especially if they do not feel confident about the significance and worthiness of their narrative. It is the subtle skill of the interviewer to frame the interview situation within an environment that sup-ports a narrative account, without imposing the interviewer's structure on the narrative.

The autobiographical narrative interview has two distinctive parts. First, the period of the main narration begins when the narrator is asked to tell their life story. During that part, the interviewer should not ask any other questions. When the narration comes to its natural end, we enter the second part of the interview, where the interviewer can ask direct questions. Those questions, however, should be related to the narrative part. This section aims to pick up on the most relevant parts of the biographical account, asking the narrator to explore them in more depth and in the form of the narrative. When this part is over, the third section of the inter-view allows for more specific questions that should nonetheless relate to the biographical narrative (see Table 4.1).

Table 4.1 The sequence of the autobiographical narrative interview

The sequence of an autobiographical narrative interview:

1. Period of main narration – built around the individual life story.

2. Questioning period, including:

    a. Internal narrative questions – queries about the events told in the narrative part;

    b. External narrative questions – queries about the researcher's specific interest relating to the biographical narrative.

Source: Adapted from Rosenthal (2008: 50)

Period of main narration and the issue of the first question

A crucial part of the autobiographical narrative interview, which is the subject of detailed discussion in the literature, is the skill of eliciting the narration by asking the right first question in the right way (Domecka et al., 2012). According to Rosenthal (2008), within the first period of the 'main narration', the interviewer explains the idea of the autobiographical narrative interview and activates the narration process by asking the interviewee, 'Please, tell me your life story'. In order to open an unobstructed narrative flow, the interviewer needs to connect with the narrator and build mutual understanding about what a biographical interview is. The interviewer should also be prepared to outline the interview procedure and address the interviewee's concerns without prompting. Below is an extract from one of the Euroidentities projects that includes a well-set first question:

I: OK. So let's start the interview. So I just told you the idea is to –erm-// you were just going to tell me about the story of your life and how you became the person whom you are today/. And /ehm/ I'm not going to interrupt you and you can just start, probably –eh-, with your very first memory

N: -Mmh mmh-

I: And then just continue as you like.

N: Yes.

I: OK. And if there's any, you know, if you're, sometimes if there's silences that's no problem. If you like need some time to think.

N: Ah. - Right, OK, so will I say who I am and?

I: Yeah.

N: Or not, yeah?

I: Yeah you can, yeah.

N: OK, well I am ...

This first element of the interview requires a relationship of trust to be established before the interview begins. The state of the interactional power balance is a very important issue. Where one party is required to share often very personal events from their life, the interviewer needs to find a way to make the narrator feel comfortable with it. This often lies in the sphere of the interviewer's interpersonal skills. It is common practice for the interviewer to share some elements of their own life with the interviewee before or after the interview.

An additional difficulty in asking the first question is the possibility of leading the interviewee's answer into the areas of the interviewer's initial interests. This is especially the case where we select the narrator because they represent a specific concept in our theoretical sample. At that point, the narrator knows about the aim of our research (as a part of gaining informed consent), and this knowledge may influence the type of story they choose to tell. For example, in the Euroidentities project, some teams and interviewers included the interest in Europe in the opening question. Individual interviewing styles, and judgements of the interview situation, were the main reasons for introducing a Europe-probe into the question:

I: So, as I told you before, this is part of a project looking at people and notions of identity. So, If you'd like to tell me the story of your life, in any way you want, in any order that you want and while you're doing it, I'll make a few notes.

N: OK

I: Things I want you to clarify after, because I don't want to interrupt you as we go along. So

N: It's going to be a little monologue ((laughing))

I: Just a monologue – however you want to say it.

N: Yeah..

I: OK. As I say, we know that you are Dutchman. If you could talk about the story of your life and the way Europe you think Europe has affected your life. I will make notes as you go along. So would you like to introduce yourself now, and start however you want?

N: OK. My name is …

An interesting aspect of the first question is that, as soon as the narration unfolds, the first question loses its impact. While at the beginning the issue of Europe may have an impact on the choice of events, due to the constraints of biographical narration (see Chapter 3), interviewees lose themselves in their own story when they are in a narrative flow. What can go wrong at this stage is the first question being too direct, as this changes the narrative communication scheme from narration into argumentation or description. In an attempt to help the narrator to start, one of our interviewers early in the study mentioned that she was interested in the narrator's travels. This resulted in an hour-long interview which outlined

the places the narrator had visited and still plans to visit. This shows how important it is for the narrative interview to start off correctly and ensure that a record
is kept of the first question, as this may shed light on the biographical content
during the analysis.

During this opening part of the interview, the interviewer is expected to actively
listen to the narration and note down possible questions and discrepancies without
disturbing the free-flow narrative. Active listening can be challenging for the interviewer (Domecka et al., 2012: 41). Probing for more detailed information is second
nature to a skilled interviewer. However, in the case of an autobiographical narrative
interview, the urge to dig deeper into biographical experiences should be restrained.
On the other hand, there are situations where the interviewee might need some
help from the interviewer in keeping the temporal structure of the events, or getting
back to the narration when the interview is interrupted.

Narrative questions

The second part of the interview includes more direct questions. These are based on
observations from the first part of the interview. They should be asked in a manner
that encourages the narrator to go back into storytelling mode, including more
details and clarification on how it fits the bigger picture. This stage of the narrative
interview also shows the narrator that you listened and heard the story and that you
have found it interesting enough to ask for more detail. It is general practice here
to ask biographical questions first, usually starting with earlier experiences and following them to the most recent. External questions should come last, mostly
because they tend to turn into argumentative and descriptive modes of communication, after which it is very difficult to get back into narrative mode again.

Analytical procedures in the autobiographical narrative interview method

Together with a particular interview technique, the autobiographical narrative
interview method requires a specific analytical framework that captures the narrative structure of the life story. The analysis focuses on the sequential patterns of life
events that run throughout the biography and specific process structures that provide an insight into the power relationship between individual agency and social
structures. The analysis focuses first on the overall narrative shape of the story and
then investigates particular trajectories that support the biographical construction
of the story.

Structural sequences

The autobiographical narrative interview transcript is a self-contained textual frame, with clear indications of the story's beginning and end. Each element of that textual frame carries analytical meaning. The beginning of the life story, referred to as the preamble, sets out the main threads of the life story that carry on throughout the narrative. The biographical coda, or the life story's ending, usually ties up those threads and brings the narrator to the present situation. Analysing preamble and coda alongside each other often reveals interesting symmetries. The following two extracts come from an interview with Dean, an international NGO worker from the UK, who was interviewed as a part of the Euroidentities project. In these two extracts, we can identify the main biographical threads that his biography is constructed around.

Preamble

I: Tell me your life story as, you know, you think it unfolded.

Dean: Sure. Well, I guess like everyone, I'll probably start when I was born. I was born in London but I when I was six weeks old I moved to Nigeria. With my parents uh who were uh working as VSOs at the time.

I: A VSO is?

Dean: Voluntary Service uh Organisation, Voluntary Service Overseas and in fact, and my father subsequently worked in Nigeria, so I went there and we lived there 'til I was about three. And, I don't remember much about those first things in Nigeria but I do, I do feel that, you know, it and the other subsequent travel has sort of shaped me. But those first three years – were in Nigeria. Now while I was in Nigeria, and I've never worked out exactly when, but my parents divorced and because my mother met another man while we were in Nigeria together.

And so about the time that I was three, four – my parents, well my parents divorced – and from my point of view its been a very amicable divorce, there hasn't really – there's no obvious sort of difficulties on my part, but we'll come back to that ((fast)). So I came back from Nigeria and I lived with my mum in London and we stayed here until I was about nine and then we moved to Ireland. And we moved to Ireland with my step father because my step father got a job at the university in in Dublin. I was ((5 sec)) I think you know my,- I don't have many memories of those, at least I don't consciously, I kind of don't have a conscious memory of the of those sort of early years. I have sort of subsequently been to therapy and they've said, you know it seems like there were lots of problems happening and things and maybe that's the reason why you haven't, you know. You don't remember certain things, but well

I don't know. But I one of the big things that shaped me in those early years was I had a medical condition, which I still have.

This preamble starts in the way that biographies usually begin, with the statements 'when I was born' and 'when I was a child'. At the same time, it brings to the surface the three main threads that will constitute the most important biographical trajectories of Dean's life. The first is associated with his international development work that was 'shaped' by his early experiences of international mobility. This trajectory highlights a wider connection between Dean's parents' commitment to international development and his own career choices. The second is his parents' divorce, which set up a difficult relationship between Dean and his parents and a traumatic relationship with his step-father. These relationships turn out to be the source of hardship and conflict in his life, where he struggles for control over his own biographical choices. The third trajectory is his struggle with a medical condition that he feels has negatively impacted his sense of agency, causing feelings of shame and disempowerment. In the coda, the same threads appear, but from the perspective of accomplished life challenges.

Coda

Dean: And the big point for me was that I've always been very scared of self-catheterisation. Which is what I need to do to control, for me, to give me back control rather than always just flopping in front of the consultant. You know, I actually, this is very important, – but I've never been able to do it. I wasn't able to do it because … it had huge associations for me of times when I'd been hospitalised and they'd force catheterised me, which was really painful and, you know, awful stuff. But before we went to Bangkok, you know, the scarring was continuing the problems were recurring and I realised that I was going to have, you know, I mean, there were people in Bangkok that I could deal with but you know this wasn't really very sensible. I had to deal with this. And they'd been saying to me for a while, you know, you should really consider self-catheterisation – and I finally decided that yes I would and the nurse showed me how to do it and I did it and it wasn't as awful as I thought and it gave me a huge, well, freedom for one and control over my own illness and, // was really the thing that, you know, I thought well, I can go to Bangkok now because you know I can control this and I took a whole load of catheters with me. And I still do and you know every couple of weeks I self-catheterise. And it's fine, it's just become part of, you know, my life like injecting insulin or something, you know. It's just something that you do and it's not a big issue, but for me it was huge and the fact that I got beyond it makes me feel very, makes me feel good about myself.

I: You can control it.

Dean: Yeah, in control which for me is very important. I've always wanted to be in control. ((laughing)) One of the very silly things about me being in control is over my office, you know, in the back yard[1] and the fact that I've got it you know the way that I want it. And I get very, jumpy when Ann goes in there ((laughing)). Because – she never turns things off quite the way it should be and she leaves things around and it's just, you know, so I have to go in after her – and clear it all up and put it back the way I like it.[...] So I think I mean I can't think of anything else really. /Ehm/ I don't know, do you have any questions, or anything that you think?

In the coda, Dean combines his fight for independence from a difficult medical condition, with the ability to take his dream job and move to Bangkok with his family. In his attempt to conquer his fear, he gains a sense of agency that allows him the freedom to resolve other elements of his biography, including building stable family relations and progressing his international career as an NGO professional.

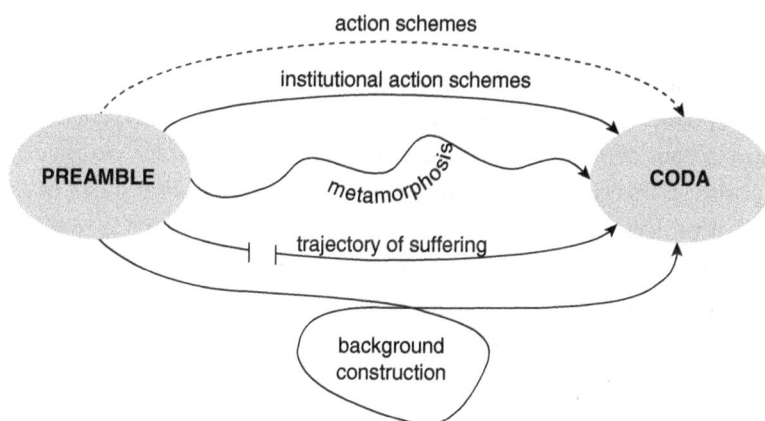

Figure 4.1 The analytical structure of the autobiographical narrative interview

The biographical preamble and coda enclose the narrative structure of the story and create the framework for the analysis of specific threads that entwine with each other, creating an intricate system of dependencies (see Figure 4.1). This system includes conscious and unconscious aspects of biographical work (Kohli, 2005) that cannot be accessed via direct questions. This aspect of autobiographical narrative interview analysis is the main analytical advantage of unstructured biographical data. The next step of the analysis is to investigate the narrative forms of the specific biographical threads.

---

[1]The office is at the back of the house, in a separate 'small garden house'. Dean refers to it as a posh shed.

Identifying narrative process structures

The autobiographical narrative is built as a sequence of narrative units, with the particular events captured in the form of the biographical thread. The biographical thread can be understood as a story within the story, where the specific thread comes into the forefront of the autobiographical narration to indicate biographical changes through time. The autobiographical narrative interview method focuses on the narrative forms of those biographical threads. It looks closely at 'how these events were told' to capture the process that the individual went through. The original terminology used by Schütze refers to these as process structures. In his work, he distinguishes four main process structures – action scheme, institutional action scheme, metamorphosis and trajectory of suffering – that capture the relation between the narrator's agency and conditions in the wider social and cultural context. The process structures capture perceptions of power throughout the unfolding life story, either in the form of individual empowerment or a sense of powerlessness.

Biographical action scheme

The biographical action scheme is used by the narrator when speaking about planned and executed actions. These refer to individual choices made by the narrator that are possible because of pre-existing opportunities. Action schemes indicate a situation of confidence and control over one's life course, where plans and dreams can be positively executed. This type of process structure often looks like a small biographical project, where the individual claims responsibility for making things happen. The extract below comes from an autobiographical narrative interview with Sarah, a Brazilian who was a mature language student at a British university at the time of the interview. Her narrative is full of projects mapped out to achieve her greatest goal, to recapture her Italian roots and move to Italy:

> But all in all we've had a very interesting life because we [Sarah and her husband] are driven by projects. Obviously we didn't stop the [living in Italy] project, we start again with fingers crossed a new project and I decided to learn the language and I started to learn the language just listening to RAI, you know 'RAI televisione', the Italian channel in Brazil, so I learned a lot and I learned more Italian in Brazil than I learned there, when I lived there [...] and I had a bright idea because it's me, to start a new career so, and I started to start nursing. [...] And I studied nursing for 3 years and for me it was a project as well because the Italian government they were taking nurses from countries which offered in, which was a programme just designated to Italian people living abroad. [...] It was my case. They are

intentional to get the best nurses abroad, Italian ones, which was my case
to go to Italy and to get a job straight away in – the health public sector in
Italy. And I start to study because I am such impatient we started this project
and to how can I say to be a nurse because amazingly I had such a desire to
do something quite a challenge for me. [Sarah, 44, Brazil]

Interestingly, Sarah's project leads her to study Italian in the UK, where her son
moved to pursue his studies. Sarah's investment in personal projects that are constantly adjusted due to changes in her family relations gives the impression of
personal drive and grit, but it follows a biogeographical thread of international
mobility. The biographical trajectory that is told in the sequence of action schemes
indicates Sarah's ability to identify the conditions and restrictions set by social
structures, such as the ability to speak the language, and find spaces where she can
gain a foothold to keep moving in the desired direction, that is her plan to become
a nurse to better fit the Italian migration system.

Institutional action scheme

An 'institutional action scheme' refers to a situation where the narrator sees the
source of their decision-making process within prevailing institutional patterns and
guidelines. This type of action scheme carries notions of control over one's life,
while simultaneously revealing the complex structure of available social scripts,
which the individual is encouraged to follow. These can encompass educational
trajectories or career patterns, but also power relations within organisations, communities and families. The following extract comes from an autobiographical
narrative interview with Jakub, who went to France on an international study
exchange. During this time, he mastered the language and entered the professional
world of IT specialists in an international company:

After the Bachelor's degree, they already valued me at the university. Because
in a couple of classes particularly the IT ones, like Access, like IT-classes, such
as, I don't know, even the statistics and math, I had [top grades]
[...] So at university I've made quite a name for myself. And so they told me
'OK, you can apply to' [for an internship]. And so I submitted my papers
to one of the companies. To X. It turned out that the X corporation had its
international headquarters in Lyon. So I applied there. And it turned out
that they were looking for someone precisely for this, this programme, as
among others, they had some project to run in Poland. And so they thought
'man, we've got a Pole. Fantastic, we're taking him!' [...] I won't deny, this
internship opened many doors for me. Because, well, X in France is just like

some big corporation. [...] X was a company that would open all the doors for you in France. And I managed to be taken on, to their technological centre. So, as a young guy, I thought I couldn't have done better. [...] But remember: I still had [to work in a] hotel. Well, I decided not to quit the hotel, because even though we worked at that company, but they paid us some close to nothing. 100 Euro a month, so really, ridiculous for the work we were doing. Well, but I treated it more in terms of an investment. I thought, OK, I'll bear this. I discussed it at the hotel. At the hotel it was all right as well and they were understanding. [Jakub, 32, Poland]

A narrative's institutional action scheme often feels like getting on a slide: there is intention at the beginning of the process, but then things take over. The individual enters the framework of opportunities, where one thing leads to another by the force of inertia. These opportunity structures are often institutional and include well-developed progression patterns, such as education or professional career. Jakub still has a sense of his accomplishments, such as good grades and professional qualities. However, there is a strong presence of the structural factors, such as the internship programme that links his university degree with a major corporation in France, then the international project framework that expanded into the Polish market at that point in time. Institutional action schemes are a good indicator for 'roads well-travelled' and social mobility.

Metamorphosis

Biographical metamorphosis is the pattern that occurs at times of intensive personal development, when the narrator is encountering and experiencing new and unexpected possibilities. Biographical metamorphosis is a complex process structure, which often attaches meaning to biographical experiences in terms of values and convictions. It includes a complex set of changes in response to certain external circumstances, together with a process of embracing and internalising new social structures and new biographical paths. The extract below comes from an autobiographical narrative interview with Dean, the international NGO professional working in the field of international development who was mentioned in the section on preamble and coda. We already identified this as one of the main threads of his life story. The extract below shows what he considers to be his turning point:

So at nine I went to Calcutta, to India, and spent a month with him [father] and I got the shock of my life [...] I think was very important in a very positive way in my life in Calcutta was that one day, you know, I was living the high life, we had servants, we had a big house, we had a chauffeur driven car, you know it was really, it was like, you know, colonial times, yeah. [...] I was going to lunch with him one day and was being taken by the chauffeur in the car to his office and the window was, the air conditioning in the car had broken down and the windows were open, and in Calcutta there are lots of railway lines criss-crossing the city, so you have to stop quite regularly to, you know, wait for trains to pass, and we stopped at these lights and the chauffeur was gesticulating at me to wind my window up and I didn't really understand why and, you know. And suddenly the, this person who was begging shoved the stump of his arm into my face and was begging for money. And I was so shocked. I mean it was absolutely a frightening, frightening thing, a shocking thing. And you know shooing him away and all that. But the interesting thing was that, from then on, I began to notice, really, really notice, the poverty, the deprivation, the way that people were living and I, you know it. You can see these things and you can really see these things and of course they were there all around me before but I suddenly start to notice. And I think, you know, it was at that point that I really started to ask myself that question, you know, of why. You know this, of this issue of injustice and why is this happening. Why have I got everything, you know, that I have, in a material sense, and these people have nothing? And it just seems so unfair and that has affected me for the rest of my life and affected me in the job that I've gone into and the way that I view things. And it was a huge, huge uh issue for me and that really, in many respects, is my first kind of proper memory of my, of my childhood. [Dean, 46, UK]

Linguistically, metamorphosis will include language around conversion or conviction and often aligns itself with a set of moral values. Anthropologically, we can spot narratives of passage between one state and another. Metamorphosis is focused on finding inner strength, here understood as an expression of agency, but also highlights structural conditions in which this type of agency emerged. In the social sciences, this relation is very interesting. It offers an insight into the interactions between the established structural norms and individual convictions in contributing to wider social change.

Trajectory of suffering

The last form of the biographical process structure is the 'trajectory of suffering'. This term is directly translated from the German and often criticised in English-speaking discussions for misleading the reader into thinking of suffering as a type of trauma. This process structure indicates instances where the individual experiences loss of control. The trajectory of suffering will include painful or even traumatic experiences (Schütze, 2008), where choices are taken away and the personal situation is spiralling down. In terms of content, a trajectory of suffering may include experiences of war, episodes of sickness or alcoholism as well as being the victim of crime or becoming unemployed. By using this narrative form, the individual indicates a social situation in which the narrator needs to fight to preserve their emotional and social integrity. The extract below comes from Pauline, who is from Northern Ireland and decided to settle in Denmark with her Danish partner after a successful international career. In her narrative, she mentions the difficulties of gaining a foothold in her new situation:

[A]fter Sweden I tried to live in Denmark for four months. I couldn't find a job and I was unemployed and I was kind of thinking, you know, I've got a degree and all, I've done so much and I've, like – got this experience behind me of working in Sweden and I can't get anything in Denmark and I had kind of just walked into Kai's life [partner] and lived in his flat only knew his friends, you know, I just felt like I'd given up so much and I couldn't [...] it was starting to bring in this not so nice side to our relationship [...] that was a really tough time. And I – I actually put on loads of weight [...] Because I was just eating, I wasn't exercising so much and [...] that was one the toughest times in my life. So, probably up until that point I had just all good experiences, really. [...] and I just felt like I was kind of riding on a very high lucky wave. And like in psychology I was always drawn to different psychologists like humanists or people who would have put out a sort of positive spin on, on things. So our sense of being active in your life, rather than passive. And I always felt like you could be really strong and you could change, like, anyway. But that, that experience has really, it knocked me a bit because it was, like, I lost control. I always thought you could control life. [...] I think I had lost, you know – a sense of who I was, because I hadn't, you know, I had no identity, people would ask me what I did and I'd say I was unemployed and then they'd give me loads of ideas how to get out of it and all this... [Pauline, 31, N. Ireland]

As a process structure, the trajectory of suffering analytically indicates situations where the individual has become detached from specific social structures. In Pauline's case, having entered an unknown linguistic and cultural context, she lost her connection with her family, her friends, the job market and even her own body image. This process structure points out the vital importance of social connections for individual wellbeing, and exposes the mechanism of social exclusion, where individual agency cannot engage with the relevant social structure.

Background construction

The process structures outlined above have one distinctive pattern. They are sequential. As small stories within the larger biographical narrative, they also have a beginning, middle and end. The three narrative constraints to storytelling apply in the narration of particular biographical threads; they have to be self-contained and logical structures. But autobiographical narratives include multiple biographical threads and sometimes, in an effort to make sense of events, this logical, sequential structure needs to be adjusted. This type of adjustment is referred to as 'background construction'. In the narrative sense, it indicates the moment when the narrator realises that, in order to fully explain certain events, they need to go back in their timeline and include additional events that will help the listener to fully make sense of the situation. This narrative adjustment carries significant analytical weight. It usually indicates a high emotional load that the narrator has pushed to the back of the life story narration. The events included in the background construction are of key analytical importance; they indicate that some of the events are not fully processed and have the potential to threaten the individual's sense of self. The following extract comes from an autobiographical narrative interview with Monika, a young Polish woman living in the UK (for an in-depth analysis of this particular case, see also Svašek and Domecka, 2013). She indicates in the preamble her strained relationship with her family, especially her mother and sister. She highlights the fact that her migration has been an attempt to separate herself from a very dysfunctional family dynamic. She narrates the unequal treatment of the two sisters, an abusive mother and an absentee father who migrated to the USA. When she comes to the point in her story where her mother physically abuses her when she is heavily pregnant, Monika needs to explain to the interviewer the depth of the conflict. This background construction is what follows:

Ah, I'll go back to something earlier, there was such a situation that... my sister had been living for a month, I guess, a month, before she went to the States and I got to know about that unfortunately when she was already in the States that she was in the States. She was working in the mornings and once I got so nervous because I was knocking on her door, and knocking, and knocking and no one was responding. We were living in one tenement building, a private one. There were only... it belonged to my mum and her sister. And her sister was living in one half and we were living in the second half. So I rushed to her, I ran there and I say – 'Tell me where my sister is' and she started laughing – 'So you don't know anything? She's in America'. It was as if I got a slap in the face. Just... well, I don't know, I felt... again in my life I felt terrible. And I asked her – 'Why? Why no one told me?' She just shrugged it off saying that my mum decided that if she had told me, I'd have called the airport and said that she was smuggling some, I don't know, drugs or something and she would have had to stay. Only one reaction – I turned on my heel and just a regular war started between me and my family. [Monika, 35, Poland]

This background construction contains very painful memories and difficult experiences. Only one sister was chosen to go to the USA to live with their father, while the other was left behind without the slightest indication of options. This type of betrayal, as well as the cruelty with which she was treated, is used to indicate the turning point in her family relationships. From that point on, she highlights that there was nothing but war, in which she was kept hostage by remaining dependent on her mother for accommodation and financial help. Monika's biography is her story of escaping in a physical sense – by migrating to a different country – and in an emotional sense – by pushing away painful memories and cutting off all her relations and investing heavily in her own family life. The background construction disturbs the sequential flow of her story and, by doing so, she indicates unresolved aspects of her biography that can be a valuable source of knowledge for the process of individual coping strategies as well as adjustments to structural change.

Distinguishing the process structures makes it possible to compare biographical experiences between different autobiographical narrative cases. Typologies based on the way in which individuals themselves choose to narrate their experiences – especially experiences associated with transnational mobility – capture different sides of the social phenomena in question. They develop an understanding of these phenomena, placing them in a complex framework of relations between individual and social structures.

Tip from the field

Be aware of multiple analytical frameworks

The autobiographical narrative interview method incorporates a coherent analytical framework that can nonetheless interact with other analytical frameworks, including sociolinguistics, psychoanalysis and symbolic interactionism. These extended analytical frameworks can add a further dimension to the analysis and expand the terminology used to describe the phenomenon in question.

Making generalisations from autobiographical narrative data

The analytical frameworks of biographical sequences and process structures in the autobiographical narrative interview method are useful tools for the investigation of internal and external dynamics, patterns of social change as well as cognitive and emotional processes of meaning making. This type of framework can be used in a variety of academic disciplines, including social psychology, linguistics, health and education studies as well as sociology and anthropology. As mentioned in Chapter 3, depending on the research design, this methodology can be used to answer a variety of research questions, and when combined with a relevant analytical framework, the research can generate different types of findings and generalisations about the nature of the process (Gobo, 2008b: 421). At this stage of the research process, you should expect to frame your findings within the ongoing academic debate you wish to contribute to, and formulate an argument that is supported by your findings.

There is no 'golden path' on how to draw generalisations from qualitative data, and this skill is best learned by critically engaging with the work of others in your field, either by becoming familiar with other studies, or cooperating during the research process. Below, we present four studies that build on the autobiographical narrative interview method and make generalisations in a variety of ways:

- Study 1 outlines the importance of biographical inquiry in the **understanding and processing of war trauma**.
- Study 2 outlines the **generational processes of remembrance** in response to the historical event of displacement.
- Study 3 engages in **comparison between the narrative process structures** used to narrate experiences of international migration.
- Study 4 focuses on the **therapeutic role of autobiographical narrative interviews** in the field of criminology and prison studies.

Study 1

Pressure and Guilt – War experiences of a young German soldier and their biographical implications, Parts 1 and 2 (Schütze, 1992)

This is *the* classic study by Fritz Schütze published as a set of two journal articles.

Method and design

The study is an analysis of one autobiographical narrative interview with the German soldier Hermann, born in 1918. Hermann did not support the Nazi ideology but, like many others, was enlisted as a soldier during the Second World War. The interview transcript was 120 pages long and strictly followed

(Continued)

the autobiographical narrative interview research method. The reason for the interview selection was to explore the process of guilt and remorse caused by participation in war without the individual's ideological commitment.

Study findings

This study was set to investigate the thesis posed by two prominent psychoanalysts, Alexander and Margarete Mitscherlich (1977), that post-war Germans are not able to repent and mourn their involvement in war crimes. In their thesis, they claim that, in order to protect their sense of self, those individuals who committed crimes in the name of the ideology (which forms part of their super-ego structure) would have to deny and repress their war experiences. But the question arises about non-committed German soldiers, who still participated in and witnessed war crimes. Schütze's findings illustrate how feelings of guilt and pressure are hidden within the biographical narrative structure. The narration of the military service itself focuses on the sense of adventure, camaraderie and survival. It touches upon military realities, such as hierarchies and individual autonomy. The moral aspects of the conflict are not present. This is where the Mitscherlich thesis holds. But in the biographical analysis, the guilt and pressure associated with war experiences appear and resonate in the form of background constructions told on the back of other, difficult biographical experiences. According to Schütze (1992: 358):

> by living through biographically extreme and crucial crises in their later lives, Germans were forced to recollect and to think about encounters with instances of collective moral deterioration and of suffering inflicted on the victims by the Nazi military and oppression apparatus.
> They were then finally able to 'translate' the meaning of moral deterioration into a future of their own individual lives during the Nazi and war period.

Generalisations

This study contributed to the development of a theory that tested the assumptions of psychoanalysis as applied to the Second World War generation in Germany. Its generalisation strength lies in the identification of the process by which we can explain one more variation of the complex socio-cultural phenomenon associated with collective guilt. The importance lies in the sequential analysis of the whole life story, including later experiences that help process what happened in the individual's past.

Study 2

Biography and memory: The generational experience of the Shoah survivors

Method and design

The study used extensive archive and biographical material in the study of experiences of Holocaust survivors, and included 20 autobiographical narrative interviews with individuals who left Poland shortly after the Second World War, settled in Israel and, at an older age, decided to journey back to Poland to revisit childhood places associated both with their memories of childhood and the trauma of the Holocaust. The study compared and contrasted the cases to uncover thematic overlaps.

Study findings

The analysis of autobiographical narratives focused on the thematic as well as structural analysis of 'biographical work' undertaken by Holocaust survivors to reconcile biographical continuity and process the split between their childhood experiences in Poland, the trauma of war and the process of settlement in Israel. This process is taking place at an individual and a collective level, as many of the experiences are part of the cultural narratives of Holocaust survivors and the Jewish diaspora. Thematically, the return stories focus on several topics. Among the individual aspects are language issues, such as the abandonment of Polish and the learning of Hebrew, a change of name, as well as identity work, entanglement in the re-emergence of traumatic memories and attempts to recognise the places and people known from childhood. In terms of collective aspects, themes centre on visiting places of collective remembrance, such as Auschwitz, and their intergenerational transmission. The analysis of autobiographical narratives points out 'the need to see one's biography as a coherent whole, which in its final phase, manifests itself in a desire for completeness and need to come full circle' (Kazmierska, 2013: 414), including the complex set of relations between old and new geopolitical and personal relations and between individual and collective trauma.

Generalisations

The study focused on the biographical aspects of 'the returns' to highlight the need to reconcile the biographical chasm between what was and what is. Kazmierska (2013) highlights these processes in the context of post-war geopolitics and the wider discourses of post-war displacement. The study used a biographical approach to make generalisations about biographical work that internalises generational social change from a long-term historical perspective.

Study 3

Guest, trader or explorer – Biographical perspectives on the experiences of cross-border mobility in Europe (Eichsteller, 2018a)

Method and design

This study used 91 autobiographical narrative interviews collected across seven European countries (as a part of a big collaborative research project). It investigated the experiences of international migration in the context of the European Union. This study looked at three narrative process structures – action schemes, institutional action schemes and trajectory of suffering – to investigate the impact of power relations between the individual agent and social structures on the migrant's identity.

Study findings

The study distinguished three archetypes of migrant stories. The first, the guest story, is told from the point of view of someone whose agency is subjugated by the social structure of their new country, thus often displaying a trajectory of suffering structure. Stories of this type indicate the hierarchical nature of receiving societies, the individual's drop in status as well as a restriction of personal freedom. The second, the trader story, is embedded in the context of international organisations, which ensure the individual's professional status in the receiving society. Stories of this type are firmly embedded in the narrative of institutional action schemes and tap into established transnational mobility programmes that seek to integrate migrants into their receiving country. The third, the explorer story, follows the process structure of the action scheme and indicates a situation where individual agents can gain a foothold in an international context, often jumping between different national circumstances. The conclusions drawn by this study focus on the nature of power relations between transnational agents and the social structures in receiving countries. The study discussed aspects of individual rights in a national and international context and how these affect the individual's willingness to follow traditional and non-traditional social scripts and manage biographical risks. Finally, the study pointed towards the emergence of alternative forms of belonging that favour organisation-based belonging over place-based attachments.

Generalisations

The study generalisations explored the differences in how the process of migration is internalised within the biographical narrative. It illustrated the exploratory power of narrative structures in the investigation of different points of view, which show how complex migration experiences can be, and how they affect the biographical sense of self.

Study 4

The Triple Bind of Narration – Fritz Schütze's biographical interview in prison research and beyond (Szczepanik and Siebert, 2016)

Method and design

The study was conducted in four medium-secure prisons in Poland in 2011–2012. The researcher interviewed 23 male repeat offenders using autobiographical narrative interviews. The study aim was to understand the process of repeated offending and the formation of habitual offender identity.

Study findings

The analysis of the study focused on the repetitive patterns of offending and highlighted the role of intimate relationships in events that lead to an interruption of criminal activities. The researchers highlight the therapeutic character of the autobiographical narrative interview. Szczepanik and Siebert (2016: 294) argue that 'in engaging in biography work narrators gained an understanding of their own actions and often for the first time discussed difficult moments in their lives: they attempted to justify their crimes and commented on their decisions to act in certain ways'. The researchers noted that biographical narrative helped the interviewees to recognise the repetitive nature of their criminal career and break away from the usual process of rationalisation and neutralisation of their criminal behaviour. They also noted the important role of the interviewer, who was recognised as an outsider to the prison system.

Generalisations

This study focuses on the therapeutic value of the autobiographical narrative interview method in the context of the prison system. The generalisations are built around the concept of biographical work that the individual engages in during the process of narration and its contribution to a rehabilitation process that encourages self-reflection and recognition of social links outside criminal networks and the prison system.

Summary

This chapter aimed to introduce the reader to the autobiographical narrative interview method. We outlined the theoretical background, the development of the method and current applications. The chapter outlined the procedures of data gathering, including the structure of the autobiographical narrative interview technique, and offered some indication of the interviewer skills required to gather the necessary data. We also illustrated the analytical procedures focused on understanding the narrative structure of the interview and identifying process structures that uncover biographical meanings embedded in the narrative. Finally, we discussed the application of analytical frameworks in drawing generalisations and presented four examples that use the autobiographical narrative interview method in a variety of research designs to answer different research questions.

Questions to consider

1. What is the value of narrative in investigating social phenomena?
2. What can we learn from the analysis of narrative and process structure?
3. What is the role of analytical frameworks in drawing broader theoretical generalisations?

Don't forget to use the additional resources to support your research in Appendix 3!

5

NARRATIVE ETHNOGRAPHY

Objectives

By the end of this chapter, you will be able to:

- Understand the impact of structured data on the narrative form of the biographical interview
- Understand the impact of the analytical framework on data quality and the study design
- Recognise the diversity of approaches within the biographical narrative field of study and their relevance to the research questions
- Identify and analyse the relevant narrative environments: intimate relationships, local cultures, jobs, organisation and status
- Understand the concept of intertextuality and its implications for your research
- Understand the patterns of making generalisations out of biographical narrative data.

Countering the serendipity in biographical research

Biographical narratives give an exciting insight into relations between the individual and their social world. They capture events in time, both historical, such as the impact of social changes and historical events, and biographical, such as identity evolution observed through the biographical stages of life. Biographical narratives entwine places, senses, physical and social realities, and the process of sense making and emotional attachment. They are incredibly rich sources of 'unstructured' data that, when used well, can provide researchers with a wealth of information. This intertwined character of the narrative, combined with extensive information, means that some of it will be judged relevant for the particular research project, while the rest can seem quite serendipitous and less than systematic. It takes skilful analysis to tackle unstructured biographical narratives. It takes practice to understand how many possibilities this type of data can provide for social science inquiries across different disciplines.

Contemporary research, however, especially projects that depend on external funding, can rarely afford the open-ended research questions and freedom to go wherever the serendipitous biographical data may lead. These research projects require more control over the research process, and this control can be exerted in two ways, either through structuring the biographical data or by imposing specific analytical frameworks. Both strategies aim to bring some order to the biographical narrative research that will align with the study's more specific aim. Both approaches have an impact on the quality of data and robustness of the analysis. It is a researcher's informed decision on the research design, research question and form of analysis that will decide how much control over the biographical narrative process and analysis is needed to deliver the project objectives. But intervening in a biographical narrative and application of particular analytical frameworks can also have serious consequences. Biographical narratives that are too structured may not yield enough detail or relevant information to successfully carry out the analysis, and it is rarely possible to re-do the interviews. The application of firm analytical frameworks can narrow down the visibility and complexity of the phenomena. This type of interference can be compared to the use of chisel and hammer on a rock sculpture; it can create a stunning effect, but it cannot be undone. With knowledge and experience, research can shape the data and analysis, but mistakes can also have a dramatic effect.

Interventions in a biographical narrative research process are also a matter of degree. Changes to the interview technique can be either minimal or highly structured. Analytical frameworks can be built around specific, biographically relevant aspects of life or reflect the scope of more abstract theories. In the process, it is possible to cross the invisible line between qualitative and quantitative research designs – where the focus shifts from the range of variation in the experiences, to the strengths of their representation in the sample or the presence of patterns and associations (see Chapter 6). Control applied precisely over the research process can enable larger samples, introduce more synchronous mixed method research designs and aid analysis using computer software, such as NVivo, Atlas.ti and many others. This allows biographical narrative data to form a valuable part of the social science landscape across a range of scientific disciplines. This chapter and the next represent the evolution of research approaches and biographical methodologies. This chapter (5) outlines research procedures that fit well within the qualitative paradigm, while Chapter 6 introduces some more structured approaches and possible links with the use of cross-case comparative designs, such as qualitative comparative analysis (QCA).

This chapter will first give an overview of the biographical narrative research field, including the narrative ethnography approach, and then discuss possible modifications to the data collection and data analysis. Finally, we will examine a number of biographical narrative studies and discuss how they employ biographical methods to make scientific generalisations.

Exploring methodological approaches to biographical narratives

The biographical narrative method is one of those research techniques that is constantly re-discovered across disciplines and research interests. It typically reflects the researcher's need to gain a deeper understanding of the world through the eyes of the narrator, to unearth motivations, hidden unconscious meanings, and the impact of certain social changes. To gain these understandings, researchers often turn to biographical accounts and attempt to apply the new analytical frameworks to this type of data, find new shades of meanings and make new theoretical connections. In this context, the application of biographical research can be mapped out across the scientific world and most of the social science disciplines. It can seem like each approach and discipline have contributed something to the evolution and dynamic nature of biographical research (Holstein and Gubrium, 2011a). Below, we introduce three distinct biographical narrative approaches and their basic assumptions to show various methodological solutions. This list is by no means exhaustive; the approaches have been selected to highlight methodological innovations in approaching biographical narrative data.

Narrative ethnography – finding environments that frame biographical narratives

Narrative ethnography, which we introduced briefly in Chapter 2 (pp. 24–26), is an approach developed by the American scholars Holstein and Gubrium (Gubrium and Holstein, 2008, 2009; Holstein and Gubrium, 2011b), and it is one of the most comprehensive approaches to biographical narrative research. As an analytical method, narrative ethnography is based essentially on the assumption that life stories are embedded in and shaped by the wider social and cultural context in which they are told. In its conceptual origins, the method builds on the foundations of the Chicago School and especially the work of Everett Hughes. Narrative ethnography approaches life stories as accounts that provide insights into their narrators' social world, with special emphasis on the individual's 'going concerns' (Hughes, 1971), understood as spheres of everyday life that carry immediate relevance to everyday life. The idea of going concerns focuses the analysis on changes and processes occurring in what Gubrium and Holstein (2009) refer to as 'narrative environments'. These relate to 'the work of maintaining particular ways of framing and doing matters of relevance to participants. Such concerns vary in size from families, friendships, support, and recovery groups, to schools, nursing homes, and therapeutic enterprises' (Gubrium, 2005: 526). Depending on who tells and who listens to the story, biographical narratives set life events around socially and culturally relevant circumstances, such as important relationships and local cultures, jobs and organisations, and status (Gubrium and Holstein, 2009).

In the context of designing your research project, understanding the nature of these 'narrative environments' helps narrow down the research questions and link the findings to the wider literature. We will discuss the actual style of analysis in the section below, but for now, imagine that you are interested in the family relations of the individual, and further narrow it down to issues around the consequences and impact of domestic violence. Within that framework, you can focus on all the biographical elements of the biographical narrative that frame the family structure, its emotional and economic realities, the acts of violence, and finally their impact on the life and relationships of the narrator in their adult life. In the context of other relationships, this all links with institutions, such as schools and social services, the notion of stigma and low self-confidence. The empirical material can then be compared with what is known from other studies on the subject. In this way, the use of biographical narrative is focused on the specific social problem that is a direct outcome of your methodological strategy. In particular, it encourages appropriate case selection featuring the phenomenon you seek to investigate; the design of the narrative interview that may steer towards the issue you are investigating; and a relevant analytical framework that connects your findings to the wider body of knowledge.

Furthermore, narrative ethnography sees narratives as a system of assumptions about society and the individual's role, which are conveyed within biographical narratives. The framing of biographical 'going concerns' is thus a reflection of greater narratives, which exist at a more abstract level of society. You may notice, for example, that many people will recall domestic violence events in a similar way, excusing the abuser and blaming themselves. This tells you more about the society these people are living in than about the experience itself. According to Gubrium and Holstein (2008: 250), narrative ethnography is concerned:

> with the production, distribution and circulation of stories in society, which requires that we step outside of narrative material and consider questions such as who produces particular kinds of stories, where they are likely to be encountered, what their consequences are, under what circumstances particular narratives are more or less accountable, what interests publicise them, how they gain popularity, and how they are challenged.

Within that context, biographical narrative research can offer truly unique insights into the social world and broader social change.

Life stories as a blueprint of identity and belonging

The second example of biographical narrative research practice that can be used to research social realities has been developed by the American scholar Charlotte Linde (1993, 2001, 2009) in the field of management studies. According to Linde (1993), life stories naturally navigate towards biographical turning points, or rather the events that the narrator feels are worth reporting. Events such as education, marriage, illness, divorce, childbirth, career milestones and ideological conversions constitute the natural and culturally specific components of biographical narratives. Linde's approach focuses on the way the narratives, and biographical narratives in particular, 'transmit the part of social knowledge that concerns history, values and identity. This is because the narrative consists of events and evaluations: what happened, and what its moral meaning is' (Linde, 2001: 163). Furthermore, Linde's approach is very much focused on the way people claim and negotiate group membership. She highlights the fact that biographical narratives will change to reflect the changes in identity and belonging. For example, we see this phenomenon in the narratives of religious conversions, highlighting the point of transition and splitting the biographical narratives between life before and after the life-changing event.

The approach in this sort of research project is very much focused on different types of knowledge. Linde suggests that narrative is a good way to study the tacit or unconscious types of knowledge about the social world. According to Linde (2001), tacit knowledge is 'frequently used to describe any form of non-quantifiable knowledge, particularly the knowledge about social interactions, social practices, and most generally, how a group or an institution gets things done' (2001: 160). Linde is particularly interested in how individuals incorporate their own life stories to fit a wider narrative. She applies this methodological model to the study of organisations, such as big commercial companies that promote specific 'organisational cultures'. However, this approach's potential can easily be extended to any organisation with a strong identity, such as a university, or to a student, medical or religious community, or the police, to name just a few. Linde (2001) argues that:

> We use these life stories to claim or negotiate group membership and to demonstrate that we are in fact, worthily members of those [groups]. Part of becoming a member of any institution, formal and informal, is learning to tell the stories of that institution and learning to tell one's own stories in a way coherent with those of that group. Part of what one needs to know to be a member is what the stories of the group are, what events in the past are judged to have relevance to the present, what values the stories exemplify, and when it is appropriate to tell them. (Linde, 2001: 163)

Linde's analytical approach offers a unique way of framing the biographical narrative analysis that is focused on the ongoing interaction between the individual story and wider social narratives and the way individuals adjust and redefine how they see and present themselves to fit into a context, so as to belong. Interestingly, this particular feature of the biographical narrative is also used in therapeutic settings. For example, in the Alcoholics Anonymous 12-Step programme, people struggling with an addiction are asked to tell their life story three times at different stages of the programme and to re-work the story to evaluate and highlight different elements of identity and belonging as a way to recovery.

Sociobiographical method – how we cope with the world

The sociobiographical method is embedded within the BNIM model (see Chapter 2) developed by two British scholars, Prue Chamberlayne and Tom Wengraf (Chamberlayne et al., 2002, 2004). This analytical model focuses attention on two aspects of a biographical narrative account: the life lived – the objective events, such as education, marriage, divorce as told in biographical sequence; and the story told – the subjective layer of narrative that gives an insight into the emotional and subjective part of narration, containing the meanings and justifications. In the parallel analysis of both aspects, the sociobiographical method aims to understand a particular individual's 'life journey' and its links with a wider social world. The Social Strategies in Risk Society (SOSTRIS) project, for example, was interested in the practices of social exclusion affecting economically vulnerable groups, such as unemployed youth and redundant industrial workers.

The application of this analytical framework focuses on searching for 'resemblances and differences between life journeys, as we move between what seems specific to an individual, and what seems to represent a social pattern' (Chamberlayne et al., 2002: 2). This approach focuses on the diverse social strategies that individuals develop as a response to specific social challenges, such as unemployment, lone parenthood or the shift to 'work from home' employment in the time of a pandemic. The analytical framework is based on the principles of hermeneutic case reconstruction (Breckner and Rupp, 2002: 292), which means that it aims to reconstruct 'those partially conscious, partly unconscious patterns that indicate in what way a person has moulded their perceptions and reactions specifically as a result of a difficult situation in life'. The sociobiographical method thus untangles the emotional aspects of the life challenges and their assumed social aspects. For example, lone parenthood can be an assumed problem from the social policy perspective. However, the individual life strategies analysis may indicate that some support networks, such as the family network or access to affordable childcare and health care, can make a key difference in tackling this problem. This type of analysis is a valuable resource for social policies that can accurately identify the point of policy interventions.

Building your analytical toolkit with an open mind

All approaches presented in this book, and many others, have developed a distinct take on biographical narrative research that caters to specific research interests and disciplines. This creates unique difficulties within the biographical narrative research field. In our experience, several university work colleagues have been involved in biographical narratives at some point in their career. However, as they are often located in different disciplines, we rarely interact or even know about each other. The specific analytical approaches tend to gather within tight-knit research communities that may remain ignorant and dismissive of the work done in other countries and disciplines. But as you can already see, most of the biographical narrative methods build on similar premises, while differing in their interpretation and application. They can and should interact more, and we hope to encourage both experienced and young researchers to look beyond their own practice in search of new developments and perspectives.

The broader field of narrative studies also has a lot to offer in building a methodological toolkit. Biographies are a unique type of story and expanding your understanding of how stories are structured, told, represented, and why we tell them and how we listen to them should be a part of every research project. Below, we have a selective and by no means exclusive list of scholars whose contribution to narrative studies has been useful to the development of biographical narrative studies:

- Sociolinguistics – Anna De Fina, Deborah Schiffrin (Bamberg et al., 2011; De Fina et al., 2006; Schiffrin, 1996; Schiffrin et al., 2008)
- Visual sociology – Roswitha Breckner (Breckner, 1998, 2010; Breckner and Rupp, 2002)
- Sociology of stories – Francesca Polletta (Polletta, 2012; Polletta et al., 2011)
- Education – Michael Bamberg (Bamberg, 2006, 2011, 2012)
- Psychology – Dan P. McAdams (McAdams, 2008, 2010, 2012).

Tip from the field ——————————————————————

Know your toolkit

Sometimes you may find that your research question leads you in a direction that your analytical approach is not best suited to. In this case, it is important that you are open to other analytical solutions that may help you to uncover the previously 'hidden' aspects of your data. As a researcher, you need to understand that any problem can be tackled with multiple research tools, and it is your responsibility to choose the best tool for a job.

Data collection – how to structure the biographical interview

In the previous chapter, we outlined the procedures for the 'unstructured' type of biographical narrative interview and discussed the merits of an uninterrupted style of interview. In the original three-part interview, there is a third part that always allows for some direct questions that can be used to gather more information to address the research question. However, sometimes this interview form seems too bulky and time-consuming to apply to a specific research project. There is always the temptation to make the interview more focused and more manageable to suit a specific research problem. Depending on the level of intervention, we may cross the line between the narrative form of the interview into the semi-structured life history interview methods. These decisions have long-lasting consequences and should be made with a degree of caution.

One of the most important things to consider when using the biographical interview structure is the commitment towards the narrative form of the interview. Most of the biographical research traditions and their analytical frameworks insist on the narrative element of a biographical interview. Letting the narrator tell their story in their own words allows for insight not only into their life events but also into their words, that is the way things are said. Qualitative analysis will depend strongly on the narrative material that explores the complexity of narrative realities, structures of power and conflict. However, there are a few ways of introducing more structure to the interview while still keeping some elements of the narrative. This can be done by directing the opening question or giving a narrator some options to structure their narrative.

Tip from the field

Narrative is a precious qualitative resource

Some features of the biographical narrative interview, such as length and perceived lack of focus, may tempt inexperienced researchers to abandon the narrative type of interview in favour of the direct 'question–answer' type of exchange. This type of questioning is more likely to elicit argumentation, rather than narration. While you get a direct answer, you will probably lose most of the 'unconscious' meanings and values and hear what the interviewee thinks you want to hear. There are research questions suitable for this more structured approach, and it is your choice as a researcher to judge the best approach. However, our argument is that narrative is the most precious qualitative resource and, when possible, you should aim for this type of data.

Directing the opening question

We can imagine the situation in a project regarding domestic violence when the narrator chooses not to include this episode in their biography. Analytically, that act in itself would be telling us something about the biographical work of the person, but it is difficult to report on the findings based on the absence of the episode from the data. Apart from the selection of the interviewee, it is possible to introduce a probe into the first question, to direct the interview to highlight a specific line of inquiry. For example, you may reinforce the fact that your project is about domestic violence and within that context, you would like the narrator to tell you their life story. This should be done in a measured way, as the risk of this approach is that the narrator will focus entirely on this aspect of the story to the exclusion of all the other biographical elements. This tends to happen when, as a researcher, you cast narrators to play specific roles, and they in turn, to help you, act them out for you. Saying that, if you indicate by your behaviour and questioning that you need a narrative of the 'domestic violence victim', most subjects will play that role for you; but you cannot and should not assume that this is who they are in real life.

Helping the narrator to structure their story

The other way of structuring the narrative is to give a narrator a framework that will accommodate the process of narration. You might ask for the life story to be told as a book, with the key elements given as a sequence of book chapters. Allowing the narrator to think about the story's overall structure before telling it also opens up an interesting bridge to expanding narrative biographical methods. There are several innovative approaches (see Chapter 6) that use different methods to unlock the narrative and storytelling – for example, a walking interview technique (O'Neill et al., 2015) that aims to elicit a narrative while walking and talking about meaningful places (see also Chapter 8); drawing life-course maps (Schubring et al., 2019); or utilising meaningful objects or audio-visual props (O'Neill et al., 2015).

Analytical procedures embedded in the analytical framework of narrative environments

Considering the diversity of analytical approaches, three of which we have outlined above, there is a limit to how many analytical procedures we can illustrate in practice. Analysis is a creative interpretive process and it is impossible to anticipate every step of it. We have selected the narrative ethnography approach to illustrate some of the analytical procedures, but we also indicate the points of cross-over where other approaches could provide a valuable alternative. The data used in this section come from the Euroidentities project (see Chapter 7, Study 3 for a full description). They relate to the various aspects of transnational experiences that activate a whole series of adjustments and identity changes that modify aspects of belonging.

As discussed at the beginning of this chapter, narrative ethnography uses the concept of narrative environments as an analytical tool. Based on that assumption, Gubrium and Holstein introduced five types of environments which 'reflexively shape the realisation of the problems in question, and mediate their sustenance of transformation' (Gubrium, 2005: 257). Life stories consist of: stories of family relationships – between children and parents, siblings and intimate partners; local cultures which include friendships as well as local communities and networks; jobs – in terms of professional identifications as well as the organisation of work; organisations – such as educational institutions, churches or nursing homes; as well as status-related statements which reveal the structure of values and achievements. Within each environment, different types of dynamics and adjustments occur. Depending on the research design, you will either focus on the individual processes within the case or compare and contrast several cases, as you can see in the illustrations of analytical procedures below.

Intimate relationships

Relationships and social ties within the family and with significant others, reinforced by intimate and emotional elements, are powerful means of shaping individual lives. Within the context of autobiographical narratives, relationships become one of the most significant indicators for the investigation of social aspects of belonging (Gubrium and Holstein, 2009). The ties between people shape and influence individual plans and social expectations, thus offering an insight into the formation of a personal sense of continuity and coherence. Along with the roles and expectations associated with the life cycle – from child to spouse, parent and grandparent – relationships change their shape and significance. Different types of relationship involve different levels of personal freedom and opportunities, different sets of social responsibilities and rights as well as different biographical costs and benefits.

Transnational biographical narratives contain a wide variety of transnational practices addressing these issues of intimate relationships. A narrative, ethnographic study of personal relationships offers an insight into the mechanisms of establishing and maintaining an emotional connection between people and negotiating belonging in changing international contexts. To illustrate this element of intimate relationship narrative, consider the case of Kinga, a mature Polish student currently living in the UK. During her narrative, she only briefly mentions her short marriage to a Japanese man. Kinga was an English teacher in China, and after her return, she met her future husband in Poland. Their marriage in Poland was a good one, but things changed when they decided to move to Japan. The move caused a shift in the relationship dynamic that left Kinga unable to adjust. In her narrative, she says:

> I also think that it depends on where a given couple is. My experiences with my ex-husband were totally different when we had been in Poland. He was living in Poland for quite a long time. And the relation between the same partners looked completely different in Asia. I personally think that the role of the woman in Japan is very – I don't know those are my private opinions, and I really don't want to sound racist, but it could be said that a woman

does not count much in Japan. There is not much she can say, and nobody really asks her about what she thinks. And it really does not matter what kind of education you have and what you are doing. It is a totally different relation than in Europe, and the thing is that it is changing dramatically, at least in my experience. [Kinga, 31, Poland]

This fragment of Kinga's narrative is very rich. She is engaging in cross-cultural comparisons, pointing to the changes in gender role between the cultural contexts that had a detrimental effect on her marriage. She highlights that her husband lived in Poland for a long time, and this implies that their relationship followed the cultural patterns and gender norms that were familiar to her. The move to Japan was, however, a culture shock. In strong words, she expresses perceived inequality and loss of her status within the Japanese context. Her wishes and opinions were disregarded and lacking power. This is especially telling when compared with her narration of her time spent in China, where her role of teacher was respected. The same did not apply in Japan, where she was also teaching English. She mentions that her education and occupation did not give her any social leverage. In the end, the marriage failed, and Kinga went back to Europe. This type of analysis of an intimate transnational relationship points to a shift in power, here in terms of gender, between spouses in the process of moving between countries. Similar patterns can be observed in terms of language disparities and adjustments to extended family structures, such as relationships with parents and siblings.

From the point of view of family relationships, a glimpse into the generational structures of transnational family life can be interesting, for example the effects of mobility on both children and parents. As an illustration, let's look at the case of Gwilym: a Welsh man married to a Swedish woman. During their marriage, they lived with their three children in both Wales and Sweden. Their family relationships feature complex negotiations around language. Gwilym sums up his family dynamics in the following quote:

Charlotte [his wife] felt at that time she was losing her language and we decided, well I think I pushed her into talking Swedish with, with our son. So then I was talking Welsh to my children and English to my wife, but Charlotte was talking English to her husband, Welsh to her daughters and Swedish to her son. And oddly enough the girls picked up the language with their little brother, so they speak Swedish, and now we've all learnt all 3 languages so whenever we speak now it, it can seem to an outsider a terrible mixture. [Gwilym, 55, UK]

This 'terrible mixture' just highlights the internal dynamics of this transnational family, where three languages are used to negotiate individual relationships between parents and children. Speaking one's language within a family context can be a part of negotiating an external sense of belonging. At the time of the interview, Gwilym's two daughters were living in the UK, while his son decided to stay in Sweden. Gwilym mentions that what for him was just an episode (10 years living in Sweden), for his children was half their life. Now this transnational family needs to accommodate multiple countries of residence into the family dynamic. This type of analytical procedure would focus on the intergenerational aspects of family life, looking at intimate relationships related to childhood, parenthood and grandparenthood, where the attachments and experiences contribute to the transformation of individual life.

Intimate relationships are a fascinating narrative environment to study. How people make and narrate emotional and social connections with each other is a rich research field and can encompass diverse research questions, from intercultural relations, gender roles and parenthood to conflict, dependency and violence.

Local cultures

Every local culture has its own set of rules, applied in the form of tacit knowledge, which regulate membership of the group and social positions in the local hierarchy. The local culture narrative environment presented in life stories often addresses issues of belonging to a place and community. In the context of biographical research, we can see that these ties to the local culture emerge naturally throughout the life cycle, starting in the process of primary socialisation, and are passed down to new generations of community members. This narrative environment also contains the primary gateways for participating in the social structures of everyday life. Friendships and access to local networks are the dimensions of social life shaping the structure of opportunities and limitations; they also have a strong hold on the areas of individual and collective interests, participation and values (Gubrium and Holstein, 2009). Gubrium and Holstein argue that local culture stories are not the big, all-encompassing narratives of society often associated with the narrative environment of status (see below), but the individual stories of everyday struggles that aim at gaining respect. Analysis of this narrative environment can be particularly useful for studying youth cultures, grassroots politics, civil societies, and communities.

As we are using the data from the research project interested in transnational mobilities in Europe, we conceptualised local cultures within the context of migrant groups that deal with intercultural communication issues while navigating their own and other national cultures. Narrative analysis of transnational life stories in this narrative environment context enables us to grasp the emergence and life of 'migrant' neighbourhoods, communities based on shared international experiences, and relations between the 'native' communities and transnational newcomers. Below, you can see a short extract from the interview with Jakub, a young Polish professional living in France. Jakub finished his degree at a French university and started his career in a high-profile company. As he navigates the international and national aspects of his identity in France, he recognises different types of 'migrant' communities and how he can use the notion of respectability to self-position himself within that cultural landscape. Jakub says:

> I mean, you know, you meet Poles because they are Poles. And you know the French from work, from university, from the outings with mutual friends. At first, we stuck more with the Poles. [...] There are two groups. There are people who work in some professions professionally, and there are girls who do babysitting. How do they differ? Well, you know. For me, going for this babysitting thing when you have already graduated from university in Poland, that is a bit stupid. Because if you have your studies, then well you know, you work in your profession, right? With all due respect for those who are doing it, because it is a job, and a tough one too. And those girls sit there, waiting for I don't know, some French prince charming, who'd take them and all that, so, I think, they're hurting themselves a bit. [...] I spend quite some time with the people I work with. So we have our own crew at work. And it's really not a problem to make those connections, even with different nations, no problem. It's enough if you're quite open. [Jakub, 32, Poland]

In his narrative, Jakub makes a distinction between two groups he belongs to: people he meets because of his professional affiliations; and people he meets because they are Poles. He distinguishes the two groups of Poles in France, clearly differentiating who gains more respect and why (he even uses the term 'respectability'). In this short element of biographical narrative, Jakub maps the landscape of his social connections. He narrates how he is negotiating his identity as an international professional and Polish citizen in France to gain respectability on the one hand and access to local networks on the other. This type of analysis can indicate the hidden power structures within local communities as well as the processes of networking and mobilisation of social and cultural resources. It can also indicate the body of local knowledge about how things are done within these communities, and what type of 'respectability' symbols are needed to access these communities and networks.

Another example of local cultures as a narrative environment is found in celebrations and rites of passage. These life events are all about other people, family, friends and a local community who engage in activities that re-enact cultural scripts and foster social traditions. Narrative analysis of such events gives an insight into relationships and the importance of shared experiences. In the context of transnational narratives, it also shows the importance of biographical elements in facilitating intercultural dialogue. Below, we present a short extract from a biographical narrative interview with Pauline from Northern Ireland (UK). At the time of the interview, she is completing her PhD in Denmark, where she lives with her husband. She had worked all over Europe and made many friendships all over the world. For Pauline, her wedding was the only opportunity to bring all the important people in her life together. Pauline narrates this event as follows:

> Our wedding was amazing because it was like, the one time in my life
> when everyone was in the same room. You know, that was, I looked down,
> and I could see the French ones there, the Dublin ones there, the ones
> from home, the ones from Denmark, the ones from Ireland. There were 11
> nationalities in a room. And that was so nice. It was, like, that was oh, it was
> [like my mum] had said to me on the day at our wedding, she just felt the
> sense of pure love. And it did. Like, that day, it just felt, like, you pick up
> these wee gems of people from everywhere you've gone. And it wasn't just
> about me and Kai [husband], you know. We're the ones there that should
> be just about, you know, you and the person, but it was me and Kai and
> everyone. [Pauline, 31, Northern Ireland]

Pauline's account of the wedding is the map of her international experiences. She uses an expression of 'wee gems of people' as these relationships are precious to her. However, she is also aware that as she is the only link between all of those people, this wedding celebration is the only life event that will bring all these elements of her life together. This type of analysis has the potential to explore the nature of celebrations in biographical perspective – as a rite of passage, but also for the continuation of cultural traditions, and community norms in their traditional and non-traditional forms.

Organisations

The narrative environment of organisations and social institutions is another analytical lens you can apply to the analysis of biographical narrative interviews. According to Gubrium and Holstein (2009), an organisation mediates the main concerns and structures of many activities in everyday life. The authors argue that 'contemporary life has come under the purview of countless establishments – schools, churches, hospitals, nursing homes, recreational clubs, sports leagues, and political parties. They provide particular ways of giving voice to and dealing with, everyday matters' (2009: 173). The analysis of this narrative environment is focused on a number of important aspects that intersect with Linde's analytical approach (Linde, 2001). Becoming a member of an organisation implies a recognition of entry criteria that are often formal, such as education credentials or previous professional experience. Clear organisational procedures for membership in these narrative environments, along with an often formal code of practice, make them important gateways into new networks and communities. For example, becoming a university student will require a certain level of qualification and successful application process, then the student needs to adjust to the new role and expectations and become a member of the student community that identifies with the specific institution they attend. Understanding and adapting to both the organisation's formal and informal cultures will determine the sense of belonging and position within the organisation.

Organisations represent very clear social structural aspects of biographical narratives, where individual agency is negotiated with the use of membership rules, both formal and informal. The analytical procedures can seek to untangle the formal and informal aspects of organisational belonging, the process of socialisation into organisational membership, and how people modify their own identity to fit a specific type of organisational membership. The narrative environment of the organisation allows for an interesting study of compliance as well as nonconformity within the context of biographical choices. Biographical experiences often contribute to the ability or unwillingness to be fully embedded within a certain organisational context.

Some of the most exciting research subjects in this direction are studies of total, or almost total, institutions (Goffman, 1990) that encompass the majority of individual everyday life experiences, such as prisons, closed hospital wards and closed religious organisations, including sects and convents. As an illustration, see below the extract from a biographical narrative interview with Matilda, a nun from the UK. Matilda was interviewed as a part of the Euroidentities project because she spent a substantial amount of time in France as well as other countries all over the world. In the following passage of her biographical narrative, you will see that these transnational experiences are completely overruled by her 'mission' and belonging to her religious congregation:

Interviewer (I hereafter): So was it a sort of, a coincidence that your congregation that you joined was French?

Narrator (Matilda; N hereafter): I think it was as simple as the only one I knew. [...] I think I was so naïve I probably didn't realise how important it was. In fact, some of the Irish sisters had half regrets that they hadn't joined an order that wasn't French because, you know, French was, is the congregation language; so we all learned French.

I: When you were in France, you were in the convent and had an enclosed life. You didn't even venture out into society of France; you were always within your Order?

N: Really, yeah. Well, when I went over there for the academic year I attended the university, and I helped in the boarding school in France, but no, I never went off wandering around Caen by myself. Later we took a party of girls to France; we organised a trip to France, we took a bus-load of girls to France. And that made me see another side of France, which I hadn't really experienced although we stayed in our own convent [...] I, to be perfectly honest, I'm fairly ignorant about it, too. My experience of France is very limited. I mean, although I've been to France several times, it's always to a convent and you can't judge the whole of France by a convent, can you? [Matilda, 64, UK]

Matilda's narrative is fully embedded in the convent organisational narrative. She is committed to her mission which by extension is also the mission of her congregation. The up-close study of her biography shows a young girl with the need to belong to something bigger and the organisation that allowed her to expand her education, taught her another language, allowed her to travel internationally and work in education. Matilda's narrative is full of fulfilment that stems from her commitment to the mission and sense of belonging.

This type of analysis focuses on how, throughout the narrative, we can trace the synchronous relationship between the individual and organisation, and distinguish any points of dissonance between them. Furthermore, we can investigate the biographical events where the individual chooses or is forced to venture outside the clearly defined roles of organisational membership, and how they might adjust and build a different type of belonging, such as in the case of released prisoners or children who went through the social care and foster systems.

Jobs

Perhaps after intimate relationships jobs are the most prominent theme in biographical narratives. This narrative environment will encompass stories associated with employment, including instances of work opportunities, changes, conflicts as well as successes and failures. For researchers, it is an invaluable source of information on how well people navigate cultural, economic and social structures as well as providing insight into larger social factors, such as the importance of career and the social impact of being unemployed. According to Gubrium and Holstein (2009), it is also useful to see jobs in the context of the differences between occupations, which are skills-based but transcend specific cultural settings, and professions, which require time to build up the position and be recognised as part of the relevant professional group. Naturally, depending on the organisation of work, a biographical narrative will highlight the relevant organisational elements and career pathways.

As an illustration, in biographical narratives gathered as part of the Euroidentities project, work abroad is one of the main pull factors for international mobility (with education in second place). Transnational work experiences inevitably shape the individual's sense of continuity and coherence, thus constituting the issues around identification and belonging.

To illustrate a job narrative environment that highlights both career continuity and a transition between jobs, see below a quote from the biographical narrative of Dean, who is an NGO worker focusing on issues of poverty and domestic child labour in developing countries. Dean started his career at a well-known charity (anonymised as AAA in the text) and built an international reputation for himself. His career has grown within this institutional environment, but he hasn't adjusted well to organisational change. At the time of the interview, he had decided to start a new, more specialised charity with his wife, Ann. He says:

> Well, yeah, the charity was, it's all happened very quickly. So I left AAA, I left AAA under a cloud, really, because I was feeling a bit jaded about the issues and starting to feel a bit unhappy about the organisation because for many years I'd seen the organisation and the issues as synonymous. And, I know it sounds silly, but it was very important for me to be able to differentiate and say OK there's an organisation and it's got its problems, and I like working there, but there are these issues, and then there's this issue which, you know, I'm really engaged in, [...], but OK I've had enough now, I've got to go. [...] And we were just, you know, we'd spent the day out, and we were in a café, and Ann [wife] just started to talk about setting up a charity and saying, I just think we could. I can't remember how the conversation started, but she started the thing going – and initially I was very standoffish, quite cautious. And I don't think this is a good idea, you know, I'm not sure, but let her carry on. It starts to work, and I think, actually, I think she's right, I think this could, there might be something in this. And then afterwards, I mean I have gone through with this, peaks and troughs, where I've thought, – well I'm not sure whether this is a good idea and then thinking, well yeah, actually it is. And I mean all this time moving on – and actually, the hardest thing of all is to make the decision. [...] But where we are with our careers and our personal life it just fits, it really fits. [Dean, 46, UK]

In the above quote, Dean is highlighting the speed of the decisions, both to leave work and to start a new, independent organisation. He contrasts this with the time it took, presumably quite a long time, to build the careers of both him and his wife to the level where they are able to build their own charity projects. Interestingly, there is a continuity in terms of his career progression; he builds his expertise in the professional world that then allows him to pursue independent work and successfully navigate the transition between jobs.

This type of analysis is very useful for an investigation of continuous patterns of employment – with the organisation of work and the pathways for career progression as well as moments of transition – between jobs, between education and jobs, and between biographical experiences of employment and unemployment, including instances of maternity leave, medical leave and retirement.

Status

The final narrative environment employs the concept of status, here seen as the narrator's evaluation of what type of practices and experiences are worth placing within the life story. This narrative element is particularly important, considering that the main constraint of narration is to position oneself as the hero of one's own life story. According to Gubrium and Holstein (2009: 150), 'status shapes expectations, actions and reactions to what is tellable, by whom, and what is hearable, and by whom'. In the analysis of the biographical narrative through the narrative environment of status, we would focus on the justifications and claims contextualising the opportunities, rights and responsibilities of the narrator and the instances where these advantages have been denied. Research projects that investigate biographical narratives that focus on status aim to explore the way people orient and self-position themselves within and against larger cultural and social narratives. The analysis of status is often associated with the notion of success and failure in the eyes of the narrator and their narrative way of presenting it to the researcher.

To illustrate status at work, let's look at the following quote from the biographical interview of Andrew, a South African dancer who, at the time of the interview, was living in Northern Ireland. During his career, Andrew travelled a lot but settled in Northern Ireland when he met his wife and started a family. In his narrative, he is negotiating both his South African origins and race in the context of Northern Ireland. In his interview, he says:

> Never wanted to be European nor I wanted to choose this place, it sort of, relationships and life just sort of chose that. But now that I'm here I think about that differently. At the same time, I do have increasingly a sense of – and I think that just happens to people in my position where I sort of feel more like, I have this imaginary sort of global identity thing that I think I have, you know. But I don't really know what that is, you know. Like I sort of, there's a naïve part of me that feels the sort of like global citizen sort of thing because I don't really belong anywhere. And so then you create this other thing, but, you know, like the problem is you can't escape the material reality that I now live here and have to choose whether my kid goes to an

integrated school, a Catholic school or a Protestant school. So that's, I can be as global a citizen as I want in my head, I have to deal with Northern Ireland's little parochial problem. On a day to day basis. I have to choose which area I live in. You know, so I can think as global as I want, but you're also constrained by your reality just as if we move back to South Africa I can come back as this person who's travelled and been different and got a global sense of who I am. But I'm going to have to negotiate race because it's like in your face and it's in, you know. [Andrew, 41, Republic of South Africa]

From an analytical point of view, Andrew negotiates the interaction between internal and external identities. His international experience gives him a 'bird's eye view' perspective as a 'global citizen'. He sees himself as someone who can draw elaborate comparisons and unpack the issues of belonging and geopolitics. This label of 'global citizenship' can be identified as a status symbol. However, Andrew also recognises the local realities and external identities he is embedded in. He mentions religious tensions in Northern Ireland that he needs to navigate as well as his race. Those symbols of belonging or elements of identity that set you apart are analytically linked with status. The individual can achieve the position of status within the community by becoming a valuable member of that community or by assuming the role of recognisable 'stranger'. In Andrew's case, he embraced his ethnicity and unique international experience to transform them into assets in his professional career as a dancer.

Analytically, status is a more challenging narrative environment than the other environments, but often more rewarding to study. It allows insight into the systems of power relations within social structures. Status can be embedded in the categories used to make comparisons within groups and between them. The narratives of status would focus analysis on expressions of the 'right way' and 'wrong way' of achieving things, assuming that they highlight cultural patterns reflecting value systems, for example types of moral norms, such as civility and solidarity, used to justify the power structure within and between groups, communities and societies.

Narrative environment and intertextuality

Looking at the biographical narrative content and structures via the lenses of narrative environments is a good way of framing the analysis, especially if your project relates strongly to one of these environments. But as you can probably already see, the biographical narrative text is likely to include the elements of more than one narrative environment. The stories of organisations may overlap with the stories of jobs and career paths, and local cultures may cross over to intimate relationships. Status, in particular, can be a part of any justification. We can see it in the narrative account of Jakub when he draws the line between different groups of Polish people in France – professionals and au pairs – or in the narrative of Kinga, whose status as a woman in Japan was so different that it destabilised her marriage and led to her divorce. This means that we need to treat the biographical narrative as *intertextual*. According to Gubrium and Holstein (2009: 186), 'analysing such narratives as intertextual productions mean that any episode of storytelling should be viewed as sharing the empirical stage with other stories'. Depending on your research question and research design, you may select only the aspect of the story that is relevant to your research or acknowledge other contributing factors and their relational nature.

Furthermore, the intertextual nature of biographical narratives means that the specific environments will pop in at different places within the narrative. That means that 'all forms of accounts can be reflexively related to prior narratives as well as to future narrative horizons. … It means looking within situations as well as transsituationally for the ways in which narrative auspices – past, present, and anticipated – shape accounts' (Gubrium and Holstein 2009: 186). For example, within the narrative of intimate relationships, you may find that accounts of the relationship between the narrator's parents in childhood shaped their later intimate relationships or were the reference point for their future style of parenthood, that should or should not be modelled on their childhood experience.

Intertextuality is an important feature of this type of analysis and poses a significant challenge not only for the researcher but also for the research audience. Most of us need to present evidence in support of our research findings. As we did above, some of this evidence is to present the quotes as support for the analysis. But a single quote can rarely encompass the complexities we discover within the text and even then you may need to justify your choices – why this particular quote? Is the quote comparable to other accounts? How unique is the quote? There is no universal solution to that problem; it will depend strongly on your discipline as well as the level and experience of the audience. In those disciplines that regularly work with text, such as sociolinguistics, you may be able to present longer quotes. Audiences familiar with qualitative analysis will expect a variety of medium-length quotes that show diversity within your sample. And the most challenging audience which has a limited understanding of qualitative research may need shorter quotes, used for illustration purposes, and more explanation on how this type of evidence is being interpreted.

Tip from the field

Help your audience understand your evidence

The presentation of empirical material to illustrate your research findings can be challenging. You should remember that a quote always needs to be introduced (paragraph before) and discussed (paragraph after); it does not speak for itself.

(Continued)

The type of quote you choose to illustrate your findings, in terms of length and content, will depend on your audience. Be aware of the traditions within your discipline and your audience's level of knowledge.

Making generalisations from narrative ethnographic data

As analytical procedures and theoretical frameworks diversify to accommodate more structured data-collection techniques and narrower research questions, we encounter different ways to make broad generalisations. The scope of these generalisations will depend on the academic discipline and the positioning of biographical stories within the larger project design.

We have selected the following studies to illustrate the diversity of applications as well as the procedures for building generalisations. They may be used as guidelines as well as an inspiration for other biographical narrative research projects:

- Study 1 comes from the field of social work and shows how biographical research can be used to explore biographical complexities within the therapeutic environment.
- Study 2 is an excellent illustration of an evaluation project that investigates identity changes and attachments associated with major landscape change.
- Study 3 illustrates the application of biographical methods to the exploration of gendered discursive labels among women who participated in the national socialism movement during and after the Second World War.
- Study 4 showcases biographical research with groups facing social exclusion, such as Roma and Sinti, and the importance of education in overcoming discrimination and stigma.

Study 1

How Do People Change Their Lives? The role of the narrative interview and the biographical trajectory for social work and pastoral care in the United States (Jindra and Jindra, 2019)

This study outlines the potential of the biographical narrative interview method for social work and pastoral care in the USA.

Method and design

The study aimed to explore the biographical complexities of homeless people who are currently part of a six-month residential programme called

'Grace Ministries' delivered by the evangelical Mennonite Church. The study interviewed 17 residents using autobiographical narrative interview methods. For this publication, the authors selected two individual cases that illustrate the contrast in general attitude towards the religious and communal elements of the programme. The study aimed to understand the biographical trajectories that led to the episodes of homelessness and how those trajectories affect their assimilation in the Grace community and potential for recovery.

Study findings

Comparing and contrasting analysis of the two cases suggested that both biographies had things in common. Difficult childhoods without the presence of biological parents, with the elements of neglect and abuse and the use of drugs in teenage and young adulthood years, led to problems with law enforcement, an inability to keep employment, and the loss of a social support network that contributed to the homelessness. There were also significant differences. The biographical interviews highlighted that Narrator 1, who was more committed to her recovery, had 'stable' moments in her past biography. She frequently referred back to these moments in her narrative, whereas Narrator 2 did not. Narrator 1 was single and committed to personal and religious growth within the community, whereas Narrator 2 had a dependent child and treated the stay in Grace as temporary housing for himself and the child. Some of the variations are also associated with gender differences between the two narrators.

Generalisations

The authors of the study were particularly interested in the importance of personal trajectories (see Chapter 4 for the trajectory of suffering) and their impact on recovery. Based on the available evidence in the field of social work, they concluded that the willingness of the narrator to engage reflectively with traumatic and difficult biographical experiences in the therapeutic setting, indicated by the relatively more detailed narrative patterns, is an important step towards accessing resources and help within the residential setting, such as Grace Ministries. In contrast, an unwillingness to engage with traumatic biographical events and a lack of reflectiveness contribute to a more instrumental approach to recovery, that may have lower chances of success. This study indicates that an understanding and application of biographical narrative interview may enrich practice by helping practitioners of social work, pastoral care and pastoral theology to gain a better sense of the needs and strengths of people under their care.

Study 2

A narrative method of learning from an innovative coastal project – Biographies of the Sand Engine (Bontje and Slinger, 2017)

This study was published in *Ocean & Coastal Management* and is an example of the interdisciplinary application of biographical research methods.

Method and design

The study was designed to evaluate the impact of an innovative environmental project on the people who are directly affected by its design, construction and everyday work. This coastal project took place in Holland, where, in order to prevent floods in the coastal areas, there is a constant need to replace the sand that the sea has taken away. The Sand Engine was a pilot project where an enormous 21.5 Mm^3 of sand was deposited in one place, creating a small peninsula. The Sand Engine uses wind and sea to carry the sand along the coast to replenish the beaches that are natural anti-flood protection. The project was a success, but the researchers were aware that this was built on cooperation with local actors, and that to replicate this outcome in other places they needed to understand the 'human' element of this innovative solution.

The researchers decided to apply an adapted biographical narrative approach. They were interested in the biographical stories that related to the different elements of the project – its timescale, involvement and perception. They used autobiographical narrative interviews with 15 people engaged in the project (a snowball selection). They also designed a validation procedure, where they presented the initial findings from the biographical narratives to 44 conference participants. They used a survey to weight their findings and find which biographical patterns were most recognisable within this community.

Study findings

The study identified three types of narrative that related the personal experiences to the wider narratives of the Sand Engine project. First, the recognition that this project was 'something unknown that needed to be implemented in the region' type of narrative highlighted novelty for the region, but also some uncertainties associated with scale. Second, 'an iconic departure' narrative focused on an innovation that has addressed the ongoing environmental problem without causing too much disruption and resistance within the local community. Third, 'a stage in an incremental process' narrative represented a normalisation of the Sand Engine project, as the natural continuation of the costly maintenance projects that had been done before.

A 'validation' survey indicated that over 70% of the sample (n = 44) that constituted the wider public to the project recognised two or three of these narratives and most of them (57%) identified with the third narrative, 45% with the second narrative and 2% with the first.

Generalisations

The project framed the findings in terms of what we can learn from the narrative understanding of the project and how these perceptions can be managed in the future to ensure the successful implementation of other, similar environmental initiatives. Bontje and Slinger point out that narratives 1 ('unknown') and 2 ('iconic') relate to the different positioning of the project at local–global scales. For the local people, this is an 'unknown' process, that can cause changes and resistance within the community. In contrast, the project is 'iconic' on the global scale (being unique in Holland and worldwide). The authors argue that the second type of narrative managed to overshadow the first because it promoted the 'positive' resonance of coastal safety, the impulse for positive business and natural environmental outcomes. This contributed towards the positive perception of the project and lowered the community resistance to change. The researchers argue that understanding competing narratives and their management can be crucial for new environmental projects.

Study 3

Biography and discourse – A biography and discourse analysis combining case study on women's involvement in National Socialism (Pohn-Lauggas, 2017)

This study investigates the evolution of National Socialism discourse based on interpretations of events associated with Nazi political ideology during the Second World War and after it in Austria.

Method and design

This study outlines three main levels of discourse that address the issue of participation in National Socialism – first and at the most general level, as a special discourse that can be traced throughout the public narrative, evolving through a 'victim myth' to a 'co-responsibility thesis'. The second level – inter-discourse – produces imagined links between public narratives and perception of the events on an individual level, represented by popular interpretations of the events. Finally, the third level of everyday discourse can be observed in personal narratives, including biographies. In this study, the research question

(Continued)

seeks to find what first-level discourses are incorporated into the third-level discourse and why, indicating which parts of the public narrative are absorbed into everyday discourse.

The study design tests one particular special discourse that is currently prevalent at the inter-discourse level, called the 'gendered victim discourse', and seeks its presence in three autobiographical narrative interviews.

The study incorporates a discourse analysis of special and intra-discourse levels and biographical analysis of particular cases.

Study findings

The 'gendered victim discourse' relates to contemporary attempts to present all women who lived at the time of Nazi occupation as system 'victims' given the impossible task of rebuilding Austria and the Austrian nation after the atrocities of the Second World War. This discourse was reinforced by the establishment of a one-time payment of 300 Euros for all women who had had a child since 1951 and did not exceed a certain level of income. This programme painted an image of women/heroes/mothers without addressing their possible involvement in National Socialism or the crimes associated with it. According to the researcher, this double label of a victim of war and a victim of the Nazis is a convenient type of discourse that removes any blame and grants the status of war hero. The women use the national victim discourse in relation to their life stories, at the same time transforming them in order to interpret their own actions and those of their families as activity that played no role in the establishment and maintenance of the Nazi regime.

Generalisations

The absence of 'gendered victim discourse' from the biographies is explained by the fact that this discursive framing of the past does not adequately address the events and realities of the war and post-war periods. For these women, this time period carries important biographical significance and adopting a single 'woman/hero/mother that rebuilds her nation' label allows them to address these formative life experiences. Furthermore, the 'victim' discourse that seems to be widely criticised in the official public and academic debates, in favour of the 'co-responsibility thesis', seems to resonate strongly with the women's own biographical narratives and reinforce this way of justifying their involvement with National Socialism. According to Pohn-Lauggas (2017), seeing which of the discourses are represented in biographies and which are not gives valuable insight into the persistence and resurgence of certain types of discourse at the national level.

Study 4

Education, ethnicity and gender – Educational biographies of 'Roma and Sinti' women in Germany (Reimer, 2016)

This study was an outcome of a doctoral thesis. It is concerned with the educational trajectories of Roma and Sinti women in Germany, embedded in the context of over-coming patterns of discrimination, oppression and marginalisation. Reimer argues that educational experiences for women from these minority groups can be life-changing, but that their educational trajectories are complicated and distorted. The study's research question focused on exploring what complicates these educational trajectories for Roma and Sinti women.

Method and design

The study is based on autobiographical narrative interviews with 16 Roma (East-ern European travellers who arrived as guest workers) women (from a minority persecuted by the Nazis). All of the women spent their adolescence in Germany and went through the German educational system. This particular publication builds on two contrasting case studies.

Study findings

The study findings point to patterns of exclusion from German mainstream society and competing gendered cultural patterns between a traditional family model and educational institutions. The author observes that early experiences of feeling dif-ferent are common in the biographical narratives, along with a need to fully belong to a close-knit family, where the girls are expected to be wives and mothers to the exclusion of all else. According to the study findings, educational institutions are often the only gateways to emancipation, but they fail to accommodate the biographical trajectories, such as early motherhood.

The study finds that the most successful educational trajectories of Roma women often benefited from educational environments outside of formal educa-tion. Voluntary work and Bible study groups were mentioned as a way of returning to mainstream society after an unfinished formal education.

Generalisations

This study highlights that there is a gendered element to the study of education trajectories among minority groups. The interaction between traditional gender roles and formal education is often permeated by the feeling of alienation that pushes girls out of school, and this needs to be addressed in policy and social work practices. The study also highlights the importance of other, non-formal educational groups that allow minority women to come back to education and use it to pursue better employment options and greater independence within family networks as well as mainstream society.

Summary

This chapter was dedicated to the narrative ethnographic approach to biographical research. A broad and diverse approach, it spans many academic disciplines and theoretical traditions, including sociolinguistics, psychology, sociology, health and education studies, among others. A narrative ethnographic approach to biographical data allows for greater control over the data and analysis, and removes some of the serendipitous nature of autobiographical narrative methods, allowing for more precise research questions and research designs. Researchers can control the research process either by structuring their narrative data-gathering methods, or by focusing on a specific analytical framework that is well aligned with the overall research question.

In this chapter, we discussed three examples of narrative ethnography. The *narrative environments* approach, as outlined by Gubrium and Holstein (2009), prioritises analysis of the relationship between the individual and broader social structures that takes place in a number of narrative environments, including intimate relationships, jobs, organisations, local cultures and narratives of social status. The *life stories* approach of Linde (1993) is focused on the narrative process of knowledge exchange, both tacit and implicit, between the individual story and larger, structural-level narratives. Linde's approach focuses on how people change their biographical narrative to justify different aspects of belonging. Finally, the *sociobiographical* approach that builds upon Chamberlayne and Wengraf's BNIM framework (Chamberlayne et al., 2004), aims to uncover the processes individuals employ to deal with changing life circumstances and historical events.

We illustrated some narrative ethnography analytical procedures that may be used as an inspiration as well as an introduction to analysis of the biographical narrative text. We invited you, our readers, to familiarise yourselves with the relevant studies to observe diverse ways of designing a study, and to draw wider generalisations. We encouraged researchers, both novice and experienced, to venture outside of their designated academic discipline and narrow traditions of biographical research, to engage in interdisciplinary methodological discussions that will take advantage of the enormous diversity of approaches within the field of biographical narrative research.

Questions to consider

1. Have you considered how much you need to control what other people are telling you during an interview? Can you tell the difference between what you want to know and what other people want to tell you?
2. How would you ensure that your questions elicit narration, rather than argumentation?

3. The analytical approach you choose to apply narrows down your focus; is this an advantage or disadvantage for your research project?
4. How would you present evidence that is suitable for your audience?

Don't forget to use the additional resources to support your research in Appendix 3!

6

LOGICAL SYSTEMS, QUALITATIVE COMPARATIVE ANALYSIS AND QUANTITATIVE CODING

Objectives

By the end of this chapter, you will be able to:

- Understand why researchers use methodological innovations to explore biographical data
- Observe how we can manage the complexities of biographical narrative and life-course data on the level of biographical data gathering and data analysis
- Understand the implications of imposing a structure on biographical data
- Understand the role of data coding and its implication for data analysis
- Recognise the strengths and limitations of using CAQDAS in biographical research
- Recognise the difference between qualitative coding and quantitative coding
- Understand the main principles of qualitative comparative analysis and its implications for biographical data analysis
- Identify the strengths and limitations of methodological interventions for biographical research.

Biographical narrative research, when done correctly, has everything qualitative methodologies cherish – unstructured form, layers of meanings, intersecting social categories and intertextual relations between themes, subjects and emotions. Within that narrative richness, there is a potential for the skilled researcher to uncover new meanings and new relations that answer important questions about the nature of relationships between individuals and their social worlds. Biographical narrative research, however, is also a part of academic and policy environments, where it needs to withstand scrutiny with respect to research transparency, replicability and generalisability. There is increasing pressure from audiences and publishers, policy makers and other users of qualitative and quantitative methodologies to expand and innovate using biographies. These innovations often face resistance and scepticism, indicating that work with qualitative and narrative data is a craft that cannot be reduced to predetermined analytical steps or simplistic cause–effect dichotomies. However, within the qualitative research field there are innovative approaches that can be applied and modified to fit biographical narrative methodologies. They aim to accommodate a larger number of cases by simplifying the narrative data, and to employ coding frameworks aided by computer software for the kind of analysis that may point to unrealised connections, associations and structures within the cases and between them. These types of methodological innovation, if successful, promise to increase the applicability of biographical research and its relevance within both academic and non-academic environments.

This chapter tackles the issue of managing complexities of biographical data throughout the research process. First, we discuss the implications of structuring biographical data and the links between the biographical narrative and life-course research strategies. Second, we explore the analytical approaches that include qualitative and quantitative coding of the data and the potential for use of computer-assisted qualitative analysis software packages, such as Atlas.ti, MAXQDA or NVivo. Finally, we consider the application of qualitative comparative analysis (QCA) tools in the analysis of biographical data.

Managing biographical complexities

In the preceding chapters, we discussed at length the challenging nature of biographical narrative methods that embrace the unstructured type of data, and open-ended analysis. As scientific methods and methodological tools develop, they can be adopted into biographical narrative research. Methodological innovations offer exciting opportunities, allowing for larger samples, the incorporation of biographies into more elaborate and complex research designs, as well as comparative insight into individual biographical narrative research practices. This chapter presents three such methodological innovations, namely 'data reduction' using structured and semi-structured interviews; analytical reductions that use coding frameworks, often supported by computer software; and, finally, the quantification of qualitative data for the purpose of QCA.

Life course research – structuring biographical data

Embracing the complexity of autobiographical narrative style interviews has much to commend it, including the individually unique narrative structures and processes that can be analysed in a variety of ways. The problem with the unstructured form of the interview, however, lies in the lack of focus, which might be particularly problematic for some research fields and research questions. Imagine a research project that is investigating the health habits of those individuals who seek a specific treatment. These habits develop over a lifetime and are often embedded in a series of coping mechanisms for difficult situations, shaped, for example, by community perceptions of body image and socio-economic opportunities and limitations. This life-long perspective lends itself to biographical methodologies, but not necessarily in the shape and form of an open-ended biographical narrative interview. This type of research problem would require some moulding of the narrative form in an attempt to force the biographical account to follow the sequential life-long process, but with a specific theme in mind.

This approach, referred to in the literature as the life-course approach, is not a new development. It has a long research tradition in many disciplines, such as health studies, clinical psychology and international development. According to Caetano and Nico (2019), the life-course approach shares many similarities with the biographical approach. At its core, the life-course perspective 'should be understood as an explanatory theory that proposes the use of the past experiences as a means to study the trajectories of individuals' (2019: 364). In many respects, it uses the biographical framework or the 'life course' in order to employ the right terminology, as a container for all other everyday life events. Within that framework, which assumes sequenced trajectories of events, researchers aim to track significant changes or quantify certain occurrences. This opens up a number of research opportunities that would satisfy the requirements of some of the research problems. For example, in international development studies of poverty, researchers are interested in the life trajectories of people who either lifted themselves out of extreme poverty, or fell back into poverty. Analysis of their life stories aims to uncover types of drivers, maybe environmental ones, such as drought or lack of fertile land, or social ones, associated with a lack of education or inadequate health facilities, that alone

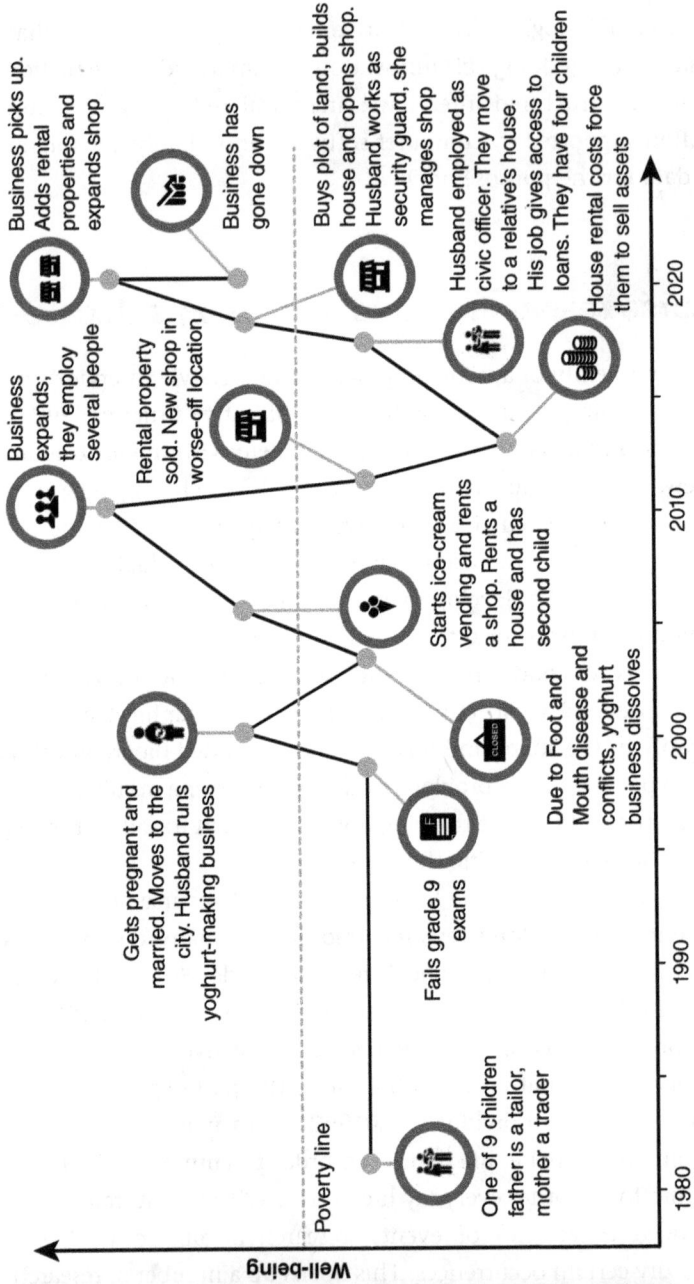

Figure 6.1 Visual representation of life-course interview plotted against study-assigned poverty line

Source: Chronic Poverty Advisory Network (CPAN)

or in combination might direct these poverty trajectories. With a greater number of cases, it is even possible to weight certain factors or their combination in patterns of likelihood of occurrence, to determine which factors are more relevant and should be prioritised for policy intervention.

To generate this type of data, we need the type of interview that directs the interviewee into a specific thematic framework and makes sure that we preserve the sequenced account of the theme. To achieve this type of data, the researcher needs to control the interview process with the use of semi-structured and structured interview techniques, asking some direct biographical questions. For example, '(While talking about nutrition) can you tell me about your childhood ... what did you eat?', followed by 'So, in your adult life, is there more food available, or less? Do you get more or less food than you did as a child?'. This way of structuring the interview usually keeps the biographical sequencing, for example by asking separate questions about childhood, adolescence, adulthood and older age, but funnels the themes of the interview into the specific area of everyday life that is relevant to the overall research question.

Depending on the skills of the interviewer and the overall recording of the data, this type of interview can still be considered a narrative interview. Within the confines of the direct question, there might be a space for the flow of narration that would allow for in-depth qualitative analysis. The quality of data here is influenced directly by a sensitivity in the question wording, timing, interview recording and transcription. There are a number of ways in which this type of data can be formatted for analysis. For instance, the answer may be **recorded as a simple fact** – 'Interviewee said that there was more food'. Interestingly, those facts can be plotted against a biographical timeline, creating the scope for life-mapping approaches and visualisations (see the Study 2 example in Chapter 9 and Figure 6.1). This type of recording creates only a few data points within each biographical unit, but allows for the analysis of a large number of cases.

Life history interview mapping is a visual technique that allows us to trace well-being trajectories, here associated with poverty levels in relation to a poverty line established by panel data analysis. The technique identifies turning point trajectory drivers, such as economic shocks, that affect the long-term poverty trends of households:

1. More qualitative orientated analysis interview transcripts can include detailed **interview notes with the occasional direct quote** that may be relevant for further analysis. For example, the interviewer will record that 'the amount of food has not changed, but the type of food eaten leans more towards highly processed food'. This technique relies on the skill of the interviewer to capture the subtleties and nuances of the account that can be recorded for further analysis of patterns between cases.

2. Analysis focused on narrative patterns may include the **detailed transcript of the interview**, whether simple transcription of content or more advanced recording of the socio-linguistic interaction (including pauses, hesitations and interactional notes on the rapport between interviewer, interviewee and the wider context). Here, the analysis may follow some aspects of narrative analysis, but this type of data recording is more suited to analysis within individual cases and between a limited number of cases.

Tip from the field

Reduce your data

We encounter many students who follow the tradition of their field in the design stage and conduct the life-course type of interview only to discover later that their data could be deeper and that certain types of analysis are not available to them due to the structured character of the data. The thing to remember is that it is possible to reduce the data from the narrative biographical interview form, especially if we know exactly what we are interested in. However, it is not possible to build a structured interview into the narrative form without conducting the interview again. Therefore, understanding the relevant methodological strengths and shortcomings at the early stage of the research project will determine what you can and cannot get out of your data and analysis.

The life-course approach can be applied in research projects with large samples that can be analysed using quantitative methods. This type of analysis increases the generalisability of the findings and makes it a desirable research companion in many mixed method research designs (see Chapter 9). This approach also has some significant limitations. According to Caetano and Nico (2019), life-course approaches have demanding rules for the operationalisation of variables and theoretical frameworks. An explanatory framework needs to be devised that can then be captured within the data. The interview questions need to be specific enough to capture the nature of the topic – for example, 'what did you eat as a child?' needs to be translated into a caloric and nutritional value of the specific food in the answer, and then the answer to 'Has there been a change in what you eat now?' may be an indicator of socio-economic improvement, or of moving between rural and urban areas. Additionally, the scope of the change is an issue. If the project aims to track changes in nutrition, how can the degree of change be captured in the interview? All these research elements have to be part of the initial design of the interview and analytical frameworks from the start, leaving very little margin for error.

Furthermore, according to Dannefer (2003), life-course approaches struggle to account for diversity in biographical patterns. When looked at in detail, the 'stages' of the life course become more nuanced. For example, 'when adolescence ends and adulthood begins' may look different between specific generations and between different cultures. Additionally, life-course research finds it hard to account for the autonomy of the self, or what is also referred to as agency. It assumes that the individual always lives in some configuration of social institutions, for example family and community, that frames everyday life choices. However, events such as migration, where the mobile individual removes themselves from the social control of these institutions, introduce too much diversity and create too much contrast for the framework to handle. In the nutrition example, asking a migrant interviewee about changes in diet between childhood and the present does not measure the same thing as the identical question put to a more settled individual.

The life-course approach is often criticised by disciplines and researchers who advocate the importance of subjective accounts, narrative depth and subtle, humanistic types of analysis. Our position is that each methodological tool is suited to different types of research problems and research realities. Therefore, focusing on possible synergies between approaches, with the application of both qualitative and quantitative methodologies, may expand the field of inquiry without damaging individual research paradigms (Nico, 2016; Caetano and Nico, 2019). Understanding both traditions, and their strengths and limitations within specific research contexts, with an open mind, will be beneficial for both traditions. Study 1 is a good illustration of this type of development in practice.

Study 1

The Life History Interview Method – Applications to intervention development (Goldman et al., 2003)

This study was part of intervention planning for the Harvard Cancer Prevention Program which focused on working-class and multi-ethnic populations.

Method and design

The study collected 15 open-ended, semi-structured interviews. The sample for the study was purposive and aimed to include an ethnically diverse group recruited from the project sites associated with the Harvard Cancer Prevention Program.

The interview script included topic areas that represented the main research interests, including demographic data; description of the typical day; eating habits and cultural influences on diet; physical activities and cultural or contextual

(Continued)

influences on activity; sources of stress, coping mechanisms and support; and occupational health and safety concerns and experiences.

Interviews were recorded and detailed interview reports (including the interview notes and interviewer observations) were analysed using the approach known as immersion/crystallisation that involved group discussions, including the anthropologist leading the project, research assistants and project investigators.

Study findings

Analysis of the data identified six recurring themes within the topic areas and across them, including: immigration and social status; social support; stress; food/nutrition; exercise/physical activity; and occupational health and safety.

The authors explore these themes to show the variety of experiences that can affect practices relevant to cancer prevention initiatives. Immigration and social status themes indicate that people from varying ethnic backgrounds can have very different expectations when coming to the USA, and that change in one status can affect how they access health care systems. The social support theme explores the role of trust and family and community networks in the process of gaining a sense of security. The stress theme highlights the tensions within the family and pressure within the job environment. The theme of food and nutrition focuses on different rituals and cultural norms, but also highlights the impact of shift work on the different size and time of meals. The exercise and physical activity theme points to an assumption that engaging in physically demanding labour is a sufficient form of physical activity, and shows that some people were actively avoiding sports for fear of injuries. Finally, occupational health and safety indicates poor environmental conditions and helplessness in addressing these issues on the part of management.

Generalisations

These findings were then used to plan 'context-rich, non-stereotyping intervention strategies and educational materials for the multicultural, working-class participants in the Harvard Cancer Prevention Program' (Goldman et al., 2003: 572). One of the main highlights for the staff of the programme was the opportunity to reflect on their own assumptions about the migrant population, and not to assume that participants were poorly educated. Identifying struggles with language resulted in the employment of multi-lingual field staff. Attention was also paid to preventative messaging, for example in the context of shift work where information about meals and physical activity had to be changed to accommodate the life realities of this particular group.

Data coding and using qualitative data analysis software

Data coding, in one form or another, is a natural part of the analytical process that organises ideas to uncover patterns within the data. This type of organisation can include finding the thematic threads throughout the data, or noticing the differences in accounts of events between men and women, or people of different ethnicities. In the research methodologies that analyse texts, such as narrative and discourse traditions, from the moment the researcher picks up the highlighter to indicate the importance of the passage, and the pencil to make a note of why this passage of text is important, they engage in the process of data coding. In the last two chapters, we highlighted certain parts of text to draw attention to the 'important' aspects of the narrative. In short, data coding is a process of breaking down the data, so as to put them together in a different way (Corbin and Strauss, 1990). Disagreements about data coding are not about whether to do it or not, but about how to make the process of disassembling the data and assembling study findings scientific, transparent and meaningful. Imagine that your piece of data is a model of the Eiffel tower made out of LEGO and that data coding allows you to take it apart to analyse its construction (without instruction). There is a possibility that you may go too far and break it down to the single bricks. That would tell you how many bricks were used to build it and what types, but would you be able now to replicate the building process? You may also focus on colour coding the bricks, or analysing the main sections of the building, but you still need to be able to understand the principles of balance, weight distribution or proportions, and make notes on the process of disassembling to be able to say something meaningful about the process of construction. Either way, you need to know how you want to proceed and what type of analysis would be most beneficial for your study *before* you take it apart.

This type of analysis, especially when enhanced by the use of computer software on larger data sets, requires a level of confidence and knowledge that may make some researchers hesitant to use advanced techniques in data coding. Within the biographical narrative traditions that pride themselves on the more humanistic analytical procedures, that sentiment is quite widespread. Merrill and West (2009: 144) argue that analysing narrative data:

> is deeply intuitive, subtle, intersubjective as well as a challenging process: intellectually, epistemologically and in terms of researcher's self-knowledge. This may defy computerisation. We feel, from our experience of attempting to use computer-based analysis, that it can also overly objectify as well as simplify the analytic process and risk devaluing and dehumanising the subjects at the heart of the research, including the researcher.

The problem with data coding in the narrative research traditions is a conflation of meaning between data coding and data analysis. Coding is a tool of the analysis, allowing the researcher to break down interview texts into more manageable chunks. Analysis is about the ability of the researcher to identify the chunks we are searching for and how they can be used to answer our specific research questions. To use our previous LEGO metaphor, simply because you can disassemble the tower down to the level of the single brick does not mean that you should.

The role of CAQDAS in enhancing qualitative analysis

Discussions about coding in qualitative research methodologies have been brought into sharp focus by the rise of computer software. Computer-assisted qualitative data analysis software (CAQDAS in short) refers to computer packages such as NVivo, Atlas.ti, MAXQDA, Dedoos, QDAMiner that are used to facilitate data organisation and analysis. Among this variety are commercial, licenced software packages, as well as publicly available open-source programmes. The principles they operate on are very similar, but they differ in terms of interface design and additional research tools. For a detailed overview of CAQDAS software packages and research practices, we recommend *Using Software in Qualitative Research: A step-by-step guide* by Christina Silver and Ann Lewins (2014).

Tip from the field

Accessing CAQDAS

Some of the best-known software packages, such as NVivo, Atlas.ti and MAXQDA, are quite expensive. If you are a student, a university staff member or an employee of a research institution, there is a chance that your affiliated organisation has a licence for one of these packages. If not, you can access them for free for the trial period of (usually) 30 days, which means that if you plan your work in advance you can code and analyse a small research project for nothing.

Biographical research projects and computer coding

For the purpose of any qualitative research, but biographical narrative research in particular, you should understand the relationship between the qualitative software you are using and your analysis. The software is only a container for your data and it is up to the researcher to build the analytical framework that will, in the final stages of the analysis, reveal the patterns within the data that can be used as evidence to support your argument. You can already observe this aspect of the research process in other methodological approaches to bio-graphical narrative data. In Chapter 4, we illustrated how the way things are said in the unstructured flow of autobiographical narrative can be used to under-stand power relations. In Chapter 5, we used the framework of narrative environments to narrow down thematic analysis of the narratives. All of these, and many more analytical frameworks, can be built into a CAQDAS project. The choice of which one to use will depend on the research question and other analytical considerations.

Building analytical strategies for biographical research projects will take place on several different analytical levels (Silver and Lewins, 2014: 17):

- **Data coding level** means carefully viewing and reading the relevant material. As you are going through the material, you will annotate when you identify and reflect on interesting aspects, which is equivalent to marginal scribbles in the text version of the analysis. It is at this level of analysis that biographical research needs to produce analytical notes that ensure that the sense of biographical continuity and coherence is not lost in the analysis. Biographical sequence memos and trajectory notes should be used to secure the data from too much fragmentation.
- **Data indexing level** is the process of highlighting and coding relevant sections of text or audio depending on your analytical approach. You might build the coding framework based on either 'thematic codes' or 'process structures'. This level of analysis will also retain the attributes of the biographical research unit, such as age, gender or research site.
- **Conceptual level of the data** is concerned with the interrogation of patterns, relationships and connections within and between the data. Well-coded data will allow you to sort coded 'quotes' according to specific attributes (age, gender, research site) to spot the differences between biographical research units. For example, how men and women talk about their marriage may be an important analytical tool for a project that focuses on changes in family life.
- **Making analytical connections** is the level of the analysis which highlights the importance of stepping back and making links with the wider context of the study. At this level, you are expected to insert your study findings into a conversation within your field of study. This may take the form of interrogating your data to fit a particular theory (deductive analysis); focusing on your own theory building (inductive analysis); or employing elements of both – going back and forth between theory and data (abductive analysis).

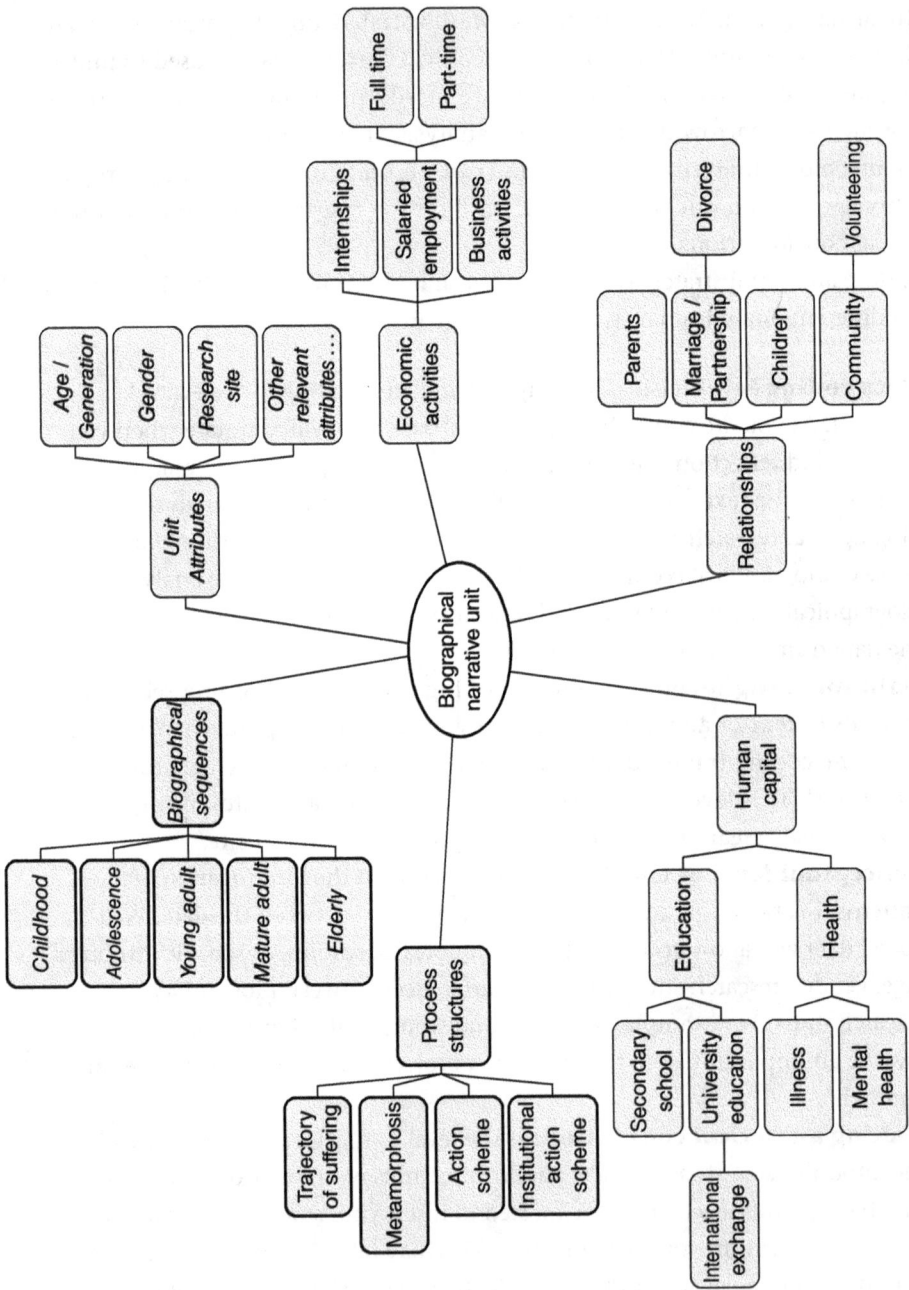

Figure 6.2 Biographical coding framework

The process of analysis will take place on all four levels simultaneously. Your observation of the data will point you to specific concepts and theories and, at the same time, certain theories in the field will direct your attention to a specific way of coding the data. This process is very dynamic and multidirectional, and the use of qualitative analytical software allows you to contain and manage this complexity.

An example of coding

Not many researchers present the coding framework of their studies, as this is what happens behind the scenes, 'in the kitchen'. The final product rarely displays this part of the process as it tends to get messy and evolve as the project goes on. The coding framework in Figure 6.2 was created to illustrate some of the biographical issues that may guide you in creating your own analytical frameworks that reflect your particular research questions.

Looking closely, you can see different types of coding that illustrate the different levels of analysis. Data-level coding may include observations on economic activities, relationships or experiences with social institutions, such as schools and health-related issues. They may expand in the direction that reflects the research question. If you are interested in international mobility, you may focus on international exchanges within the university system, international employment and international relationships. The indexing level in biographical research may include biographical sequencing, indicating parts of the narrative taking place at specific stages in life – for example, tracking employment for narrators in their youth and early adolescence to highlight the trajectory of employment progression. If you are interested in biographical process structures (as explained in Chapter 4), you can also code these specific elements of the narrative. Finally, to enable you to make meaningful cross-case comparisons you can attach attributes to your cases. These can be used to compare, for example, the accounts of economic activities in different biographical ages (youth, early adolescence) by gender, or research site. When designed well, this type of coding framework will allow you to make meaningful observations and conceptual connections that can enhance your analysis.

Tip from the field

Coding is a skill you should learn before the project and hone during the project

Coding with computer software is becoming an important part of qualitative research training in many universities. But as with many skills taught in school, students usually find it difficult to use coding software in their own individual

(Continued)

research projects. It takes time and practice to learn how to upload documents, create coding frameworks and then manually code the data. It is tempting to take a shortcut and do it in the 'intuitive' way, especially with the project deadline looming near. This is because the **true value of qualitative coding, either by hand or using computer software, comes at the end of the analytical process**. You can spot the difference between male and female responses, or review the variety of experiences that fall into your conceptual codes, and enhance your analysis, but in our experience not many students get that far into the process. Some of the reasons are time constraints and lack of confidence. For that reason, it is good to plan for both. **Make sure that you have time to learn your software, discuss your coding frameworks with your supervisor, and trust that the process will lead you in the right direction**.

Advantages and limitations

Computer-assisted qualitative analysis is associated with the rise of the big commercial software programs. These are constantly updated, adding new research tools, such as instant transcription of voice recording; analytical tools for video recordings; and text-based tools, such as word frequencies, word clouds and sentiment analysis. The marketing of these software packages points to 'theory building' and 'hypothesis testing' tools that increase the analytical power of qualitative analysis. But, outside the visually powerful rhetoric, essentially CAQDAS is a clerical tool. According to Kelle (2008: 456):

> CAQDAS allows the exploitation of qualitative data more fully. But this is achieved not through the development of computer-aided analytic techniques unfamiliar to qualitative work but through the mechanisation of clerical tasks used in hermeneutic science for hundreds of years.

These clerical aids help to structure data material and allow for quick retrieval of the raw material to support analysis. This frees up head space to follow analytical patterns and create broader theoretical links.

The robustness of analysis supported by qualitative software increases with the scale of the research project. It offers the ability to manage larger samples and more cases, to work collaboratively with many research partners and to manage hierarchical data projects where the data collection, data processing and data analysis are done by different people within the project. This does not mean that smaller projects cannot benefit from the support of CAQDAS. They also provide learning opportunities to hone research skills that are transferable to bigger academic and non-academic research projects. Another benefit of using a qualitative analysis software package to store both data and analysis lies in the ability to retrieve relevant information quickly and efficiently. This is especially important in long-term projects, such as PhDs and larger, more collaborative investigations. Sometimes, for the purposes of publication, you will be asked for additional evidence or extra pieces of analysis. That may happen months or years after the project has finished and most of the information stored in your head will be gone; but with sufficient coding and analysis, you should be able to efficiently identify the relevant information.

There are also limitations to the use of CAQDAS in biographical research. One problem is data fragmentation. Hollway and Jefferson (2000) argue that computer-based analysis can fragment data into a clerical type of coding that will neglect deeper understanding in the hope that somehow the computer will generate some solutions. For biographical analysis, there is the possibility of losing the overall biographical sense of continuity and coherence that is the cornerstone of the analysis. This echoes Kelle's (2008: 455) observation that focusing too much on software procedures may result in 'reifying the code and losing the phenomenon'. The final limitation of computer-assisted analysis of biographical narrative data is the danger of losing the nuances and subtleties of the narrative, especially when they are contradictory between different biographical episodes and between individual argumentation and narration of events. For example, marriage can have a good side, even though the person is divorced. When you focus only on the divorce, either as a personal attribute or when coding the texts relevant to the experience, you will lose the parts of narrative that mention 'the good times' or the natural progression of the relationship, and focus instead on the argumentation outlining the reasons for the divorce. These limitations have significant implications for biographical narrative research projects. They have to be addressed early on by the implementation of additional analytical procedures, such as memos and annotations, that will counter some of these issues.

Quantifying codes and links between conditions and outcomes – QCA

The type of coding we have discussed in the previous section can be described as qualitative coding, where the researcher creates analytical categories through interpretation of the data (Charmaz, 1983: 111). As we follow deeper into coding practices, we arrive at the point that makes it possible to utilise the computational power of software in more and more cases. What started as qualitative coding can be transformed into a version of quantitative coding where we apply 'preconceived, logically deduced codes into which data are placed' (Charmaz, 1983: 111). This shift between qualitative and quantitative coding can also apply to biographical narrative and life-course data, which would lead to a direct conversion of the qualitative data into quantitative code-based analysis, which can then be supported by certain number-based procedures to seek patterns and typologies of associations between biographical conditions and biographical outcomes (Kelle, 2008: 455). For example, to simplify this analytical pattern, in the study of divorce we can identify a set of conditions, derived from theory and other studies, and seek their presence (or lack thereof) in the data. We can investigate relationships with and between parents, and other significant relationships, within the biographical account, and try to identify those conditions which alone or in combination have led to the biographi-cal outcome of being divorced. The outcome we are searching for is a confirmation or rejection of our hypothesis on what conditions are likely to lead to divorce. This is the general logic of the deductive analytical process. Furthermore, we can use some additional measures, such as strength of associations between the conditions and outcomes to support our analysis.

The QCA approach stands for qualitative comparative analysis and can be applied in this type of study. QCA was developed by Charles Ragin (2008) and has its own open-source software (fsQCA) available on the website of the author, together with a set of resources for analysis. Qualitative comparative analysis is a technique which aims to apply a more rigorous and mathematically sound form of reasoning to qualitative data. The technique employs some of the assumptions of Boolean algebra, set theory and fuzzy logic. QCA was created for the analysis of 'deep' qualitative data units with a large number of possible variables and a lim-ited number of cases under investigation. In this section, we will discuss some of the aspects of QCA that make it relevant to biographical narrative research.

Biography as a deep data unit

The principles of QCA are built on the assumption that researchers have access to a limited number of cases that are considered to be deep data units. In his original study, Ragin (2008) uses the example of nation states/countries as the unit of study. He is interested in what conditions lead to the emergence of democratic governance systems. There are a limited number of states to investigate, therefore a statistical analysis of the comparison between states is not feasible. But states are deep data units, meaning we know a lot of what happens within states. Ragin argues that with their history and complex economic systems, states provide sufficiently deep units to allow for the testing of outcomes – for instance, survival or collapse of the demo-cratic system – based on a number of theory-derived conditions, such as literacy and legal opposition. For biographical researchers, the autobiographical narrative in particular can be treated as a deep data unit, where configurations of biographical conditions are examined in order to understand the dynamics between individual and social biographical elements. QCA relies on an in-depth knowledge of cases, that can be used for theoretically derived hypothesis testing. However, the researcher needs to be aware that not every biography is a deep analytical unit. Highly structured biographical data or data with only a superficial level of narration will be too shallow to capture some of the meaningful complexities within and between cases.

Defining outcomes and conditions in the biographical context

The QCA approach is case-specific. Rather than focusing on a specific variable, it focuses the analysis on the configurations of conditions within cases. This can be compared to analysis of the recipe for a cake. The researchers are not interested in how many cakes have flour in them, but in what combination of ingredients and baking practices leads to this specific sort of cake as compared with the variety of other possible cakes. Baking metaphors aside, on the basis of a deep knowledge about biographical cases, the researcher identifies possible conditions or ingredients throughout the set of cases, and the QCA computer software (fsQCA) analysis helps to identify the strongest patterns and create typologies. According to Small (2011: 77), 'the core ideas behind QCA are to treat each case as a particular configuration of traits and to identify the sets of traits necessary for a given outcome to occur'. The QCA approach provides insights into the configuration of conditions (or bio-graphical experiences and practices) within and between biographies, treating each biographical case as a single analytical unit.

The vital part of the analysis is then a process of identifying what in the biographical unit will be treated as a condition and what would count as an outcome. In this con-text, the outcome is rooted in your research question. You may look into the biographies of people and research what conditions lead to divorce, such as personal incompatibili-ties or conflict (sufficient conditions) and what conditions lead to the lack of divorce, such as mutual support structures (necessary conditions). The outcome would be that in the sample some of the biographies are of people who are divorced (outcome pre-sent), and some are of those who are not (outcome not present). In the next step, you will identify the list of conditions based on biographical experiences and through a series of decisions you will quantify those conditions as either 1 – condition present, or 0 – condition not present. It is also possible to assign a gradient between 0 and 1, to highlight the intensity or relevance of this condition to the biographical unit. (For more guidance on the specific techniques of this, see Ragin, 2008.)

Next, QCA focuses on identifying explicit connections between case elements – establishing configurations – and searching for commonalities in the configurations across cases. Ragin (2008) emphasises two general strategies which allow for combinations of causal patterns within complex data to be detected. 'The first strategy is to examine cases sharing a given outcome and attempt to identify their shared causal conditions' (2008: 18). This approach is appropriate for the assessment of necessary conditions – a combination of elements which needs to occur in order for a certain phenomenon to take place. 'The second strategy is to examine cases sharing a specific causal condition, or, more commonly, a specific combination of causal conditions, and assess whether these cases exhibit the same outcome' (2008: 18). Following this style of reasoning, a pattern of a sufficient combination of elements can be identified. The outcome of the analysis is two typologies: one of sufficient conditions and one of necessary conditions that show the level of association with the outcome.

Deep knowledge of the biographical cases is necessary to understand and make both typologies of conditions meaningful for your research. They need to be interpreted and embedded in your theory to hold any explanatory power. This is the only way you can claim that your generalisations – the hypothesis confirmed or rejected – can be distinguished from the accidental associations that are features of the particular data set. This step is the most important aspect of QCA, where the qualitative skills of data interpretation meet more quantitative methods of data analysis.

Size of the sample

In the world of quantitative research, having a small number of cases limits the application of statistical models that are interested in patterns of causality and generalisation to a larger population. The most significant advantage of QCA, and the reason to apply it to the analysis of biographical data, is that this analytical technique is well-suited to small-n studies. The number of conditions which can be tested in the data set depends heavily on the number of cases under investigation. The exact number of conditions cannot be larger than the number of cases, and Ragin (2008) points out that the best proportion between the number of cases (n) and the number of conditions (k) should fall in the following function: $n<2k$. In the context of some biographical studies, 20 or more deep biographical cases will be sufficient for QCA analysis.

Quality measures

According to Rihoux and Ragin (2008: 12), 'a well-executed QCA should go beyond plain description and consider "modest generalisations": QCA results may be used in support of "limited historical generalisation"'. Qualitative comparative analysis does not have the generalisation power of a statistical, probabilities-based analysis, but offers an analytical tool for rigorous and systematic analysis of data which would otherwise only be available for interpretative methods. Instead of measuring the strength of correlation, it assesses the coverage and consistency of complex patterns across the data; these two measures report on the strength of empirical support for a specific combination of conditions.

First, the **consistency measure** 'gauges the degree to which the cases sharing a given combination of conditions agree in displaying the outcome in question' (Ragin, 2008: 44). Consistency indicates how closely a configuration of conditions is approximated. Second, the **coverage measure** assesses 'the degree to which a cause or causal combination accounts for instances of an outcome' (Ragin, 2008: 44). Both of these descriptive measures provide a picture of fit between the analytical model and the data; thus, if there is a number of condition configurations, coverage would be lower, but consistency would be higher and vice versa. The coverage and consistency number falls between 0 and 1, and Ragin (2008) argues that the number should not be lower than 0.75. Both consistency and coverage measures depend on the data set and the conversion of qualitative data into quantitative measures. We would argue that a data set that has been built upon narrative data may have lower measures of consistency and coverage (approximately 0.6) as some configurations may come as a natural feature of the narrative, rather than as an actual association of conditions.

Study 2

QCA analysis of cosmopolitan practices in biographical narrative perspective (Eichsteller, 2013)

This is a small illustration of the QCA model selected from a PhD thesis entitled 'Becoming a citizen of the world: A sociological study of the biographical narratives of new cosmopolitans'.

Method and design

This study used 25 autobiographical narrative interviews with people with significant transnational experience to investigate cosmopolitan practices. The QCA outcome was defined as a general cosmopolitanism index (GCI) that classified 25 biographical cases on the spectrum between local and global, based on the intensity of international movement and self-positioning of the narrator within the biographical narrative, as either insider or outsider within the wider social environment. The study identified over 21 biographical conditions, such as childhood experiences of mobility, a general biographical orientation to see and visit multiple places, cultural dispositions that include linguistic abilities, and the ability to adjust to new situations or a willingness to take risks.

(Continued)

This example showcases the testing of one hypothesis based on Szerszynski and Urry's (2006: 117) proposition that even simple 'sensations of other people and places create an awareness of interdependence, encouraging the development of a notion of "panhumanity", combining a universalistic conception of human rights with a cosmopolitan awareness of difference'. This hypothesis operationalised cosmopolitanism as the interaction between physical mobility (MOB), here represented as spending more than a year living abroad in one or more countries, reinforced by the individual eagerness to explore and consume a variety of places and cultures (PLACON), alongside development of the transnational individual's narrative perspective (PERNA), which allows them to position themselves either inside or outside of the specific physical, cultural and social context.

Study findings

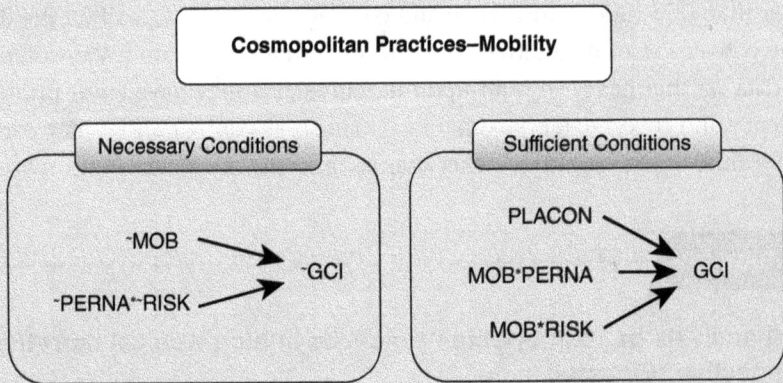

Figure 6.3 Necessary and sufficient conditions for cosmopolitan practices according to mobility (solution coverage of 0.82)

The outcome of the QCA analysis can be seen in Figure 6.3. QCA analysis indicates three possible combinations of conditions which would be sufficient for the development of cosmopolitan practices. International mobility combined with a narrative perspective that embeds the narrator outside of the cultural context and a willingness to take risks were well observed within biographical narrative cases and would support Szerszynski and Urry's (2006) hypothesis. Furthermore, the analysis of necessary conditions points to a lack of mobility, on the one hand, and an unwillingness to take risks, combined with the lack of an external narrative perspective, on the other hand, as factors that would lead to the absence of biographical cosmopolitan traits. Interestingly, the final pattern of sufficient conditions that links the consumer perspective on visiting places and meeting people with a cosmopolitan outlook resonates well with the notion of tourists.

This pattern was then examined further in the specific biographical cases displaying that particular pattern.

Generalisations

This QCA analysis indicates a strong association between extensive mobility and cosmopolitanism as well as openness to new places and people. This is further supported by a development towards the comparative outlook, the ability to make connections between cultures, languages and social systems. The analysis also points to biographical accounts of risk taking and independence that drive cosmopolitan individuals to seek out new places and new experiences that may be contrary to the traditional notions of identity and belonging. All these biographical features support Szerszynski and Urry's (2006) interpretation of cosmopolitanism within the biographical framework.

Strengths and limitations

QCA is a type of analysis that explores deeply the relations between biographical events and specific biographical outcomes. It is a technique that, when executed correctly, can reveal unexpected links and complex connections that can easily be missed when we rely only on the individual researcher's interpretations. It can be used as an extension to qualitative coding and the fsQCA software is relatively easy to use. QCA enhances cross-case comparisons well and suggests new lines of inquiry. But this technique also has important shortcomings. The sense-making process, especially in biographical narrative data, may be confusing as some of the patterns may be just an artefact of the data and not an actual association. The selection and operationalisation of outcomes and conditions can be restrictive, with some cases displaying some conditions strongly, whilst, in others, they are there only by implication or interpretation. According to DeMeur, Rihoux and Yamasaki (2008), QCA also displays some limitations in the investigation of time and sequences which require a creative approach for biographical narrative analysis. Some conditions may evolve over time, for example the intensity of international mobility.

We argued earlier that QCA analysis is balanced on the line between qualitative and quantitative analysis, thus opening itself up to discussion within both research method paradigms. While this is positive for methodological discussions and can lead to innovative solutions and methods development, this in-between position can be difficult for empirical studies. Researchers need to address both qualitative and quantitative sets of problems and often need to translate the findings for two different, academic and non-academic, audiences. QCA analysis may be more convincing to some, as it uses a more quantifiable language of condition, outcomes and associations; but, at the same time, without the qualitative explanation of these patterns, it loses its analytical edge. This balancing act between qualitative and quantitative data and analysis may create some difficulties at the later stages of the project – for example, when reporting findings and producing publications.

Summary

This chapter focuses on methodological innovations applicable to biographical narrative and life-course research that can be used to manage the complexities of biographical data. We have discussed techniques for structuring biographical data and walking the tightrope between open-ended narrative and structured interviews to obtain analysable sequential biographical accounts. We also explored the application of coding frameworks that often come on the back of qualitative analysis software packages, such as NVivo, Atlas.ti and MAXQDA. We argue that, as with all other analytical tools, use of both qualitative and quantitative coding to explore biographical complexities comes with a number of challenges. Data fragmentation and distortion of biographical trajectories and sequences are particularly relevant concerns for biographical researchers, and they prompt valid criticisms. Our position is that with an appropriate level of knowledge and confidence, these tools can be adapted to biographical narrative analysis, allowing for more focused theory testing and an increase in the number of investigated biographies. Finally, we presented an example of the qualitative comparative analysis approach that brings analysis of biographical narratives into the territory of quantitative coding that can be used to explore deep data units, including biographical accounts, with the help of hypotheses used to identify logical relationships between conditions and outcomes.

Questions to consider

1. What are the advantages and disadvantages of structuring the biographical interview?
2. What is the difference between qualitative and quantitative coding in biographical research?
3. What are the risks involved in using software packages for coding and how might they be addressed?
4. How can biographical research prevent data fragmentation during analysis?
5. In what ways do methodological innovations, such as QCA, challenge research practices in biographical research?

Don't forget to use the additional resources to support your research in Appendix 3!

7

DESIGNING A PROJECT USING
BIOGRAPHICAL METHODS

---Objectives---

By the end of this chapter, you will be able to:

- Understand the concept of 'research design'
- Appreciate the significance of well-defined research questions
- Apply different logics of interpretation to make design choices
- Evaluate designs for small-scale as well as large-scale research.

> Design is a logical task undertaken to ensure that the evidence
> collected enables us to answer questions or to test theories as
> unambiguously as possible. (De Vaus, 2001: 16)

This book is not simply about data collection for biographical research. It aims
to cover the entire research process, including the purposes of research, issues
of design, and approaches to data analysis. How do we get from our interest in

a research topic to a research question, and how do we plan a project to make sure that we achieve a satisfactory answer to the question? What are the choices in research design using biographical data? This chapter discusses issues around project design, building on the earlier discussion in Chapter 3. It presents findings from research projects which focus mainly on one of the analytical models covered in Chapters 4–7, and discusses issues regarding the research process, the presentation of findings, interpretation, and how evidence can be applied to wider debates about society and social change. We will use examples of projects (including student projects) and research project vignettes to explain the process of designing research.

The term 'design' suggests an active process or plan to specify a product or process. In social research, the term implies that the researcher has to engage in a planning process which involves choices guided by: (a) the commitment of the researcher to a particular understanding of the object of their study; (b) a research question or questions; (c) sources of data; (d) a method of interpretation; and (e) the presentation of results. A number of commentators (De Vaus, 2001; Gorard, 2013; Blaikie and Priest, 2018; Flick, 2018) highlight the need for these choices to be driven by a design logic, a logical approach to the connections between the component parts of the research process. A researcher's general view of reality – their sense of what it is relevant, valuable or meaningful to investigate – will govern their approach to the subject matter of their research. These commitments are recognisable in the way that researchers orient themselves to particular social theories (critical theory, structuralism, feminism and many others). They may also be expressed in political values like emancipation or prioritising policy impact. Orientations are important because no research method or technique of investigation is self-validating. In Chapter 2, we discussed some of the characteristics of biographical research, including its underlying commitment to subjective meaning, a relational understanding of data and the necessity of interpretation (as opposed to a search for facts and causal explanation). These attachments are vital in deciding how to frame research topics and determine what biographical research can or cannot do. For example, biographical data could help us to understand the phenomenon of attempted suicide, but it would be unsuitable for research designed to test the hypothesis that the suicide rate in year A was higher than year B because of certain factors. In other words, researchers' commitments will lead to research questions being framed according to a 'way of knowing' the subject. Figure 7.1 is a graphic representation of the relationship between an orientation to the subject matter of the research, a commitment to the framework of interpretation, and methods.

In this book, we have deliberately adopted the descriptive phrase 'way of knowing' instead of the technical term 'epistemology'. Although research methods training typically refers to epistemology, we have found it to be more confusing

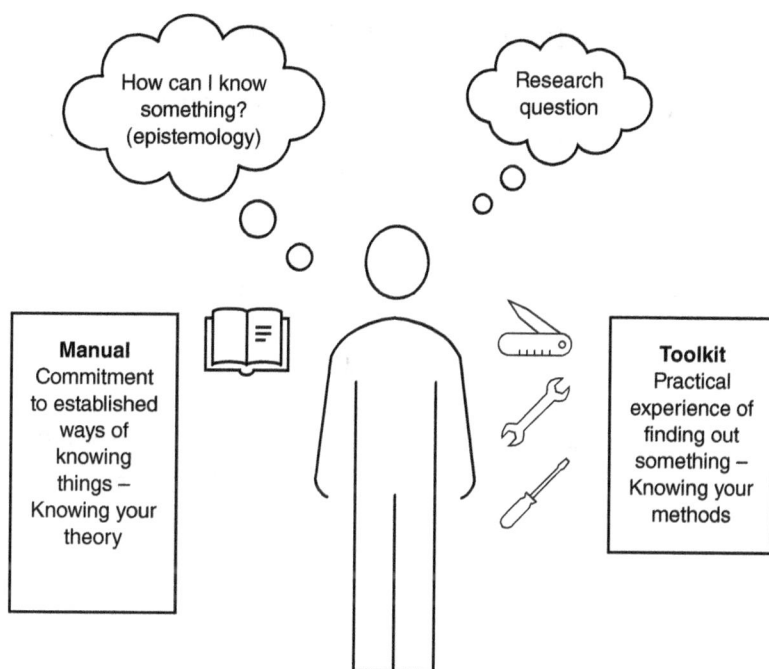

Figure 7.1   Knowing your research subject

than enlightening when students are expected to enter into philosophical questions about the nature, origin and scope of knowledge, epistemic justification or the rationality of belief. While these are important matters in a sub-discipline of philosophy, the vital message is that the social worlds of human beings can be known in different ways. There is no single best way of knowing. We agree with Becker (1993: 218) who, writing from a vast experience of social research, says:

> Epistemological issues, for all the arguing, are never settled, and I think it is fruitless to try to settle them, at least in the way the typical debate looks to. [...] They are simply the commonplaces, in the rhetorical sense, of scientific talk in the social sciences, the framework in which debate goes on.

It is a common mistake to assume that the choice of research methods (between quantitative or qualitative, for example) is directly linked to a researcher's commitment to a particular theory or type of explanation. Actually, the difference between qualitative research and quantitative research exists at the level of methods, not at the level of theoretical orientations, which is why we pay some attention in this book to examples of biographical research that use or work in combination with quantitative methods.

Research questions

In Chapter 3, we explained that the use of biographies in scientific inquiry requires that we understand what type of research questions can be answered with the help of biographical research. Here we consider this issue in more depth and with examples. How we set about framing research questions is not simple. Questions are shaped by assumptions and theories. As we saw, biography is particularly pertinent to questions about (1) the interplay between agency and structure, (2) the interplay between biographical and historical time, and (3) trajectories of individual and social change. Our questions should play to these strengths. The function of a research question in a research design is to turn a research topic into a logical procedure for collecting data that will provide new, true information and understanding about the topic. To be a good question, it should meet certain criteria:

- It should be specific to the topic. If it is too broad, it will not be answerable in a meaningful way. If the question is too narrow, it will yield a limited or even trivial answer.
- A good research question will have a clear connection to previous knowledge and understanding of the topic. It will add to, complement or challenge what we already know. Research is rarely so pioneering that no one has been there before.
- The question should be formulated in such a way that the shape of the answer (which might be positive or negative) will be clear before the findings are apparent. It means that the question should be formulated concisely and without ambiguity.
- Similarly, the question will imply what type of data you need in order to produce an answer.
- Good research questions in biographical research will reflect the strengths of the method, namely its access to the interplay of agency and structure, and the ability to perceive the impact of time and space in human experience.

─**Tip from the field**─────────────────────────────────

Practise your research questions

Practise formulating research questions capable of being addressed through a research project using biography (e.g. from current news topics about social issues), bearing in mind the above criteria.

It is instructive to read extended accounts of research to see how the research question is derived, revised and expressed. Journal articles are usually too compressed to have anything but a sanitised version of the process, but more extended descriptions are sometimes available in books or theses, where the authors reveal the twists and turns on the road from a research topic to their developing understanding of an issue through refining their concepts, to the specification and re-specifications of their research questions – all before they start to collect data. An example from our own experience of doctoral supervision will help to illustrate this. The research is by Eileen Tilley (2020) and it uses a biographical narrative approach to trace how Welsh-speaking identities are negotiated through time and in different social spaces. The focus is on adult learners of Welsh as a second language. Tilley, a second-language speaker herself, notes the ambivalence of the position of adults learning Welsh, and challenges to the legitimacy of 'new speaker' identities. Against this background, she initially states the theme of her research as 'second language learners' lived experiences of learning and using Welsh in north Wales'. This is obviously not a question, although it is a relatively specific, bounded topic. Picking up on the discussion in previous research about the active negotiation of new linguistic identities led Tilley to revise the original statement and put it in the question form: 'How do second-language Welsh speakers in north-west Wales negotiate their social identity in the process of learning and using Welsh?' She mentions that 'the term "new speakers of Welsh" appeared to be an unfamiliar concept in some academic contexts, and that [she] did not have sufficient confidence in the extent of its currency to include it in the research questions' (Tilley, 2020: 68). To have adopted the term would have restricted 'who counts' as a language learner. This example shows a deliberate and thoughtful approach to the research question against the background of previous research, a logical framing of the main question, and close affinity to the characteristics of biographical method.

Keeping in mind the discussion (in Chapter 3) of sampling for biographical research interviews, which distinguished between key informant sampling and theoretical sampling, we can now turn to the issue of research designs and how we might go about choosing one.

Alternative designs for biographical research

The unit of analysis in biographical research is the individual life story. In the vocabulary of research design, this is synonymous with a 'case', although the term case can be confusing because it is used in a variety of ways in methodological discussions. In a quest to bring conceptual clarity to the notion of a case, Gerring says it simply 'connotes a spatially and temporally delimited phenomenon of theoretical significance' (2017: 27). The concepts of a life and a life story do have a theoretical foundation in biographical research, time and space are integral to them, and the boundaries of the life span and individual person are clear, hence this is an appropriate definition. Adopting this approach, the question of research design concerns the relationship between cases, the evidence we collect about each case, and the relationship between the case and its context. A research design is therefore a specific arrangement of these relationships motivated by the purpose of the research question. We will now describe some of the options available.

Single case study

We saw in Chapter 2 that some of the pioneering studies using biography focused on a single case study (notably Thomas and Znaniecki, 1919). Many subsequent studies have been produced using a single case. In criminology, the Jack Roller (Shaw, 1996 [1930]) and the Professional Thief (Sutherland, 1988 [1937]) are iconic accounts of the genesis of crime and delinquent behaviour based on a single informant. In other disciplines, single cases feature in migration research (Riemann, 2003; Schütze, 2003), holocaust studies (Rosenthal and Bar-On, 1992), social work (Wengraf, 2004) and many other areas. To see how Wengraf uses the single case of an agency manager 'Lola', to present some key themes in work with homeless people, see the description in Study 1. Autobiographies and autoethnographies focus by definition on an individual case. The most obvious strength of the single case study is the amount of depth that it allows for understanding and interpretation. It is not unusual for interviews to be several hours long or to occur in a sequence over time, supported by other documentation of the narrator's life. The data derives from a profound and intensive relationship between the interviewer and the interviewee, which helps to ground the interpretation and enhance its validity. A study based on one interview can therefore be a good choice of design, even if it is open to the criticism that it has poorer prospects for generalisation than a larger set of interviews. The criticism is sometimes misplaced because research published as a single case is typically embedded in a context which includes previous studies on related topics, other interviews or various kinds of contextual data which make it possible to look at the interview text from the outside in as well as from the inside out. For example, Wengraf's Lola case was part of a research project which used biographical narrative interviews with other managers, front-line workers and clients. Platt reminds us that Stanley, the Jack Roller, is one informant from a study of 200 similar cases, and 'the functions performed by the case cannot be seen within the covers of Shaw's book, but only by looking at the wider program' (Platt, 1992: 22). In theoretical discussions about case study method, these additional cases which constitute the informal background are sometimes called 'shadow cases' (Gerring, 2017: 139) because they are not foregrounded in the interpretation and are not part of a comparative design.

Comparison of two or more cases

Many biographical researchers use a small number of cases (two may be sufficient) to add a comparative dimension to their study. This 'cross-case' approach has several advantages. It may highlight contrasts across similar cases or similarities across contrasting cases. This type of design is a regular feature of 'grounded theory' methods (Charmaz, 2014), where the intention is to develop a better understanding of a phenomenon by comparing two cases chosen for their relevance to the theory the researcher is trying to develop. The cases are selected according to the categories and data they contain rather than how they might represent a larger population. We can appreciate the logic of two-case comparison in the following brief examples. Within the Euroidentities project (see Study 3 in this chapter; also Miller and Day, 2012: 255), two language teachers, both female, were interviewed. One was a teacher from England running a business English language school in Germany. The other was from Denmark, teaching English and Danish in northern Germany. The research topic was identification with Europe and the interview data contained relatively small amounts of information on this subject. However, in revealing comments about national differences, the responses showed how mobility between countries highlighted the relevance of Europe. The first teacher says she feels more European in Germany than when she is at home in England, and the second teacher says she feels more Danish and less European when she is in Germany, but more European on returning to Denmark. This lack of symmetry in the responses demands an interpretation, given the general similarities in their professions, gender and working in Germany. In this example, the cases are theoretically sampled for their overall similarity while offering some contrast in the topic of concern to the research. The two cases give particularly good purchase to explore the role of national culture and language in the formation of collective identity.

Cole and Knowles (1995) conducted a study of two school teachers who exchanged their respective positions in Canada and New Zealand for a year. The researchers used narrative interviews and written diaries with both participants to explore how the different exchange settings affected the teachers' professional development, against the general background of their life stories. Their experiences of an unfamiliar national education system created a rich source of data for contrast and comparison, but the authors show that the teachers have unexpectedly similar stories to tell (in narrative structure more than content) about their teaching experience, professional relationships, socio-economic conditions and travel. Extended quotations from the two narratives are juxtaposed in parallel columns to highlight these comparisons. The theoretical framing is 'the exchange experience' and the study concludes that there are close parallels in how the two teachers made sense of their experiences within and outside the classrooms – supporting the idea that international teacher exchange programmes are beneficial for pedagogical practice as well as personal development. This is an example of a two-case study with cross-case comparison, a longitudinal element (the life story and one year of intensive observation) and within-case analysis.

The social settings in the two examples we have just considered are relatively complex. The participants are involved in pathways which represent different experiences of education and training, different countries of origin and national cultures, and different experiences of mobility. This has unfavourable consequences for generalising from the case. But what happens if we try to compare cases that are deliberately chosen to be as similar as possible, a design logic which is used, for example, in twin studies in other areas of science? In a paper from a project on young people confronting the economic crisis in Italy, Spanò and Domecka (2015) adopt a comparative case design which starts from a position of close similarity of social condition and explores the reasons for contrasting outcomes. The cases are 30-year-olds Fabio and Maria, who 'at first glance have very similar characteristics from the point of view of social positioning: both come from upper middle-class Neapolitan families, were born and raised in good residential districts of the city, and have good university degrees' (Spanò and Domecka, 2015: 3). The autobiographical narrative interviews yield rich data on their family backgrounds, pathways through the education system, professional careers and private lives. The data confirm the similarities in their generation, social class, educational attainment and opportunities, yet their stories turn out very differently. Maria has embarked on a successful entrepreneurial career in e-commerce, to make a living, and is also an organiser of cultural events, her 'passion'. She recognises the importance of her family as a source of economic and cultural capital, 'covering her back'. Fabio, on the other hand, remains without a stable position, and feels neither the need nor the desire to work, spending his time on basketball and poker. Although benefiting from his family's resources, they are too dominant in his life because he does not have to prioritise income or job quality. The project is framed in terms of a theory of the economic crisis, and the part it plays in young people's biographies. Spanò and Domecka offer an interpretation which avoids psychologising the attitudes and motives of their respondents. Instead, they highlight the crucial role played by biographical work, reflective capacity and sociological imagination, the 'soft' skills needed to make sense of one's life and cope with the economic crisis. These skills are, above all, generated through experiences that are transmitted in the family. Family capital is both a source of opportunity and a potential brake on the progression to adult life.

We have seen how comparing two (or very few) cases can be fruitful for theoretical development, encouraging researchers to exploit the benefits of very detailed individual analysis combined with a process of refining the categories used for interpretation. Finding a basis for theoretical sampling and comparison is an important design skill, given the inherent complexity of human lives and experience. We now turn to consider the type of design which has a larger number of cases and allows the researcher to play to other methodological strengths.

Tip from the field

How many interviews?

Do not assume that your project should have a target number of interviews from the outset. The number will depend on the purpose of the research (one may be enough!) and may be revised as the research proceeds.

Cumulative case studies

As the experts in Baker and Edwards' discussion paper (2012) all agree, the answer to the question 'how many qualitative interviews is enough?' must be 'it depends'. There is no rule which will give an answer to this question without careful consideration of the purpose of the research, the type of research question being asked, and the accessibility of interviewees. This is certainly true for research using life stories. A set of interviews can support research aims and objectives that are unachievable using one or two individual cases. It may only require a small number of interviews to establish that a phenomenon contains more variety or complexity than previously thought. If the subject of interest is not well defined, it may be necessary to conduct one interview after another until the range of characteristics of interest reaches 'saturation'. This term is used in grounded theory approaches and '[r]efers to the point at which gathering more data about a theoretical category reveals no new properties nor yields any further theoretical insights about the emerging grounded theory' (Charmaz, 2014: 345). In biographical research, the notion of saturation is challenging because the variety of relevant life experience can be so large that it may seem impossible to exhaust the range. This is why it is important for the topic and the research question to be well specified and not too broad. For example, a set of interviews to explore the childhood foundations of obesity in adulthood would have to be defined by criteria such as age, gender, weight, social class, place of residence, encounters with health and welfare services, and many other categories for comparative analysis to be meaningful. Inexperienced researchers are often tempted to think that 'more' interviews are 'better' but the criteria for selection are not statistical, and this does not follow. What is needed is close acquaintance with the subject matter and clear relevancy criteria. For example, in the Euroidentities project (Miller and Day, 2012) the criteria were spelled out in the concept of 'sensitised groups' – 'aggregates of persons whose life experiences could be anticipated to have caused them to reflect on their situation of living within the continent of Europe and perhaps be challenged by these experiences' (pp. 3–4). Group characteristics were defined accordingly and the groups became the frame for selecting individual cases. The scale of the topic was unusually large, so it may be helpful to return to the smaller-scale example we introduced above (Tilley, 2020), to see how the researcher arrived at the final number of biographical interviews. (The research is presented at greater length in Study 2.)

Tilley's research was cumulative in the sense that she started out with a tentative target number of interviews with ten current and ten previous learners of Welsh as a second language, all within the geographically well-defined area of north-west Wales. This was based on the understanding that 'few studies using the biographical narrative method seemed to have involved more than around 20 interviews' (Tilley, 2020: 74). Her research design was informed theoretically by the literature on second-language learning, by her own personal experience, and by the preference for a narrative method of interviewing which would generate data on learners' experiences over time. Once the problems of access were solved, the final number of interviews was 24, balanced across both groups. Analysis focused on how identities were negotiated in the various dimensions of the learners' experiences, including prior dispositions, goals in life, intimate relationships, formal learning and the wider community. The design allowed Tilley to construct an original typology of 'new speakerhood' ideal types to differentiate between the varying speaker trajectories experienced by the participants. In this way, the biographical approach brought new dimensions to speaker categorisation, which is usually based on the level of linguistic competence achieved, for example 'non speaker', 'semi speaker' or 'fluent speaker'.

Cross-national comparison

In recent years, biographical research has broadened in scope and scale, notably through a series of international comparative projects, often with large-scale funding and collaborative team organisation. Research design issues become very significant in the management of such projects, not least because funders such as the European research framework programmes require research aims and objectives, methodologies and analytic steps to be clearly set out in advance and monitored at every step. The traditions of international comparative research in social and political science were dominated until recently by commitments to causal explanation and quantitative methods. Qualitative approaches, including biographical methods, have had to justify themselves in this competitive context. Against this background, we consider some of the design and methodological issues that apply to large-scale, cross-national comparison involving biographical narrative data, using two examples.

The first is the Social Strategies in Risk Society (SOSTRIS) project which was part of the European Commission's Fourth Framework research programme concerning social exclusion and social integration in Europe (Chamberlayne and Rustin, 1999). The project was one of the first to use biographical-interpretive methods transnationally and on such a scale. It focused on six target groups in seven European countries: unemployed graduates, early retired people, unqualified youth, single parents, ex-traditional workers and ethnic minorities. The research topic of social risks was informed by the then-current theories of Ulrich Beck (1992) and Anthony Giddens (1991) which highlighted tendencies towards individualisation and reflexivity. This influenced the choice of socio-biographical and life-history methods. The selection of interviewees came from groups deemed to have lasting experiences in the six categories of exclusion. The total number of interviews was 252 (six or seven in each category). This allowed for multi-dimensional analysis of the complexity of individual strategies across countries and over time. In commenting on the methodology, the authors say: 'a problem with a research methodology which invites research subjects to set out in narratives their own definitions of their life-situations is that it may generate too many rather than too few models and categories' (Chamberlayne and Rustin, 1999: 10). In this, like other large comparative projects, more data are collected than can be analysed but until the data are collected, it is not possible to narrow down the groups and categories of interest. Inspired by theories of risk society, the project focused on 'reflexivity', the capacity of the subject to think about their own life course, to understand its dynamics and to devise strategies to overcome their difficulties. This led to the conclusion that social policy and practice need to find ways to develop this reflexivity in clients and to prepare practitioners to work effectively at an individual level.

A subsequent example was the Evolution of European Identity (Euroidentities) project, funded by the European Union's Seventh Framework research programme (Miller and Day, 2012). In some respects, the research topic was even harder to define than the theme of social risk in the SOSTRIS project, but the choice of biographical methods was made for similar reasons. It allowed a topic, people's identification with 'Europe', which had been studied previously mainly through quantitative polling and attitude surveys, to be addressed in a new, person-centred way, from the bottom up rather than top down. Autobiographical narrative interviews were designed to give access to the time dimension in respondents' lives, and the comparative design enabled analysis of the evolution of identities in seven different country locations. (More details of the project design and methods are available in Study 3.) Here, we can add that from a research design point of view, the large interview database facilitates several types of analysis: cross-national comparisons by individuals or groups, comparative thematic analysis by groups, within-case analysis of selected cross-cutting themes such as language, and theoretical development.

Study 1

Boundaries and Relationships in Homelessness Work – Lola, an agency manager (Wengraf, 2004)

This study uses a single individual's narrative to explore some key dilemmas in work with service users in an advice and housing referral centre for rough sleepers. The narrator, Lola, a former nurse, is the manager of the centre which employs four advice workers and an administrator. She has a professional social work qualification.

Method and design

The general topic of the research is the relationship between being a social work professional and a human being. It is framed in terms of professional choices and the idea that, even with training, practitioners are profoundly influenced by the need to come to terms with unresolved issues from their past. The case is purposely selected because it is considered to demonstrate very clearly the dilemmas in working with service users, how relationships are controlled and the boundary issues involved. The research questions are not stated directly but could be phrased as: how does a professional's training, life experience and expertise influence their professional practice on relational and boundary issues? Or, 'how do agency staff and their homeless clients manage their expectations and the boundary between providing or receiving a service and behaving humanely'? Part of a larger research project on agencies dealing with homeless people, Lola's case study uses an in-depth biographical-narrative interview in the BNIM tradition, which distinguishes between the 'lived life' and the 'told story' of the interviewee. The first stage (open-ended narration following a biographical question) is what Lola says about her life and the experiences she has had, including her perspective on boundaries and relatedness in her work for the agency. The second stage is the researcher's response to her telling of the story and her current perspective, enriched by further narrative questions about the topics raised. The analysis therefore starts with Lola's own narrative and self-understanding before moving on to the researcher's (rather different) perspective.

Study findings

Lola sees the agency where she works as having moved in a positive direction, from being a 'charity' to a 'professional' culture. She feels that she is well suited to her present job. Her narrative shows that she believes in challenging clients to overcome their dependencies and accept responsibility for themselves. To do this, it is necessary to challenge her staff as well, to overcome their dependency impulses and maintain boundaries. At the same time, she recognises that some boundaries may be too high and may prevent practitioners from knowing the lives of their clients and seeing them as human beings. Wengraf, the author of the study, notes that the initial narrative is relatively straightforward and optimistic. The second stage of the research explores how Lola's present professional perspective emerged from her life experience. 'The account that emerges from the follow-up session is complicated and more contradictory', the researcher says, thanks to various key incidents in her life, including being pregnant at 16, her ambivalent family relationships, and her working experiences in a home for autistic adolescents, then in a home for the elderly, later in a hospice, and most recently in the housing agency. Wengraf interprets the case as pivoting around professional boundary maintenance, on the one hand, and relatedness, or the formation of close, caring and 'holistic' human relationships, on the other. 'One of the features of Lola's discourse is that of a self-revision of a previously (normally positive) evaluation by a subsequent (often more negative) one and that this contradiction is usually neither noted nor commented upon by her' (Wengraf, 2004: 20).

Generalisation

This case can be considered as following an exploratory design. It proceeds with an interpretive analysis which leads to some general commentary on the development of institutions and the connection between bureaucracy and holistic practices. Wengraf (2004: 25) concludes:

> it is worth speculating that an emphasis on boundaries in psychosocial professional theory may correspond very well to the administrative division of labour between and within agencies and hierarchies. [...] The pro-boundary practice of the organisation is likely to predispose it towards a fetishization of boundary relations in their model of human development for their clients.

The implication for social work training is that a more complex theory of boundaries and relatedness is needed, and that case studies using biographical narrative method should help in this task.

Study 2

Narratives of Belonging – Experiences of learning and using Welsh of adult 'new speakers' in north-west Wales (Tilley, 2020)

This study by Eileen Tilley for a PhD thesis investigates the ongoing negotiation of identities of learners of Welsh as a second language in the north-western part of Wales. Some of these 'new speakers' have attained fluency, others have succeeded to a lesser extent, while certain others have allowed their learning to lapse.

Method and design

The research took place with the aim of tracing how Welsh-speaking identities are negotiated through time and in different social spaces such as the family, leisure and work. It was informed by theories of second-language learning which emphasise the self-identification of the learner and the response they receive in the linguistic community, not just their linguistic competence. The scope of the project was circumscribed by resource and time limitations which encouraged a relatively narrow geographical focus. It led to the choice of a design to allow both current learners (recruited via language classes) and previous learners (accessed by snowballing) to be included. The total sample was 24 interviewees, some of whom also used language diaries to record their experiences. Tilley's interviews used biographical narrative-interpretive procedures which delivered the type of longitudinal data which is essential to appreciate the journey into new speaker status. The data analysis was informed by the narrative ethnography approach, which made it possible to map out how identities were negotiated in various dimensions such as family life and education, the Welsh class, the wider community, and the workplace and career.

Study findings

Tilley found that the extent to which participants were able to develop Welsh-speaking identities beyond the classroom varied according to context, initial dispositions and the recognition which they were able to negotiate. It was the 'ongoing assessment of developing identities, rather than the amount of Welsh learned, which chiefly influenced whether participants continued learning or gave up, and whether they were able to use what they had learned to establish identities in the world outside' (p. 176). Individual trajectories were therefore the result of complex interactions between the dimensions and when participants talked about where they had ended up, they fell into distinctly different groups. This is the basis for the construction of a six-fold explanatory typology of 'new speakers' as well as for some policy recommendations on adult second-language learning and services.

Generalisation

The geographical focus and sample size of 24 individuals means that the study findings cannot be automatically generalised to all new speakers of Welsh. Differences in learning opportunities in other regions, or demographic variations in the population of Welsh speakers, make that impossible. However, the strength of a biographical approach is that it elicits in-depth information on the relationship between social structures (of opportunity, for example) and individual agency. Tilley's research uncovers the salient features of how new speakers relate (or sometimes fail to relate) to the Welsh language community. It is likely that these features account for the majority of variation wherever Welsh is being acquired by adults as a second language.

Study 3

The Evolution of European Identities – Biographical approaches (Miller and Day, 2012)

Method and design

The Euroidentities project was a collaborative international project funded by the European Union Framework 7 programme from 2008 to 2011. It consisted of seven partner teams, who adopted a common cross-national and comparative approach to the question of what it means to be European or to have a sense of identification with Europe. The emphasis was not on attitudes, but on the everyday experiences and processes that people go through in their lives which lead them to a sense of self and identity. The design was based on a selection of target groups who were expected to have experiences that would 'sensitise' them to the topic of living within the continent of Europe: transnational workers, the educationally mobile, farmers, and civil society organisers (dealing with cultural, environmental or peace and reconciliation issues). Data were collected through in-depth autobiographical narrative interviews (see Chapter 4 of this book) to provide details of the evolution of European identities over time. An unusual feature of Euroidentities was the large number of interviews, more than 200 by the end of the project. Analysis of the interviews deployed grounded theory methods to discover and explore the multiple dimensions in the expression of European identity.

(Continued)

Study findings

The Euroidentities project does not confirm the existence of a collective European identity as a mindset or cluster of attitudes, but that does not mean Europe is irrelevant in the lives of the people studied. Rather, by situating the question as biographical, it shows how attachments to 'Europe' are implicit and situational. They may be positive and negative. For example, single-market freedoms may be experienced positively alongside frustration with obstacles to integration in another country (such as facing the devaluation of one's social and cultural capital). Europe becomes a frame of reference for orientations which express a person's agency (or possibly lack of agency) as they navigate the complexities of work, relationships, language and culture across national borders. One important consequence is that 'national collective identities are brought down to earth and relativised by the European mental space' (Miller and Day, 2012: 261). Mental space in the biographical context is the field of orientation for biographical work. This is quite different from the idea of Europe (or more specifically the EU) as an object of collective representation, sponsored to some extent by European institutions themselves. The findings are reported at length in Miller and Day (2012), in a format which interweaves chapters on theory, methods and substantive themes, with 'case study' chapters based on one or more biographical interviews.

Generalisation

Euroidentities shows how biographical interviewing provides excellent data for exploring the complexity of European identities, offering an alternative to survey-based research on attitudes and opinions towards Europe. The strategy of comparing cases from a variety of countries across the continent is very fruitful for understanding the interactions between individuals and their social worlds. Comparing cases from seven locations and five sensitised groups generates similarities and contrasts which call for explanation. These can then be theorised and brought into contact with more data. See, for example, the article by Davis et al. (2017) which uses the notion of 'imagined communities' to interpret the experiences of Euroidentities interviewees who highlight language and language learning in their storytelling. The Euroidentities project was completed before the UK left the EU but its results, which are not particularly comfortable for EU integration policy, suggest that the mental space of Europe will remain significant for European citizens whether they live within or outside the EU.

Summary

In this chapter, we have explained the logical sequence of the research process and the importance of research design. 'Logical sequence' does not necessarily mean that it is always linear. Most projects involve false starts, revisions, problems of accessibility, and are subject to all sorts of contingencies. The most important constraints are time and resources, which can shape design decisions as much as the 'internal' issues of concept definition, selection criteria or dimensions of analysis. The expectations associated with the organisation of degrees and research in higher education institutions are bound to be influential for MA and PhD projects. The requirements of funders are important for career researchers. Yet, as we have shown, we can learn from the experiences of generations of researchers who have applied biographical methods in a wide variety of contexts and found creative ways to frame and answer their research questions.

Questions to consider

1. How would you explain the relationship between abstract concepts and empirical reality expressed in the research design process?
2. Evaluate the research question in a published example of biography-based research.
3. How will you decide how many biographical interviews are enough in your own research project?
4. If a biographical narrative interview can be considered a 'case', what is it a case of?

8

MIXED QUALITATIVE METHODS

Objectives

By the end of this chapter, you will be able to:

- Understand the concept of 'mixed methods'
- Differentiate between 'convergent', 'sequential' and other mixed method designs
- Appreciate the 'added value' of combining different methods
- Identify the choices in how to mix methods in a practical study.

A mixed methods way of thinking is an orientation toward social inquiry that actively invites us to participate in dialogue about multiple ways of seeing and hearing, multiple ways of making sense of the social world, and multiple standpoints on what is important and to be valued and cherished. A mixed methods way of thinking rests on assumptions that there are multiple legitimate approaches to social inquiry and that any given approach to social inquiry is inevitably partial. (Greene, 2008: 20)

Following on from the previous chapter's discussion of research design as a set of logical connections between a theoretical perspective, research questions, strategies for data collection, and methods of data analysis, this chapter considers designs in more complex settings. These include studies which combine biographical approaches with other, mainly qualitative, methodologies such as ethnography and policy analysis. The topic is important because social research has expanded into multiple fields which sustain a huge variety of theories, explanations, data and methods. It is increasingly common for research to draw on two or more types of data and to engage in more than a single form of analysis. While this has led to a proliferation of 'mixed methods' research (Tashakkori and Teddlie, 2010; Creswell and Plano Clark, 2017), it has also provoked many questions about the relationship between methods and the assumptions they make about the nature of society, human beings and the meaning of their actions. In this chapter, we will explore how biographical narrative research relates to ethnography, and some of its variants, as well as social policy research. A key question is: how can we ensure that mixed research designs are consistent, and analytical frameworks are compatible? The emphasis is on qualitative research which uses biographical data alongside other data and methods. We will address the issue of how quantitative research (using survey or panel data, for example) can be combined with biography in the next chapter.

Mixed methods

The term 'mixed methods' signifies the practice of combining two or more research methodologies in the study of the same phenomenon. Such practices have been used since the origins of the social sciences, but the concept itself has a more recent history which comes from the partial resolution of the past antagonisms between quantitative and qualitative methods of data collection and analysis. These disputes between the advocates of 'scientific' and 'humanistic' approaches reached their peak in the second part of the 20th century, when sociology and other social science disciplines were establishing themselves as academic fields. Today, it is less common to find sharp distinctions being drawn between scientific, positivist and quantitative approaches, on the one hand, and humanistic, interpretive and qualitative approaches, on the other. In fact, it is widely accepted that all science involves interpretation and that it can be based on quantitative and qualitative data, separately or combined.

The issues in research design using mixed methods typically revolve around choices in how methods can actually be combined. In an overview of the ways in which practitioners have defined mixed methods, Johnson et al. (2007) note that the majority of definitions relate to the mixing of quantitative and qualitative methods. They characterise the choices as positions on a spectrum, from a 'pure' version of each method at each extreme to intermediate positions that represent a mix in which either one approach dominates – for example, QUANT+qual – or each has equal status.[1] The authors' synthesis of definitions leads them to the conclusion that:

> Mixed methods research is the type of research in which a researcher or team of researchers combines elements of qualitative and quantitative research approaches (e.g. use of qualitative and quantitative viewpoints, data collection, analysis, inference techniques) for the broad purposes of breadth and depth of understanding and corroboration. (Johnson et al., 2007: 123)

In this definition, the purpose of mixing, combining or multiplying methods is to create value in the research process by broadening and deepening the research. But how can we be sure that we are not simply replicating or embellishing our results or conducting research in parallel? There should be good reason to think that combining approaches will give us a better understanding of research problems than a single approach. The mixed method debate has moved well beyond the initial attempts to find ways to justify using 'hard and soft' data, numbers or words, in the same study. The interesting questions are about the process and aims of combining or integrating different methods. A project design may connect different types of data by comparing them for similarities or contrasts, by blending them or by looking for complementarities in a dialogue across boundaries. There are several types of design to consider.

By analogy with the land-surveying technique of confirming a position by taking measurements from two other points and applying the laws of trigonometry to determine the third, *methodological triangulation* in social research refers, more loosely, to the technique of using multiple observations from different reference points to establish a more complete description of a phenomenon and thus enhance reliability (Blaikie, 1991; Mertens and Hesse-Biber, 2012). For example, survey data on life chances could be combined with biographical interviews and diaries to help interpret and evaluate policies of equal opportunities. Genuine triangulation aims to compensate for the inherent limitations or biases of specific kinds of data by bringing together alternative measures of the same characteristic (e.g. equal rights and equal treatment as measures of equal opportunity). The idea is that if different varieties of data lead to the same conclusion, they give a higher level of confidence in the result. Triangulation is likely to involve mutual validation of instruments by checking that they measure what they are designed to measure and are free from other influences. Equal emphasis should be placed on explaining evidence

---

[1] This has become standard notation in mixed method debates. Capitalisation indicates priority.

which is out of line with expectations, as well as that evidence which matches expectations. If the research strategy involves a looser relationship between methods, it is better to refer to 'multimethod' approaches than triangulation.

Creswell and Plano Clark (2017) provide a helpful classification of 'core' research designs according to methods used in the quantitative–qualitative spectrum. They suggest three basic designs which we will now explain:

- concurrent
- sequential: from quantitative to qualitative
- sequential: from qualitative to quantitative.

Core multimethod strategies include designs that seek convergence between methods, typically at the data interpretation stage (Creswell and Plano Clark, 2017, Chapter 3). *Concurrent* or *convergent-parallel* approaches work with two strands independently during the same stage of the research process, giving equal priority to both types of data (e.g. questionnaires and interviews). The researcher chooses which methods to adopt according to the research question and proceeds to collect the data and conduct the initial analysis as if they were separate studies. At the next analysis stage, the researcher compares the content of both strands to see how far they converge or diverge. A merging of the two types of data is likely to work best when the two share the same concepts, and even the same data analysis techniques – for example, quantitative analysis of interview texts as well as quantitative analysis of questionnaire responses. Convergence occurs when the results complement and support each other, suggesting that results are valid in both strands.

Different methods may be used in sequence instead of at the same time. A study using a single method is likely to generate questions which are best answered by further research using a different method. This is known as an *explanatory sequential* design. A typical version is a first, quantitative, phase, followed by a second, qualitative, phase of data collection and analysis which aims to expand on and explain the results of the first. The example given by Creswell and Plano Clark (2017: 71) is a survey intended to show the predictors of adolescent tobacco consumption which found an unexpected association between extracurricular activities and use. The quantitative survey was followed by qualitative focus group research with adolescents involved in extracurricular activities, designed to explore the reasons for this and to explain the unanticipated result. Although this is a common sequence, there is no intrinsic reason why a design has to lead from quantitative to qualitative.

A qualitative to quantitative *exploratory sequential* design works in the opposite direction. The initial phase is a qualitative study which aims to clarify and concretise the research questions. For example, it might be to ensure that the researcher's questions have meaning for the participants. It is a foundational assumption of social research that the researcher is part of the research and can see it from the participants' point of view. This phase can then be used to create a research instrument with improved questionnaire wording. The results are compared with the original qualitative findings for consistency. Research questions can be informed by many varieties of data in designs which qualify as 'mixed'. The explanatory purpose can be served by any sequence of data collection which allows for further elucidation and interpretation, including designs which combine two or more qualitative methods.

This brief overview of mixed methods highlights the fact that the concerns of many practitioners have to do with the problems of reconciling the traditions of quantitative and qualitative research in ways that are logical, practical and beneficial for the research process as a whole. The concept of 'integration' is widely used to frame the issues (Bazeley, 2018). It can refer to links between methods (e.g. sampling from a quantitative database to select participants for qualitative analysis); to connections between sets of data (e.g. responses to questions on similar topics in surveys and focus groups); to forms of analysis which complement each other (e.g. transforming qualitative data into quantitative measures); and to integration at the level of reporting, interpreting and displaying results. The concern with overcoming the disparities between the main traditions of social research is arguably less fundamental than understanding the logic of the interaction between the components of a mixed method study – which might be entirely qualitative (we will discuss this further in Chapter 9). In ethnography, for example, mixed methods can refer to the use of a variety of data sources including informants, artefacts, rituals and work practices. Methods may combine observation, interviews, documents and images. We will adopt this inclusive understanding of mixed methods in the sections which follow, where we return to issues in biographical research.

Applications of biographical methods in mixed designs
Biography and ethnography

In this section, we consider how biographical narrative research can be combined with, and interact with, ethnography. Biographical data are particularly appropriate for understanding the unique circumstances of actors' lives, reflected in their storytelling. Ethnographic data are valuable for understanding institutional contexts and their meanings. We explore the questions of method and interpretation which arise when they are brought together in a mixed design, including the relationship between ethnographic time and biographical time, types of biographical interview, and the complementarities (or dissimilarities) between ethnographic and biographical data.

Experts in ethnographic and biographical research have produced illuminating discussions around both methods (e.g. Bourdieu, 1990; Gell, 1992; Zerubavel, 2003; Cerwonka and Maliki, 2007; Gobo, 2008a). Taken together, they highlight some key distinguishing characteristics. In summary, we can say that ethnography gives priority to observation as the primary source of information. The researcher observes and listens in to the activities of social actors 'on stage', supplemented by evidence from documents, representations and material artefacts that exist in the study setting. The emphasis is on observable social interaction, not the self-descriptions of the actors involved. Biographical narrative research, on the other hand, is all about the stories that people tell for themselves, including the idiosyncrasies of experience, personal expression and topic. In both cases, the researcher as observer and listener should be reflexively aware of their own practice and of the ways in which it can influence the results.

We can easily list the most obvious differences between the two methods. Ethnography is society-centred, or at least interaction-centred, while biographical narrative is ego-centred. Ethnography is synchronic: it smooths time to create an 'ethnographic present' (Davis, 1992; O'Reilly, 2005: 215). A biographical narrative is diachronic: a reconstruction of a past life, typically as a sequence of 'lived time'. The observer is present in both methods, but in a different way. The ethnographer as observer enters the world of the study and comes alongside without deliberately creating something new. The interviewer in biographical narrative creates both a situation and a product which would not exist without their intervention. Both methods involve the presence of a researcher and all the vexed issues about how the researcher interacts with and relates to the social actors: the extent of their 'participation', the role they adopt, their standpoint, the way they acknowledge that they are 'co-producers' of knowledge, and their ethical stance.

Combining biographical and ethnographic data in the same study can follow the logic of the mixed method designs discussed above. They can be put together in complementary ways – for example, by using ethnography to immerse the researcher in the environment which the biographical narrator currently inhabits, to aid the interpretation of the biographical data and give it greater depth and validity. Each biographical narrative can add nuance to the overall picture, highlighting the different layers of social context within which the lives are lived. An exploratory sequential design could start with ethnographic research to provide a basis for selecting participants for biographical narrative interviews. Alternatively, an explanatory sequential design would begin with biographical interviews and employ ethnographic techniques to enhance the interpretation of the narratives. However, such designs are bound to be limited by the fact that time, specifically 'social time', is experienced differently in each of the two methods.

The vignette below (Study 1) describes how ethnography and biography were part of a design for research on patterns of participation and volunteering at a local level.

One of the key findings is about the different patterns of belonging in two nearby village locations. In the first village, participants shared a common social and cultural heritage of religious non-conformity, Welsh language and industrial genealogies. Many of the participants spoke of shared identities in the past tense, suggesting a collective memory (Connerton, 1989) of homogeneity that is not fully present today. The importance of history was frequently mentioned both in ethnography and biography. In the second village, history was not so much made alive in the biographies as projected into an image of the present. For example, it was the 'newcomers' rather than those more deeply rooted by long-term residence who seemed most interested in the past and the local history group. Connerton (1989: 4) hints at this complexity when he suggests, 'experiences of the present largely depend upon our knowledge of the past, and ... our images of the past commonly serve to legitimise a present social order'.

To mix biography and ethnography is therefore not a simple matter of aggregating two sets of data. We can distinguish three aspects of the relationship of time to ethnography and biographical narrative: where there is close correspondence, where there are parallels, and where there is divergence. First, there are data which involve socially produced time in the encounter of two or more individuals. This applies to both ethnography and biography. As Barbara Adam (1995) has noted, there is a similarity in the process whereby the time-worlds of participant observer and interviewers join with the time-worlds of those they observe and interview. Research has 'to contend with the invisible life-worlds and biographies which [respondents] and researchers bring to that collective time and which, in turn, influence what individual members see, understand and take to be relevant' (Adam, 1995: 72). For example, participant observation in local meetings involves an encounter in which researcher and participants' time-worlds meet for the duration of the observation. Where there is this essential similarity, it is possible to use common categories or even analytical codes such as 'early socialisation', 'family history of participation', or 'being asked to volunteer'. But that is not the whole story.

The second kind of relationship is where there is a difference arising from the nature of the constructions in the two methods. Ethnography is a representation by the ethnographer of the world of the participants based on a multitude of sources. Concepts of 'objectivity' are typically invoked. Evidence is cross-checked to see if different sources and perspectives agree. Because the logic of ethnography is to provide an account, however complex it might be, the sense of time is 'flattened' and the uniqueness of the experience of individual subjects in time tends to be obscured. Observation literally 'takes time'. In contrast, biographical narrative time is egological and the biography is the participant's own construction at the time of the interview. Temporality in the biography is shaped by the constraints of narrative storytelling as well as the events of the life story, but in the end, biography 'makes time'. In the search for more depth in the analysis in Study 1, the more these differences seem to matter. For example, ethnography confirms the story of the steep decline of nonconformist religious institutions and practices in the study localities. Nearly all of the ethnographic sources agree on this and the evidence would support a strong version of the secularisation thesis. But the study of the biographical data reveals a different story, which provides support for alternative ideas such as 'diffused religion' (Cipriani, 2017) or 'belief without belonging' (Day, 2013; Davie, 2015). People continue to believe in belonging and continue to perform belonging with reference to the religious past (Davis et al., 2021).

The third category is where the two methods are most divergent. The sense of place in biography is rooted in things that 'take place' (literally) in the course of a person's life. The biography is embodied in the narrator, but it is as conditional and subjective as that person's existence at a single point in time. There is a striking contrast between this and the material world, especially the built environment. In Study 1, major buildings such as the miners' institute or the parish church, as well as ordinary housing, are constant reminders of the durability of the social in its different forms. These objects have a time of their own which is immensely resistant to change (though interpretable in different ways) as ethnography can show. But it is quite different from the time of the narrative, and the relationship between them is oblique and changes with each new generation.

Thus, we can see that mixing methods is likely to challenge analytical categories and the assumptions we make when we use them. The example of 'time' shows that there is no single definition which can cover all its uses and interpretations. The same could be said of 'generation', class', 'gender' and a host of other categories which are part of the general currency of the social sciences. Ethnographers and biographers need to be aware that they, like other human beings, experience the passage of time through interaction, institutions and broad categories of relations, objects and events – with varying results according to the 'methods' they use. We will now turn to another, related, combination of methods which also raises major questions about their compatibility.

Study 1

Participation in local civil society – Place, time and boundaries (Mann et al., 2021)

Method and design

A mixed method study, conducted by members of the Wales Institute of Social and Economic Research and Data, was designed to capture the temporal and spatial aspects of participation and community engagement. It compares two nearby but contrasting villages, Rhos and Overton, in north-east Wales. The locations share the context of local labour markets, infrastructure and local government funding, but they are quite distinct in other ways. The first stage of the research was ethnographic observation focused on evidence of participation and community engagement, supplemented by information from historical and public databases. This was followed by biographical narrative interviews with individuals in key roles within local groups and organisations – the aim being to get some purchase on changes over time in participation in the wider context of family, employment relations, and culture.

Study findings

The biographical narratives in Rhos, a post-industrial village, are very locally embedded constructions of the lives of the storytellers in the perspective of the former mining industry, religious denominations, ancestry and 'the village' as the arena for action. They complement the ethnographic observations, and the prominent symbols of the past in the built environment of the miners' institute and numerous chapels. In Overton, in contrast, which the community council describes as a 'small but vibrant village of unspoiled charm', the ethnographic data contain fewer references to the past; history seems to be more opaque, although the village has a history several centuries older than Rhos's. The emphasis in the biographical narratives is on what makes the village a nice place to live in now. The study concludes that local voluntary association is important in forming bridges between people in 'places' and wider society, but that differing notions of belonging mean that localities are not equally situated to operate as effective conduits for participation. In Rhos, people participated as volunteers because they had a strong sense of belonging; in Overton, they often volunteered because they wanted to belong.

Generalisation

Experiences of time and space in both ethnographic and biographical data are vital to understanding the differences between the two localities in this study, which explored the relationship between ethnography and biography from one particular point of view, namely participation in local civil society. 'Social time' in each type of data is complex. Ethnographic and biographical time do not correspond in a way which would allow all the data to be aggregated and treated as if there was no substantial difference between them (for example, in qualitative data analysis software). Yet they speak to similar issues and this study brings them into a fruitful dialogue.

Autoethnography and feminist research

Definitions of autoethnography include two elements: autobiography (self-narrative) and ethnography. The approach to narrative makes autoethnography a distinctive version of mixed qualitative methods. The narrator is the researcher, and the emphasis is on conscious reflection on personal experience; positively embracing subjectivity and emotions. The ethnographic component relates to the social and cultural setting and explores links between the self and the social world, helping to explain and interpret the narrative. This is what differentiates autoethnography from autobiography, which focuses on personal dynamics more than the social-cultural dynamics that the individual confronts. As Ellis et al. explain, 'autoethnography is an approach to research and writing that seeks to describe and systematically ana-lyze (*graphy*) personal experience (*auto*) in order to understand cultural experience (*ethno*)' (Ellis et al., 2010: 1). They add that autoethnography is both process (doing autobiography) and product (writing about personal experience). The process is unavoidably a performance, designed not just to describe a biography but also to enact it with a creative, critical or active purpose. In that respect, it claims to be 'more than a method' (Holman Jones et al., 2013: 17).

The growth and popularity of autoethnography coincided with a movement in the humanities and social sciences which challenged researcher neutrality and the notion that they could build objective accounts, universal explanations of human experience or 'grand narratives' (Lyotard, 1984). In this 'postmodern' understand-ing, the alternative is to create 'small stories', localised representations of limited domains, to access the plurality of truths revealed in personal experience. This stance has close affinities with qualitative research on race, gender, marginality and minority cultures, where questions of identity are bound up with complex, con-tested experiences of culture and inequality. It strongly resists the impulse to enter a field of research with authoritative notions, to enlist and exploit cultural members for their data, and then to exit the field and write for professional or personal gain, without regard for the ties with participants. On the other hand, it is very sympa-thetic to the motivation behind much feminist research, which is committed to hearing those who are marginalised by gender and voicing their stories as a means to empower and enable.

The key steps in the research process of autoethnography from a feminist per-spective can be summarised as follows. They begin with self-narration of the personal life (or an episode in the life) of the researcher, who pays particular atten-tion to the recall of physical feelings and emotions, with all the ambiguities that involves. The research focus is often on a certain aspect of the biography, such as experiences of bereavement, while other aspects are considered contextual or sup-porting. The researcher is assumed to be a full participant in the social world they describe, and they adopt a first-person standpoint. The data are generated through introspection and via recollections which can be stimulated by documents and records, images or dialogue with others. Unlike the biographical narrative proce-dures explained previously, autoethnography does not depend on an interlocutor and does not take the form of an extempore or semi-structured interview. In the process, the autoethnographer creates 'transitional, intermediate spaces, inhabiting the crossroads or borderlands of embodied emotions' (Ettore, 2017: 4). Accounts are generally written in a personally engaged, and engaging, style – even designed to be 'aesthetically alluring' (2017: 44).

Study 2

An illness story – Autoethnography as feminist method (Ettore, 2017)

Method and design

The sociologist Elizabeth Ettore conducted an autoethnography which describes her own experience of an acute thyroid illness lasting more than two years. The approach is explicitly feminist, using data from her diaries, recollections of inter-actions and conversation, and records of feelings, emotions and bodily states. The story is recounted in the first person, an 'I' who is an older female, university professional, partner, patient, with a previously healthy body. The story begins with reflections on the personal process of recall and representation. This is followed by a sequential narrative which describes the journey from an initial consulta-tion and diagnosis with a general practitioner, through alternative treatment with another doctor to eventual 'normal' health. The process of telling the story is a way to express personal feeling and reflection on illness, bodies, emotions, gender and healing.

Study findings

Ettore describes her experience of the classic symptoms of thyrotoxicosis as a process of 'losing myself' and entering into a new illness identity. This is rein-forced by her encounter with a doctor who sees her as a biomedical 'diagnostic entity', rather than as a person whose experience of acute illness is destabilising and fracturing her notions of identity. 'If my body, ill or healthy, can't really be fully apprehended, how can my "identity"?' Over time, through consultations with other practitioners, she enters a more active phase in making sense of her illness/heal-ing journey. She comes to understand how the medical profession sees thyroid disorders in a gendered way, not simply because women are more affected by them than men, but because their susceptibility is linked to assumptions about women's metabolism, emotions and hormones. Ettore adopts a more holistic strategy for getting better, which includes a variety of technologies or embodied practices: 'I visit doctors. I have my blood taken. I take advice. I don't take advice. I rest. I take herbal medication. I learn yoga. I have jangled emotions. I express anger. I express joy. I do nothing' (2017: 54). She resists being pathologised by

(Continued)

the medical profession but willingly accepts some standard tests. Multiple, flexible identities are her response, not a fixed identity.

Generalisation

This autoethnography shows how a thyroid problem is a gendered topic. It reveals how personal experience of an under-researched illness benefits from feminist ethnography, a cultural interpretation of medical power and inequality, and from sensitivity to biographical experience. It shows how emotions play a central role in human experience and how they can be incorporated into a perceptive analysis of health and illness in contexts beyond the individual story.

Tip from the field

Autoethnography requires that you create and gather your own data

Successful autoethnography requires a performance on a stage that you design and produce for yourself. You need to make sure that you have the resources and materials to tell your story as lived experience. Such resources are likely to include diaries, observations, documents, visuals to aid recall, and records of emotions felt at the time. Do not rely solely on your recollections long after the event.

Although some descriptions of autoethnography focus on the autobiographical element as the core, so to speak, the ethnographic element is essential to link the self and the social – and the political. The adoption of a feminist standpoint enshrines the idea that 'the personal is political'. The writing of autoethnography is therefore a process of transformation. It turns personal stories into narrative representations of social interactions, subordination, cultural discrimination, trauma, 'epiphanies' and many other experiences which require ethnographic work to give them meaning in the wider context of social and cultural relations. Autoethnography could be described as an orientation rather than a single method, especially now that it has spread from its origins in anthropology and sociology to a wide spectrum of research, including studies in education, health, social work and counselling. One helpful way to understand this complexity is to visualise a triad with points to represent the self, culture and the researcher's account. While all autoethnographies combine these elements, they vary in emphasis in different studies. Chang (2008: 48) argues that there is a logic to the connections between them: 'autoethnography should be ethnographic in its methodological orientation, cultural in its interpretive orientation, and autobiographical in its content orientation'. We can see this in action in Study 2, reported above.

This overview would not be complete without mentioning that some researchers, even those who are sympathetic to biographical and feminist research, are sceptical about certain examples of autoethnography as method. While it is highly plausible to claim that 'the personal is political' in the context of feminist politics, it is another matter to translate this into a principle of research design and method. Autoethnography is driven by a concern for the marginalised and their suffering, and it espouses an activist approach to getting its message across. However, a great deal of autoethnography is written and published in an academic context, in the institutional surroundings of journals, professional conferences and books, and thus can hardly claim to raise oppositional consciousness among the oppressed. More than that, the subjects of autoethnography are not usually themselves marginalised or downtrodden in the most extreme ways, although they may have been on the receiving end of damaging racism, serious illness or other life-changing experiences. Delamont (2009) makes particularly sharp criticisms, while not denying the value of autobiography in research. Her position is that research should be ethical, analytical, not experiential, should focus on unknown worlds and attempt to make the familiar anthropologically strange. She argues that autoethnography fails to meet these standards or social science objectives, and 'that there *should* be demarcation between the ethnographer's reflexive self when there *is* a research topic, and the academic who focuses on themselves *rather than* having a research topic' (2009: 60). The response to this criticism should be to justify autoethnography in feminist research as an example of mixed methods – autobiography with ethnography – and not to err too far on the side of autobiography without ethnography.

Walking and talking

Combining ethnographic material with biographical data, as we have seen, expands the possibilities for understanding and interpretation. Within ethnography, the practice of walking and interviewing has become a dynamic and participatory way of doing research (Bates and Rhys-Taylor, 2017), deliberately using the sensory experiences of motion and an awareness of physical surroundings. The practice has the potential to bring everyday sensory experiences (sights, sounds, smells, feelings and motion) into the research process. For the same reasons, it can evoke memories and provide additional stimuli to narration. Walking while talking is particularly well suited to eliciting storytelling about movement (literal and imagined), embodiment, and attachments to space and place. The immediate access to relevant surroundings which walking gives channels the everyday skill of talking about personal experience and fits well with 'lives on the move'. It can strengthen the relationship between the researcher and self-narrator, and open up shared spaces of understanding and reflection.

O'Neill and Roberts (2020) have pioneered a method which combines walking and interviewing with a biographical focus. They describe it as the 'Walking Interview as a Biographical Method' (WIBM), a consolidation of their previous work on participatory, visual and performative styles of research (O'Neill et al., 2015). The objective of biographical work using WIBM, they state:

> is not to attempt the impossible of a 'complete individual', but rather to view the individual as evolving and moving in time and place, and stress the participatory nature of the relationship between respondent and the researcher, the co-productive nature of life accounts. (O'Neill and Roberts, 2020: 7)

The method has been applied in a variety of projects which seek to understand the lives and experiences of people who are dislocated, have made dangerous journeys, or who live in areas of social deprivation. They include: the sense of belonging negotiated by asylum seekers, refugees and undocumented migrants in the English East Midlands (O'Neill and Hubbard, 2010); the meaning of community for residents of the downtown east side of Vancouver, an area with high levels of drug use, homelessness, poverty, crime, mental illness and sex work (O'Neill and Stenning, 2013); and the role of arts and culture in facilitating processes of belonging and integration (O'Neill, 2008). In these studies, the participants are selected according to their experiences of mobility, migration or community and for the significance to them of the places where they live. They are often recruited through local community networks and arts organisations. The walking routes or itineraries are not determined by the researcher but can be based on a map of meaningful places and connections drawn by the participants themselves, landmarks chosen for their personal significance, or themed, for example, to highlight views, architectural features, meeting places, obstacles to movement, sounds or emotional connections.

The walking interview is not limited to walking and talking. It is often supported by documents (brochures, maps, drawings, creative writing), photographs and other representations. The data for analysis is thus more complex and mobile than the text of an interview. In one example (O'Neill et al., 2015: 81–86), a Kurdish artist and a photographer have a walking conversation in the centre of Nottingham. The familiar buildings are made strange to the photographer as he sees them through the artist's eyes. The artist, in turn, describes how the view from his high-rise flat evokes a feeling of space and freedom which reminds him of home in Kurdistan. More darkly, a section of wall brings back memories of being witness to a young boy being executed by firing squad against such a wall. For both, the experience is transformational: glimpsing the city through the artist's eyes changes the photographer's familiar perceptions, and the artist finds space to remember, reflect and forge a connection ('inter-subjective mutual recognition', p. 86) to his partner in conversation. Such contexts are a reminder of the potential risks that researchers and participants can face, including emotional stress and the revival of traumatic memories. Some, but not every single, risk can be anticipated and mitigated in the process of gaining consent for the research. Researchers are, however, expected to take steps to minimise the potential harm when they seek ethical approval for their project.

Study 3 (below) summarises the research on refugees and asylum seekers by O'Neill and Hubbard (2010). It reflects the growing interest in active, participatory methods which involve walking as part of the research design. While there is often a close connection to the arts, both in subject matter and ways of knowing, it is important to note that walking methods are not simply an adjunct to arts projects or policy development. They are sociological interventions, inspired by the traditions of research that connect to theories of symbolic interaction, the Chicago School, urban ethnography and others (see Chapter 2). This means that fundamental methodological questions should still be asked about the authenticity of data, the reliability or replicability of findings, and the validity of analysis and interpretation. Study 3 is an example of research which steers a careful path in representing a new, interpretive understanding of place without degenerating into a form of tourist narrative, and without losing the balance between subjectivity and objectivity.

Study 3

Transnational communities and sense of belonging – Ethno-mimesis as performative practice (O'Neill and Hubbard, 2010)

Method and design

This study, by Maggie O'Neill and Phil Hubbard, explores the topic of how refugees and asylum seekers in the UK relate to the spaces where they live, and their sense of belonging given that they experience dislocation and a lack of recognition. Walking is adopted as an embodied, spatially sensitive method which captures the complexity and ambiguity of their lives. There is an element of performance in the interaction between the ethnographer and the storyteller, which O'Neill and Hubbard (2010) describe as ethno-mimesis, a representation of the sensuousness and emotion of inner experiences alongside the biography, creating a space for telling the life story in artistic form: 'Mimesis is intended not to mimic or reflect reality, but to encourage

(Continued)

a moment of cognition through which we can develop a critical perspective that includes "empathy" as sensuous knowing' (p. 48). Participants from four cities were recruited through community organisations and networks, and invited to take part in walking events with a fellow walker (a long-term resident, councillor, etc.). Each participant followed a series of instructions which involved drawing a map from 'home' to a 'special place', using it to walk the route for about two hours, making images and recordings, then discussing the experience in a post-walk workshop.

Study findings

The authors discuss, first, how the walks facilitated dialogue, biographical reflections and shared, empathic relations. They show how physical experiences of walking are shaped by terrain, weather, traffic, the built environment and other people. All these experiences of touch, motion and perception feed into the process of collaborative knowledge production and contribute to an understanding of how far the participants make the cities their own. Second, the method encourages discovery or re-discovery of aspects of place which can be either mundane (litter and its significance) or rich with symbolic implications (sites of meeting, beauty or faith). Third, walking and talking with another person is a sociable activity and an occasion to enhance relationality: between one walker and another; through expressing the connections between the home and host countries; through mutual learning about cultural diversity; and through the process of representing the walks using images and artwork.

Generalisation

This is an example of a creative mixed qualitative methods study in biographical research, which incorporates aspects of art and performance. It offers a way to perform biographical work within a relational, multi-sensory space that is real in the lives of the participants. The study illuminates the experiences of refugees and asylum seekers in a way which challenges stereotypes and myths about belonging and integration. It is adaptable to many other populations, especially groups who share the characteristics of dislocation, transience, questioned identity and 'otherness' (homeless people or sex workers, for example). Advocates of the method emphasise that it may help participants (on both sides of the conversation) to access or say what cannot easily be expressed. It facilitates participation and creates new ways of knowing and understanding biography.

Bundling methods

If 'bundle' is a term to describe the practice of combining a package of products or services which have affinities with each other, usually to increase profit, then it can also be applied to the situation in which a number of qualitative methods are used in conjunction to explore a single topic, typically in a *convergent-parallel* way, like a woven fabric in which the threads criss-cross the data to form a complex pattern. The main difference with other mixed methods is the deliberate use of more than two or three methods and types of data. There is no limit to the number, provided the selection is justified by the complexity of patterns in the object of study.

One example of this deliberate bundling of methods is Gabb's (2009) Behind Closed Doors project which uses a multiple mixed method qualitative approach in a study of family life, where the relatively hidden areas of sexuality and experiences of intimacy are important to the investigation. While these are not new topics for researchers in family studies, they involve questions about personal interaction, emotional attachments and private behaviour which are not easy to answer, even for family members themselves. Such research requires a high level of sensitivity, trust and commitment as well as a particular attention to ethics. The research design was therefore optimised to allow the participants (parents and children) every opportunity to provide relevant data in ways they felt most appropriate. There were 10 families in the sample and the data were collected over a 6–10-week period. The main instrument for gathering data about the life course was a free association bio-graphical narrative interview drawing on biographical narrative interpretative method (BNIM; see Chapter 2). Focus group discussions were also used to explore themes which came to light in other sources of data. Participants in the study were invited to contribute in additional ways. The researchers created a floor plan of the family home and asked the participants to use stickers to represent the patterns of their emotions and behaviour in different locations. One advantage of these 'emo-tion maps' was that they could be used by children as well as adults. Combined with follow-up interviews, they generated information about feelings and connections within the household space. Adults completed research diaries which provided tem-poral information about family routines and interactions. The families were encouraged to use observation – of mealtimes, for example – supported by video recordings if they felt comfortable with that. Finally, the study used vignettes and photographs from third-party sources like a parenting handbook to support discus-sion about parent–child intimacy and other topics.

Gabb (2009: 51–52) represents these sources of data as a matrix, showing how each family and individual responded (or not) to the data-collection initiatives. Adults generally provided data of nearly every type, but the children's responses were patchier. Gabb explains how she used an integrative approach in two dimen-sions to interpret the findings: 'Through case study analysis the (vertical) relational threads of a story can be traced; cross sectional analysis brings to the fore the social-personal (horizontal) connections' (p. 43). The richness and complexity of the data are challenging, and the bundling of methods is not intended to produce tidy results but rather to reflect the 'messiness' of family living. Gabb uses a single case example to demonstrate how multiple methods contribute to a deep understanding of the topic. 'Brian' is a proud husband and father, whose written diary is more articulate than his interview contributions, where he tends to be self-deprecating about his ability to talk about himself ('I'm not very eloquent', he says). Across the methods, Brian situates most of his experiences in the father–son relationship, which he sees as changing because of the loosening of traditionally defined gender roles, but important because he is responsible for developing a shared sense of masculinity as the parent of his son. The emotion map elicited information about his understanding of the boundaries of affection and intimacy which he otherwise found difficult to talk about. In other words, we can see aspects of triangulation where the different sources of data help to compensate for their respective limitations. But there are contradictions as well as complementarities in his accounts: 'disconnections [that] illustrate the parameters that can frame our self-knowing: the uncertainties and temporalities of family relationship, the dynamic intersections between the social, historical, biographical and personal facts of our subjectivity' (Gabb, 2009: 48–49). In other words, the use of multiple methods does not add up to a neat overall composition or an internally consistent biographical narrative enhanced by 'additional' data. Instead, the bundle is deliberately left loose and untidy, better to reflect the flows and patterning of family life.

Using methods in this way to link individual actors and social processes of kinship, gender, child development, education and norms of privacy hints at applications of biographical research in the domain of applied research, social policy and professional fields such as social work, family therapy and schooling. We turn to this issue in the next section.

Biography in the context of applied and policy research

Applied, or practice-based, research is an important strand of social science. It is distinct in the way it uses social theories and methods to address programmes and procedures in practical settings. The overriding commitment is to improve services or make policies more effective. It may involve primary or secondary research, quantitative or qualitative methods, or service evaluation. Methods such as surveys, focus groups and interviews are often combined in a single study. Whether the purpose is to formulate new policy, to compare practices of implementation, or to evaluate an existing strategy, the aim is not just to understand but also to change something in society. Biographical research can have a part to play in this. In the context of migration, education, health and social care, family studies, career counselling and many other topics, biographies have been used to re-orientate research by placing social actors at the centre of processes of institutionalisation, decision making and policy formation. We illustrate the connections between biographical research and social policy with two examples. One, from the EU Leonardo INVITE project (Golczyńska-Grondas, 2008), shows how autobiographical narrative interviews can be used by professional counsellors, vocational teachers, and psychologists to counsel individuals whose careers are disrupted by major crises. You can inspect some interview transcripts which are reproduced in this publication. The second example is more far-reaching: studies in the field of European policy and integration. Both examples show how researchers with a primary interest in practice or social policy can derive valuable insights from biographical data.

Education and employment policies seek to develop systems that can prepare and support individuals right through their careers. However, careers services are generally available to targeted groups, at certain points in life, and tend to focus on information and immediate decisions. They are not well adapted to the situation of clients who have experienced a life-changing medical crisis and do not have the capacity to continue with their former occupation. They may not be able to connect easily with the routine bureaucratic services provided through education or the employment support system. The aim of the INVITE project was to create and apply a curriculum for vocational further education to address this issue, using biographical narrative techniques. The researcher partners were from university institutes and the practitioner communities, and from several countries and disciplines. They conducted autobiographical narrative interviews (see Chapter 4) with clients, the results of which were applied in social work support, and psychotherapeutic counselling. The interview is not thematic or focused on the career problem as such, but becomes a means to explore the life situation of the client and encourage them to undertake the biographical work required to understand the situation, be open to new futures and appreciate what is involved in choosing a new occupation and training for it. Counsellors learn to interpret the interview data and develop a case analysis to help their clients exploit their biographical resources for action or biographical metamorphosis. It may be a long-term process in the setting of a rehabilitation course, or it may be short term, focused on the biographical origins of medical crises or sudden unemployment. The distinctive feature of autobiographical narration is that the emergent features of the social interaction and narration are fundamentally different from the logic of the client interview in its bureaucratic form; neither the client nor the practitioner can anticipate which new topics or insights into existing problems will emerge. While the sensitivity of the approach is an obvious strength because it allows the non-occupational experiences of the client to inform possible remedies, it is not without some drawbacks: the procedures of biographical interviewing and analysis are more time-consuming than a structured thematic interview, and clients may be reluctant to disclose personal information which is not directly connected with their case. If the requisite level of trust is established, and the individual's circumstances are truly life-changing, the method can deliver benefits that will not be achieved by standard career guidance. Finding out how the individual defines and explains their problem situation in the context of their life story, without taking it at face value, opens up new avenues for understanding as well as the prospect of a more autonomous response from the client.

The second example is on a different scale: comparisons across countries of the European Union. Much policy evaluation research builds on 'before and after' designs or controlled experimental designs to establish 'what works'. A significant problem with this approach is that social policy contexts are always complex and difficult to standardise for research measurement, and another is that they do not take account of the individual experiences which either contribute to the success of the policy or obstruct the workings of the policy. The 'biographical policy evaluation method' developed by Apitzsch et al. (2008) aims to include the specific biographical conditions that contribute to the effectiveness or ineffectiveness of a policy. It uses the autobiographical narrative type of interview and interpretation against the background of a detailed knowledge of the policy field. The authors explain that 'in contrast to program-oriented policy evaluation methods, biographical policy evaluation focuses on the actually experienced effects of the implementation of the policy' (2008: 14). The original context for this combination of policy evaluation and biographical research was a study of self-employment comparing the increasingly coordinated labour market policies introduced in many European countries in the 1990s to encourage self-employment as an alternative to unemployment, especially among women and migrants. Policy measures included training, mentoring and consulting. Biographical analysis made it possible to unite two ways of thinking about the policy issue: one referring to collective traditions of ethnic entrepreneurship and the other to individual responses which prioritise self-employment as a form of self-emancipation. Subsequent research using cross-national comparisons for biographical policy evaluation in Europe includes Turk and Mrozowicki (2013). They strongly argue the theoretical case for bringing biography into the fields of European integration and European policy studies, and demonstrate empirically what European citizens experience and what courses of action they take in their interactions with EU process and structure in domains as diverse as ethnic minority policy, labour mobility, works councils, and environmental policy. Other work brings biographical policy evaluation to bear on language regimes and language acquisition (Ankiah-Gangadeen and Samuel, 2014), and on questions of intergenerational transmission in migration processes (the MIGREVAL project, accessible at http://migreval.hypotheses.org). We conclude with the example of a biographical policy evaluation of the Dublin Convention (Bartel et al.,

2020), the policy which declares that only one European state is responsible for examining an asylum application and that this is normally the state in which a refugee first arrived in Europe. In a study based on 29 biographical interviews with refugees affected by the Dublin Convention in France, the participants were invited to tell their life story (phase one) and then were asked about their experiences related to the Convention in terms of language, education and access to the labour market as well as the asylum procedure (phase two). Using this data, Bartel et al. (2020) explore, not the legal development of the Convention or its implementation, but the key biographical moments which bring the refugees into contact with it. These moments are the refugees' arrival in France, the process of integration, and times when refugees change the European state they live in after having applied for asylum. The analysis shows that the Convention does not only have an impact on the moment of first settlement and the legal process of asylum seeking. It has lasting impacts on the social integration of the participants and may actually force them to move to a new country (for example, when they experience racist attacks or are denied the opportunity to re-unite their family). It also shows how far migrants are able to exercise their own agency, even when the legal framework of the Convention is inimical to their personal strategies. The results of the analysis highlight the anomalous workings of the current policy and carry some important implications for policy makers – such as the definition of which countries are 'safe', the availability of language courses and training, and the negative impact of processing delays on long-term integration. The biographical evaluation shows that beyond the intended effect of limiting the choice of the country of arrival, the Dublin Convention often has an impact long after its formal outcome.

Summary

In this chapter, we have explored how research projects can employ two or more methods in combination, an approach known as mixed method or multimethod research. We focused on qualitative research and the question: how can we ensure that mixed method designs are consistent, and analytical frameworks are compatible? The examples we have chosen demonstrate that a careful and deliberate choice of methods will recognise how the research design needs to be framed by the research question, and be informed by detailed knowledge of the field and the strengths and weaknesses of other research. Qualitative mixed methods using biographical narrative generate rich data from a limited selection of participants: a single individual in the case of autoethnography up to tens or even hundreds of narrative interviews in the case of large international projects with teams of researchers. Large-scale projects are not 'representative' in a statistical sense, although the selection of cases will be informed by theoretical sampling principles. In general, because most qualitative research builds on the foundation that social phenomena are known through interaction and interpretation from the actor's point of view, there is good compatibility when qualitative methods are combined. In the next chapter, we will consider biographical narrative in mixed method designs which include quantitative data and analysis, often large-scale and representative, and the different challenges that researchers face when they bring together these different ways of knowing the social world.

Questions to consider

1. What is the purpose of mixing methods?
2. How would you attempt to integrate biographical analysis with other types of data?
3. What mixture of methods might you choose to examine one of the following topics:
   a. biographical experiences of mobility-impaired people?
   b. community conflicts between long-term residents and newcomers?
   c. student responses to a study abroad programme?

9

MIXED QUANTITATIVE AND QUALITATIVE METHODS

Objectives

By the end of this chapter, you will be able to:

- Understand the mixed method discussion on the 'incompatibility' and 'compatibility' theses
- Understand the reasoning for and implications of mixed method designs, including the focus on the 3Ps – pragmatics, paradigms and politics
- Consider the inner complexities of mixed method designs and their implications for biographical methods
- Understand why we use mixed method designs and the role biographical narrative methods may play in these designs, including their ability to ask both explanatory and confirmatory research questions, to provide stronger inferences and to incorporate a broader range of divergent findings.

Biographical methods can be firmly placed within the qualitative paradigm of research methodologies. Their focus on the individual 'in place' – including communities, localities, societies and mobilities – as well as 'in time' – including historical events, biographical turning points and life continuities – gives us a unique understanding of what occurred before and what happened after. This qualitative richness includes the sequence of experiences from the individual perspective that, with the use of the right analytical tools, can shine a light on the inner workings of social structures. As complex and exciting as biographical data can be, in science there will always be a need to explore and expand the sources of data, to validate them, to assess and innovate within particular methodologies, and bring them into conversation with other approaches. Within this dynamic context, we can see an amazing expansion of qualitative methodologies and their ever-growing role in mixed method designs.

Historically, according to Nilsen and Brannen (2010), biographical data were frequently combined with other types of data, including the analysis of personal documents, observation and case studies. In the early traditions of the field, biographical methods were always a part of more comprehensive qualitative mixed method designs, and by now they have evolved into the fully acknowledged 'method partnerships' that were discussed in Chapter 8. The role of biographical methodologies that go beyond the qualitative paradigm, however, is more complicated – not because of the biographical element in itself, but because they are bridging more than just differences of method. Often, the divergence lies in the basic principles of what it means to do science and what is the right way to do it. Brannen (2005: 7) outlines the grounds for the divide:

> Quantitative researchers have seen qualitative researchers as too context-specific, their samples as unrepresentative and their claims about their work as unwarranted – that is judged from the vantage point of statistical generalisation. For their part, qualitative researchers view quantitative research as overly simplistic, decontextualised, reductionist in terms of its generalisations, and failing to capture the meanings that actors attach to their lives and circumstances.

These lines of division between quantitative and qualitative methodologies are discussed differently within different academic disciplines. Some of the more 'purist' approaches would highlight what has been termed the 'incompatibility thesis' of the qualitative and quantitative matching, suggesting that there is an unbreakable link between a research paradigm, the logic of inquiry and the appropriate method (Teddlie and Tashakkori, 2009: 15). This approach would argue that if the underlying premises of the research paradigms are in conflict, which is said to be the case between quantitative and qualitative methodologies, then they should not be used together.

On this argumentation, if, for instance, a survey methodology is designed to test a hypothesis, following a deductive research logic, it cannot be combined with the unstructured type of ethnographic data that describes a loose variety of things and follows the inductive way of thinking. The incompatibility of these methods would lead to divergent or contradictory findings that would distort the researcher's interpretations and undermine the ability to generalise from the data. Proponents of the incompatibility thesis can be found in both qualitative and quantitative research communities who advocate, sometimes with good reason, that the strength of scientific methodologies depends on the preservation of the link between paradigm and method. This approach, however, can lead to the narrowing of research communities, to stagnation in methodological innovation, and to problems with the communication of academic findings to other partners, such as policy makers, industry and business.

The counter-response to the incompatibility thesis, often referred to as the 'compatibility thesis', is based on the everyday realities of social research. According to Brannen (2005), the rationale for using mixed method designs follows the 3Ps model, which includes pragmatics, paradigm and politics. First, the focus on the pragmatics of social research would highlight the fact that a critical objective is to answer the research question. In this context, Teddlie and Tashakkori (2009: 84) argue that it is 'acceptable to mix qualitative and quantitative methods in research studies that called for different types of data to answer research questions'. They stress that researchers should be able to understand the strengths and limitations of different methodologies and use them to maximise the returns from the research project.

Second, with regard to the discussions around paradigms, mixed method advocates argue that instead of trying to avoid conflicts between paradigms, the researcher should understand what elements of different methods may be advantageous for the research project and how to minimise their potential conflicts. This can be done by assigning a leading role to one method at the design stage or by sequencing the methods used at the different stages of the project. Researchers who have methodological awareness as well as the ability to combine research paradigms have developed a new paradigm of social research associated with pragmatism and consider themselves a 'third research community' (Teddlie and Tashakkori, 2006, 2009) that exists alongside qualitative and quantitative scholars and scientists.

Finally, the politics rationale is an important reason for the implementation of mixed method designs in social research. This aspect focuses strongly on the communication and application of research findings for both policy development and commercial use. Patterns of effective scientific communication need research findings that can be presented as facts and generalised to the wider population, typically as representative samples and statistical models, as well as findings that are relatable to a wide audience, presenting complex links and lived experience that relate to these facts. In academic research as well as among commercial funding bodies, this aspect of communication is very often hidden within the category of 'research impact'.

Mixing qualitative and quantitative paradigms in the context of biographical methods

The short discussion above on compatibility and incompatibility of mixed method designs touches only the tip of the iceberg that is the relationship between mixed methods. For novice researchers, the ability to combine methods in the search for answers as well as to improve the impact of the study is incentive enough to wander into this particular methodological territory. In the context of biographical narrative research, the reasons for reaching towards other sources of data and analysis often stem from an awareness of the previously discussed limitations of biographical narrative methods, such as: small samples that restrict wider generalisations; the subjectivity of the narrative accounts that calls for validation from other sources; and the inherent uncertainties of unstructured data that may, or may not, answer the specific research questions. These are all excellent reasons to expand your research project beyond biographical narrative data, but this should be done with an awareness that mitigating the limitations of one research method with the use of a different method opens your project up to an entirely different set of methodological considerations and evaluation criteria. In this context, the researcher needs to understand the implications of their chosen methodologies separately as well as in interaction with each other, and show an astute understanding of the links between research paradigms and particular methods.

The interaction between the research methods selected for the study needs to be well planned and scientifically justified. According to Brannen (2005), qualitative and quantitative mixed methods can be implemented at various stages of the project and in various configurations (see also the overview and notation system in Chapter 8). Overall design and analysis would determine the role of biographical narrative data in the project:

1. **Research design phase** – decisions at this stage of research will determine the logic of the project (Johnson et al., 2007). The researcher should decide how to order the methods in time – in sequence or concurrently – and their dominance in the design. For example, in cohort studies (see the example in Study 1 below), each person is surveyed over a period of time (QUANT), while a small sample of respondents is interviewed using the biographical narrative interview (qual). In this type of QUANT+qual research design, the quantitative

element is dominant and determines the general logic of the inquiry – deductive, focused on hypothesis testing, while biographical data are used to provide some additional context.

2. **Fieldwork phase** – at this stage of the mixed method research project, researchers must make a decision on data collection – for example, by combining a street survey (quant) with semi-structured biographical interviews (qual) and participant observation (qual) to better understand the dynamics of a group or community. At this stage of the research process, biographical narrative data can be a part of the multiple source design that will also determine the means of obtaining the data, for example by employing semi-structured biographical interviews rather than narrative interviews.

3. **Analysis phase** – at this stage of the research process, the researcher decides how to explain and interpret the data. As we have discussed throughout this book, there are always a number of ways to analyse data that may cross the qualitative–quantitative divide. They include the quantitative coding of qualitative data, or QCA technique (see Chapter 6) which renders biographical narrative data in numerical form, so that the analysis can follow the model of hypothesis testing.

4. **Contextualisation phase** – at this stage, the findings of the research study should be embedded in the broader context. In the case of biographical data, this can involve collating findings from the biographical part of the study (QUAL) with broader trends identifiable in the statistical data, for example taken from national surveys or the national census – both current and in the past (quant).

This list outlines only the basic variations of the mixed method configurations that may incorporate biographical narrative methods. Each example presented above will require additional in-depth considerations on sampling as well as data validity and reliability. Each design and combination needs to control for possible conflict and provide relevant justification for why the selected methods, in interaction with each other, are best suited to address the specific research problem.

Utility of mixed method designs with biographical narrative elements

Mixed method studies are becoming a vital part of the social science landscape. Particularly for less powerful, qualitative methodologies including biographical narrative research, pairing with a better-established method with more powerful generalisation tools, such as the survey, is a way of validating findings and adding scientific weight to their communication. In the world of competitive academic funding, publishing and impact, mixed methods offer yet another avenue to conduct innovative biographical research and creatively combine individual biographies with other methodologies.

There are three important reasons why mixed method designs are relevant for social research projects that incorporate biographical narrative methods, and can be considered to be superior to single method designs (Teddlie and Tashakkori, 2009: 33). They are: simultaneously asking exploratory and confirmatory questions; providing more robust inferences; and generating a greater variety of findings. The following three sections discuss these areas, paying particular attention to the implications for biographical narrative research practice.

Tip from the field

In the mixed method study, methodology becomes a part of the research question

This is an exciting side-effect of mixed method methodologies. In studies that employ very different methods and need to negotiate very different epistemologies, paradigms and philosophies, simply to justify their findings, the methods section becomes a vital part of the research project. It becomes integrated into the research question that reflects on how we investigate things and frame our research findings. This part of mixed method studies has implications for the development of research methodologies and research impact – it answers questions on how we can improve our research tools and methods in the future.

Addressing explanatory and confirmatory questions

According to Teddlie and Tashakkori (2009: 33), 'a major advantage of mixed methods research is that it enables the researcher to simultaneously ask confirmatory and exploratory questions and therefore verify and generate theory in the same study'. Social science research projects tend to be built around multi-levelled research questions that encompass different aspects of social reality. For example, the research question that aims to investigate domestic violence as a social problem would benefit from looking both at the general patterns within society (rates) and particular individual situations (cases) to understand the dynamics and patterns of the phenomenon. But looking both towards the general and particular requires different methodologies and different logics of inquiry. To answer this type of research question, we could look into an available crime survey that would provide answers to confirmatory questions about the social patterns of domestic violence, such as profiles of the gender, age and social class of both victims and perpetrators. This could be supplemented by biographical narrative interviews with domestic violence survivors that would provide explanatory answers on particular situations and patterns as well as insights into lived experiences.

This multi-level research question design that strictly corresponds with a particular methodology is a neat way of ordering and overlaying methods and findings to avoid possible conflict. Within this particular type of design, biographical narrative methods are commonly used to explain particular biographical patterns that include complex relations between individuals and social structures that can then be linked with some elements of the survey data. Elliott et al. (2014) is an excellent example of this type of study (see Study 1), where the research question is constructed to ask both confirmatory and explanatory questions with the use of biographical and survey data in the context of neighbourhood cohesion and mental health wellbeing.

Study 1

Neighbourhood cohesion and mental wellbeing among older adults (Elliott et al., 2014)

This study examines the link between neighbourhood characteristics and mental health. It focuses on older people in the context of active ageing and healthy participation in the UK.

Method and design

The study employs a mixed method design using the data from three British cohort studies – the Hertfordshire Cohort Study (HCS), the MRC National Survey of Health and Development (NSHD) and the National Child Development Survey (NCDS). Within all three, the researchers used the Mental Wellbeing Scale (WEMWBS) to assess levels of wellbeing across the sample. The Neighbourhood Social Cohesion Scale was used to measure the sense of belonging within the neighbourhood. The statistical analysis also included information on voluntary work, illness and disability, housing tenure, social support and participation, as well as being controlled for basic personality traits. Data were gathered between 2008 and 2011 and included quantitative surveys with 10,312 cohort survey participants.

Additionally, each cohort study included a sample of qualitative biographical interviews, 230 interviews in total, which included information on housing history as well as a sense of belonging.

(Continued)

The quantitative part of the study aimed to answer the *confirmatory* question – is there an association between neighbourhood cohesion and wellbeing? The qualitative part of the study aimed to answer the *exploratory* question on what mechanisms promote neighbourhood belonging and shape neighbourhood relations.

Study findings

The quantitative part of the study confirmed that there is a moderate association between neighbourhood cohesion and wellbeing. This association varies in different age cohorts, implying that the association is stronger in two older cohorts. This association holds even when controlling for personality traits (being introvert and extrovert).

The qualitative part of the study focused on the mechanisms of social cohesion in the neighbourhoods. The findings indicated that high social cohesion that contributes to mental wellbeing is associated with the ability to participate and volunteer in activities outside the household, including sport, church and other civil society organisations. Additionally, qualitative data pointed to the elements of neighbourhood relations that hindered social cohesion, such as the physical structure of the environment, for example very busy roads, and conflict in the neighbourhood. Biographical narratives also point to the growing importance of neighbourhoods with age; as their children leave home, narrators' need to belong shifts towards neighbours and the wider community.

Generalisations

The study argues that the use of qualitative material, along with the quantitative analysis, brings more clarity to the analysis. It gives an insight into how people conceptualise their neighbourhood, highlights the mechanisms for neighbourhood cohesion and explains the age factor in the analysis.

The authors argue that the individual definitions of neighbourhood vary – from direct neighbours to groups and churches to the wider local areas. Where quantitative analysis focuses on positive elements that aid social cohesion, such as participation and social support, the qualitative data also point to the neighbourhood elements that hinder social cohesion, such as conflict and a lack of infrastructure. The use of both qualitative and quantitative data gives a fuller picture of the link between neighbourhood cohesion and wellbeing in the context of ageing.

Providing stronger inferences

According to Johnson and Turner (2003: 299), 'methods should be mixed in a way that has complementary strengths and non-overlapping weaknesses'. Introducing mixed method designs in the research project is about creating synergy between the methods. These synergies should reinforce the chances of answering the research question in a more comprehensive way. The rationale for combining biographical narrative methods in mixed method designs is usually to explore one of the two key features of biographical narrative – the long-term time component and the deep embeddedness of the individual perspective within a social context. Each of these features can be brought in with other methods that reinforce this specific feature, contributing to the enhancement of the longitudinal and embedded mixed method designs.

Longitudinal mixed method designs

Longitudinal research designs are employed in studies of social change and capture the events over a longer time period. They are particularly well suited to the study of factors which affect the life course, life chances, employment, health and wellbeing. Panel studies are one of the most widely employed longitudinal designs, where the same group of individuals is surveyed at regular intervals, and their answers are compared over time, indicating the change in their circumstances. Biographical narrative research methods can expand on structured survey responses by adding more in-depth accounts of these changes, as well as the co-existing individual circumstances. Longitudinal designs are common in demography, where they employ the models of 'cohort studies', and in development studies with the use of 'Q^2' designs:

- **Cohort studies** – tracking a specific group of people, usually a birth cohort – people born in the same year – over their lifetime to see how the same historical and socio-economic events have shaped individual life experiences (Nilsen and Brannen, 2010). They include the repeated survey of the group supplemented by biographical interviews. This design has been successfully implemented in a number of studies throughout the UK, including the MRC National Survey of Health and Development (NSHD) panel study based on the 1958 birth cohort and the National Child Development Survey (NCDS) panel study based on the 1946 birth cohort.
- **Q^2 methodologies** – widely used in the field of development studies where they combine qualitative and quantitative methods (therefore Q^2) in tracing poverty trajectories (Shaffer, 2013). This design uses pre-existing national longitudinal surveys combined with a smaller sample of structured life history interviews (LHI) that are focused on poverty-related issues, such as food, assets and access to education. This longitudinal design focuses on life trajectories that transect arbitrary poverty lines (based on income or expenditure), identifying patterns such as sustained escapes from poverty, impoverishment and chronic poverty.

Embedded mixed method designs

Embedded research designs are employed within well-defined research settings and often follow the design of a case study. These particular designs are embedded in coherent contexts of research, such as family or community, and employ a multi-method approach to gather data intended to illuminate diverse aspects of social life and social interaction in a specific place. These designs employ biographical narrative methods to explore insider perspectives on the issues under investigation, often tapping into living memory and a sense of belonging. These mixed method approaches are common in cultural anthropology, community and organisation studies, as well as human geography. They naturally gravitate into complementary qualitative methodologies, but at the level of research design and data, contextualisation also takes in the available quantitative data, such as local and national surveys (see Study 1 on civil society in Chapter 8 and Studies 1 and 2 in this chapter).

The study by Kwan and Ding (2008) on geo-narratives is an interesting attempt to boost the power of inferences by placing two methods together within one research design (see Study 2). This study uses GIS visualisation methods employed in human geographies together with biographical narrative data that are plotted to the geographical mapping of the 'places' that elicit a fear of hate crime among Muslim women. Within the design, the researchers developed an extension to the GIS software that accommodates qualitative narrative data, including the data that have a sequential time element, to be able to incorporate time into the socio-geographical analysis and significantly strengthen the level of inference of the study.

Study 2

Geo-narrative – Extending geographic information systems for narrative analysis in qualitative and mixed method research (Kwan and Ding, 2008)

This study aims to extend the analytical capabilities of the geographic information systems (GIS) approach to narrative data by building an interface that can incorporate time into the geographical visualisation framework.

Method and design

This study collected data from 37 Muslim women living in Columbus, Ohio, in 2002 to investigate their sense of security before and after the events of 9/11 in the light of the occurrence of anti-Muslim acts of violence. The study collected a number of types of data, including the survey day – a timed account of their day; in-depth oral histories, including their account of events of 9/11; a map of their daily life; as well as photos and voice clips that illustrate the main aspects of daily geographies.

Analysis used NVivo software for qualitative coding and a GIS-based quali-tative data analysis component called 3D-VQGIS. The analysis included plotting the narrative and audio-visual material onto the time and space geo-visualisation framework to examine people's feelings and emotions of fear and safety before and after the events of 9/11.

Study findings

Study findings indicate that most of the women experienced some verbal and phys-ical abuse during their daily life activities immediately after the events of 9/11. These acts of violence were mostly in public spaces, such as at bus stops, shopping malls and department stores. This elicited some sense of fear that restricted their movement, but this change of behaviour was temporary. Several places, however, including Port Columbus International Airport, become permanently associated with fear and discomfort and this even affected international travel patterns.

Generalisations

The aim of this study was to compare emotional narratives related to place in a sequential temporal pattern – before 9/11 and after. The study developed a geo-graphical visualisation technique and software that the authors call a geo-narrative approach. It indicates that combining GIS visualisation and qualitative narrative data can be the next step in the development of this particular methodology. It points out that with the development of additional software packages, it is possible to capture more complex qualitative data types, such as these, including temporal sequences. Furthermore, integrating the multiple data types, such as pictures, audio and video materials, into a geographical visualisation mapping platform allows for the recursive and interactive analysis of narratives within GIS.

Considering a broad range of divergent findings

The third area of mixed methods that contrasts with single method studies is associated with the appearance of divergent and contradictory findings. This aspect of mixed methods is often frustrating because it forces researchers to reconcile the differences between unique outcomes of the analysis. That often means a re-examination of the data as well as a re-examination of the research tools (Teddlie and Tashakkori, 2009: 35) that is beneficial in the long-term perspective but wearisome in time-limited settings. Studies using biographical narrative data in combination with another non-narrative type of data are very likely to experience such divergence in findings. This creates opportuni-ties for discussion about underlying assumptions regarding our conceptualisation of research problems and research practice. Within that discussion, there is scope for the development of innovative and creative methodological solutions as well as conversations on methodological openness and researcher self-improvement – which should of course be a part of any research project.

In this section, we would like to present two examples of studies that incorporate biographical methods within a mixed method design and investigate the divergent findings that mixed methods can yield. The first study, by Davis and Baulch (2011), compares the findings from a Q^2 study in the field of development that examines the research tools used in the qualitative and quantitative elements of the study to reconcile differences in the results. The findings indicate that we can use the data from life history interviews to fine-tune the survey questions to pick up poverty dynamics in a more comprehensive way. The second study, by Eichsteller (2018b), compares three analytical techniques – structural analysis, narrative ethnography and QCA, and the assumptions they make regarding conceptual definitions and interpretative practices that may lead to divergent findings. This study argues that it is in the conscious and reflexive application of methods that we can judge and reconcile the contradictions in mixed method findings.

Study 3

Parallel Realities – Exploring poverty dynamics using mixed methods in rural Bangladesh (Davis and Baulch, 2011)

This study aims to examine the differences between quantitative and qualitative findings in the context of poverty trajectories in Bangladesh.

Method and design

This study follows a Q^2 design that is a combination of panel survey complemented by life history interview (LHI). The study uses data from the International Food Policy Research Institute (IFPRI) that surveyed and re-surveyed 1,907 households in 102 villages located in 14 out of 64 Bangladesh districts between 2001 and 2007. In the final stage of the project, 293 life history interviews were conducted in 161 households across eight districts. The strength of the sample lies in the ability to link the qualitative sample with the quantitative records for the same individuals and households, allowing for an investigation of the differences between qualitative and quantitative findings.

Study findings

The authors of the study highlight the disparity between the qualitative and quantitative results of the study. While the quantitative results indicate declining trends in absolute poverty in Bangladesh, the qualitative assessment reveals longer periods of impoverishment broken down with periods of improvement, which the authors refer to as a 'saw-tooth' pattern.

The analysis of the cases indicated five reasons that explain the disparities between qualitative and quantitative findings.

First, quantitative studies focus on household expenditure. Qualitative findings, however, indicate that expenditure does not accurately reflect the economic wealth of the household. A focus on assets, especially the ownership of land, seems to reflect economic wellbeing more accurately.

Second, household expenditure indicators used in quantitative studies result in clusters around the poverty line which tend to obscure the complexities of chronic poverty experiences. People are compelled to spend the same minimum amount of money to meet their basic food needs, but this does not reflect the relative severity of the household's situation. Here again, the decline in assets rather than the expenditure is a much stronger indicator. If a household needs to sell off assets to buy food, that is a stronger indicator for chronic poverty than expenditure.

Third, the authors point out that quantitative surveys often do not record aspects of ill-being – for example, domestic violence, ill health, disability and vulnerability of women-headed households that contribute to the fluctuation of poverty trajectories.

Fourth, surveys that assess poverty based on expenditure often miss changes in household size, often due to household splits.

Finally, the authors point out that it is possible that some of the differences in qualitative and quantitative findings are due to inaccurate recall of events in the life history interviews.

Generalisations

The outcome of the study suggests that we can increase the precision of poverty measurements by modifying quantitative tools. The lessons learned from this study include the need to focus on asset-based measures looking at land and livestock ownership, rather than just household expenditure in the measurement of poverty trajectories. Furthermore, gathering information on the ill-being factors, such as domestic violence, disability and ill-health, will allow for a better understanding of poverty dynamics in the context of developing countries.

Study 4

There is more than one way – A study of mixed analytical methods in biographical narrative research (Eichsteller, 2018b)

This study investigates three analytical models applied to the same type of biographical narrative data and their impact on the key aspects of analytical practice – operationalisation of concepts and interpretative practice.

(Continued)

Method and design

This study examines a sample of 25 autobiographical narrative interviews with transnational individuals living, studying and working in the EU. Data were gathered between 2006 and 2010. This study of transnational identities compares three different analytical models using a sequential design applied to the same set of data. The models are formal structural analysis (qualitative analysis), narrative ethnography (qualitative analysis) and comparative qualitative analysis (conversion from qualitative to quantitative analysis).

Study findings

The study explores the two main research problems in the application of mixed methodologies that disrupt the link between the data paradigm and the analytical approach – the use of coherent operational definitions and the transparency of interpretative practices.

Analysis of the operational definitions of transnationalism between three analytical models pointed to discrepancies in construct validities, which means that some of the methods measured different things under the same terminology, leading to divergent findings. A comparison of the interpretative practices in the three analytical models indicates that each model has a different way of safeguarding the 'objectivity' of its research practice, linked to the paradigm it is rooted in. That objectivity is, however, questioned in the interaction between these approaches, challenging the internal validity of mixed method studies.

Generalisations and applications

This study investigated the relationship between methodological procedures and implications for mixed method research practice. It served to widen methodological awareness and reflection. The comparative design is used to highlight the significance of research procedures and safeguards as well as the scope for creative and innovative solutions in biographical narrative research.

Summary

This chapter discusses the place of biographical narrative methods in the broader landscape of qualitative and quantitative mixed method designs. In the context of this overview, we highlight the complexity of the philosophical and methodological relations that still polarise research communities. On the one side, we can find those who advocate the incompatibility thesis, claiming that the link between research paradigms and particular methods should be protected and that, therefore, a mixing of the methodologies should not be encouraged. On the other hand, those championing the compatibility thesis argue that research should be about achieving the main objective of the research, and therefore should be concerned with finding the answer to the research question with any and sometimes as many methods as necessary to achieve this objective. Biographical researchers can be found in both camps, with some championing methodological purity and others foregrounding research utility. We also argued that in the contemporary landscape of academic and non-academic research, mixed method methodologies are gaining in importance and reach. They have three important strengths that Brannen characterised as 3Ps: pragmatics, paradigm and politics. They all boil down to the attractiveness of combining methods and data in the investigation of complex social phenomena, building bigger international, collaborative projects and increasing their scientific value by combining well-known measures, such as statistics, with more personal data. In this context, biographical narrative methods have an opportunity not only to be used as a complementary method in mixed method designs but also to take part in the dialogue and discussion that this type of cooperation leads to. In discussing the benefits of using biographical narrative methods as part of mixed method designs, first we showed how they can be used to answer explanatory questions. Second, we highlighted how they can bring temporal and spatial synergies with other methods to strengthen inferences and build better generalisations. Finally, we illustrated how mixed method designs with biographical narrative methods can be used to improve research tools as well as re-examine conceptual frameworks, analytical procedures and study validity.

Questions to consider

1. In your judgement, are biographical narrative methods more compatible with qualitative than quantitative methodologies; why or why not?
2. Would you agree that the growing importance of mixed method designs is an opportunity for biographical narrative methods; why or why not?
3. How might we strengthen the time aspect of biographical narrative methods by combining them with other methods?
4. How can the place and space aspects of biographical narrative methods be strengthened by other methods to answer more complex research questions?
5. What can biographical narrative research methods contribute to mixed method research projects?

10

CHALLENGES AHEAD FOR BIOGRAPHICAL RESEARCH

Objectives ──────────────────────────────

By the end of this chapter, you will be able to:

- Identify the main challenges ahead for biographical narrative methods
- Consider the impact of technology on the future of biographical research methods
- Understand the implications of mixed methods and international funding for biographical research methods
- Consider the implications of links between biographical evidence and developments in social theory.

So far in this book we have focused on providing you with the skills to understand what biographical narrative methods have to offer, to design your study and analyse your data with the creativity and imagination that can contribute to new insights within your field of knowledge. In this final chapter, we would like to bring your attention to the underlying currents within the broader social sciences that will influence the position and development of biographical narrative methods in the future. This overview is not an extensive analysis but akin to reading the sea and the weather to execute your research voyage successfully. We are pointing you to some critical methodological and theoretical developments and debates that will be likely to affect your research, and through which you will need to navigate.

First, we discuss the issue of finding your own unique identity as a biographical researcher, that will emerge in dialogue with, rather than in opposition to, other traditions. Second, we outline the main methodological advances that are likely to affect biographical narrative research and stimulate innovative approaches. Finally, we identify the major theoretical currents favouring biographical narrative methodologies and also those counter-currents where more theoretical work may be needed to connect individual accounts to the broader social issues.

Becoming a biographical researcher – finding an anchor

We started this book with a discussion of the primary challenges, where diversity within the field, in terms of approaches within different academic disciplines and across national and linguistic traditions, can become an obstacle to growth for new and experienced researchers alike. We discussed the tendencies of some traditions to claim superiority over others and the difficulties in the dialogue that come from the intercultural communication of biographies and biographical analysis. The more you search, the more you will discover that the biographical narrative approach appears to develop almost in isolation within each field of social science, arts and humanities. They will call upon different theoretical lineages, binding their academic development to their disciplinary foundations, and claiming an independent methodological development. The only point of convergence that all these disciplines seem to agree upon is a common point of origin for all biographical studies, as seen in Thomas and Znaniecki's *The Polish Peasant in Europe and America* (first published in 1918). It is a unique anchor for a research tradition that is otherwise so diverse. Tying the biographical narrative approach to this particular study acts as a beacon. It indicates that biographical research rooted in this particular tradition includes multiple data-gathering methods, values a humanistic yet scientific type of analysis, and brings individual experience to the forefront of the discussion. All these aspects are then re-homed, re-interpreted and re-applied within different academic traditions and perspectives, creating a uniquely rich and complicated research environment.

Within that rich and diverse environment of biographical narrative methods, it is sometimes difficult to find your own researcher identity. Those who enter the field from within well-established research traditions can sometimes limit themselves by not reaching outside. On the other hand, those who enter the field without any prior knowledge or guide tend to meander and get lost in the nooks between methods and specific academic disputes. Finding your researcher identity in this context is challenging, but it can also be an adventure. However, the main operating procedure should be to build that identity in dialogue with other traditions, not in opposition to them. Within that dialogue, researchers can learn and expand their methodological imagination, building creative and innovative solutions. That type of openness allows them to notice small changes and adaptations in the broader context and become better researchers in the future.

Understanding the weather – trends in methodology

Finding and relying on individual strengths in developing a research profile is an essential part of building a professional research identity. Some of the skills can be learned only during countless hours of research practice, carrying out the fieldwork, during the analysis, while writing up the data. In many ways, mastery and proficiency take time. However, as sailors do not sail only in one type of weather, researchers also need to adjust and adapt to the broader changes that affect the social world and impact on social research methods. Those challenges are transforming social research, introducing innovative solutions, and demanding new technical skills that carve new paths or compete with established social research methods. In the context of qualitative social research, and biographical narrative methods, three trends in methodology seem to be gaining in importance.

Technology and a new type of data

Technology is indisputably a game-changer in all aspects of social research. Throughout this book, we have pointed out how technology influences elements of the research project. However, the new social realities of the global pandemic at the time of writing have demonstrated that the importance and influence of technology will be even faster and more far reaching than we anticipated. The availability of mobile technologies, combined with the growing acceptance of their use, is becoming a new norm for the conduct of social research that carries new opportunities and limitations. Aspects of the research process that are particularly affected by the use of technology are:

- Data collection – technology modifies how we collect research data, expanding our ability to record interviews, from the voice only to the video interview to self-made narrative accounts. It also allows us to connect to people occupying different physical spaces, accommodating greater distances or allowing us to function with social-distancing regulations.
- Data processing and management – digital technologies also increase our ability to process data, including automatic audio and video transcription and translations of text. They enable data file management that allows for different data formats, from text to audio, video, pictures and visualisations.
- Data analysis – technology allows for complex data mining and analytical tools to support and expand the traditional narrative and linguistic analysis types. For example, *sentiment analysis* reads the emotional tone of certain words in computer analysis of large amounts of text. Furthermore, technology supports data visualisation – for example, depicting geographical and temporal biographical trajectories – and permits advanced network analysis that incorporates multiple biographical data sources.

In the context of biographical narrative, research technology also enables a new range of data that goes beyond a narrative interview. Social media accounts, for example, can be considered to provide a biographical account that, like a diary, records events in time and space with the use of additional media features – photos, videos, likes, shares, tags – that can be used for the robust investigation of social research questions (Alleyne, 2015). Mobile technologies including Geotags that track people's movements through physical space also have a potential to enhance biographical analysis. Finally, there is scope to use some of the other data produced by users of technology, generally referred to as Big Data, in ways which support the analysis of biographical narratives and life-course patterns.

The impact of technology on what we research and how we do our research reaches beyond individual skills, research techniques or even research questions. It changes the basic logic of inquiries and modifies the philosophical paradigms of science or 'ways of knowing'. Biographical research and other methodologies are built on the practical assumption that data are limited and expensive to collect. Sampling techniques and statistical models are designed to investigate social reality based on a small sample of this reality. Technology is changing the character of this dynamic. We are entering a research context where there is almost too much data to analyse, and we need analytical models and techniques that can simplify it. The new challenge is to tackle the relations and complexities of very numerous and extensive data sets, and to make sense of their correlations and associations.

The rise of mixed method designs

Another trend in methodology that carries particular significance for biographical narrative methods is the growing relevance of mixed method designs discussed through Chapters 8 and 9. There appears to be a growing consensus among research funders and research audiences that complementary methods provide more robust evidence, especially in specific applied social science disciplines, such as social policy and social justice. This has particular implications for the less well-known, or less established, qualitative methodologies, biographical narrative methods included. Accompanied, for example, by surveys that provide some umbrella of representativeness for findings, biographical methods can be used as in-depth case study illustration or explanation for a particular observed pattern. This type of collaboration widens the range for the dissemination of findings and raises awareness of the methods. It may also have limitations, when it forces the qualitative method only into the role of a case study, which is used as an aid to illustrate and support findings from other methods. These unequal relations between different methods and methodologies within the research field, additionally complicated by the politics of research commissioning and funding, can be tricky to navigate. However, mixed method designs are undoubtedly becoming more common across social science disciplines, and they can help to popularise the use of more creative and innovative methods alongside more established approaches.

International aspects of social sciences

Another development that is particularly relevant for biographical narrative research is the growing significance and status of international topics and cross-country studies in academic research. This particular dynamic within the field of social sciences is partly associated with the high status of international research funding and the growing importance of literature on the shortcomings of methodological nationalism, especially in specific thematic fields of social sciences, including transitional practices, migrations and diasporas (Glick Schiller, 2007; Amelina and Faist, 2012; Nowicka and Cieslik, 2014). Both elements, international funding and international topics, are of particular relevance to research projects that employ biographical research methods because they force us to ask the question: how can we draw comparisons or investigate agency and structure dynamics in a research project with relatively few biographical cases and many intercultural variations? We can control some of these variations via careful study designs, such as controlling for specific ages or involvement in an international historical event, or by trying to sample the biographical cases to show a range of theoretically derived representations, such as nationalities. However, the bones of the problem remain the same, and they can be answered only by acknowledging some of the theoretical currents that underpin the applications of biographical narrative research practice.

Reading the seas – currents in social theory

We have discussed at length throughout this book the nature of biographical accounts and their value for social science inquiry. They are much more than an account of who the individual is; they throw light on who the individual is within society. Analytically, biography as a text should be treated as an interaction between individual agency and the structural frameworks that either constrain or facilitate social actions. Linking analytical approaches with theoretical models, however, is always a balancing act. Biographical narrative research findings contribute to current theoretical discussions on a variety of topics, such as migration, health, education, inequalities and crime, using a limited set of theoretical frameworks that are manifestly compatible with this particular approach. Beyond this, biographical narrative approaches most often reach out to the frameworks of capitals, intersectionality and reflexivity for theoretical inspiration. They are currents united by an interest in social differentiation, distinction and the interconnected nature of social categories such as class, ethnicity and gender. But they differ with respect to some of their assumptions. Capital theory combines empirical realism with a high level of theoretical abstraction. Intersectionality theory has affinities with feminist standpoint theory and radical constructivism. In reflexivity theory, we find an actor-centred approach with the closest interdependence between concepts of structure and agency:

- Theorising biographies through the **framework of capitals** – this approach is rooted in the theoretical framework built on Bourdieu's notion of capital, which focuses on the ability of the individuals to capitalise on their economic resources, social networks, cultural and educational assets and status within social groups to execute specific social actions and gain access to limited social, economic and political resources (Bourdieu, 1986). Within the context of biographical studies, this theoretical approach focuses on the processes of exchange between some individual capital, a university degree, for example, and the place or position in the social structure, such as a place of employment. This approach has been modified and expanded to incorporate several other forms of capital, such as identity capital (Cote, 1996) and cosmopolitan capital (Kosnick et al., 2009). Drawing the link between individual capital and the position a person holds within the broader social structure is highly compatible with some aspects of biographical analysis (see Davis et al., 2017; Stock and Fröhlich, 2021).

- Theorising biographies through the **framework of intersectionality** – this approach aims to identify the overlapping frameworks of oppression and privilege, usually intersecting two or more categories of disadvantage, such as gender, ethnicity, class, age and disability. Biographical research uses this theoretical frame to identify the overlapping structural constraints that shape or direct social actions throughout the biography (Yuval-Davis, 2011; Bradley, 2015). Intersectionality is used to study inequalities and exclusion and can fit very well with biographical narrative studies (Yuval-Davis, 2011; Erel and Lutz, 2012).

- Theorising biographies through the **framework of reflexivity** – this approach is based on the concept of reflexivity, understood as a mental exercise, 'an internal conversation' in which individuals consider themselves in relation to social context. This theoretical framework is associated with the school of critical realism and the work of Archer (2007, 2011). The approach tries to understand to what extent individuals are driven by external social conditions and which aspects of their biography are driven by their agency (see Spanò and Domecka, 2015).

These three approaches represent an important current in social theory that is a conduit for biographical research: they are all focused on the individual's subjectivity. They investigate how external forces shape this subjectivity and are expressed internally in the form of agency and social action. This does not mean that biographical data give direct access to 'real' social structures; rather, we need biographical accounts to be able to infer how actors perceive the opportunities and constraints they work under. Social worlds are inherently subjective phenomena, upheld by intersubjective relations and culture, but the history of a life, the structures of the life story as told, and the pattern of the life course are all open to objective empirical analysis. All these theoretical approaches seek to explain the social and society with the focus on and from the perspective of the individual. They touch upon how individuals react while in contact with social structures – whether they are oppressed, what type of identity they develop or what type of actions they engage in – but do not theorise directly on how these social structures operate. In itself, this is not a bad thing. Current debates in social theory are interested in this type of issue. There is an intriguing question about how these theoretical currents will develop. Social sciences in the 21st century have left behind notions of an autonomous individual and essentialist references to the over-socialised or rational subject. Present theories conceptualise the subject as being an active interpreter of cultural and gender differences, an expert in identity construction, a manipulator of technical-scientific tools, and a source of creativity. To the extent that the future is going to be shaped by civilisational crises of climate, economy and health, this could change. However, there is always a risk that biographical methods will be associated only with theory-making that prioritises subjectivity and subjectivation. Combining biographical evidence and findings from biographical studies within theoretical frameworks that do address structural issues may be the next challenge for biographical researchers.

Summary

This chapter has attempted to sketch some of the future challenges for biographical narrative research and biographical researchers. We have used a nautical metaphor of navigating the seas to indicate just how many things are in flux and, therefore, how many new opportunities and challenges there are for those who are willing to venture out on that journey. First, we discussed the issue of finding your own identity as a researcher, not in opposition to other traditions and methods, but in dialogue with them, and in a spirit of constant learning and improvement. Second, we outlined some main methodological trends, such as the impact of technology on the way we do social research, noting, however, that with new types of data, we can use new analytical technologies. We discussed the impact of mixed method designs and the internationalisation of funding as a force that significantly impacts on how we are doing biographical research now and in the future. Finally, we discussed significant currents in social theory, briefly outlining the comfortable compatibility biographical narrative research shares with some subject-focused social theories, and the ongoing work to be done to link evidence from biographical research to the theories that focus on social structures.

Questions to consider

1. Do you think your identity as a social researcher is stable, or is it evolving?
2. Do you think that there is a point at which technology distracts from research rather than helps? When would that point be in your case?
3. Can you think of any other social theories that fit well with biographical evidence? Does the example you are thinking of explain the actions of a subject or processes within a social structure?

APPENDIX 1
WORKING WITH TRANSCRIPTS

The transcript is a necessary part of the analysis in biographical narrative methods. Some biographical narrative transcripts can look quite ordinary, with uninterrupted blocks of text that outline, word by word, what was said, while others can be very complex, using sociolinguistic symbols and cut-in text lines, looking more like mathematical equations than text. The type of transcription your research project requires depends on the traditions in your field of study and the type of project you are preparing your data for. Before you start to transcribe or format your text, you should consider the implications of your chosen project.

What type of transcript is necessary for the analysis?
Depth of analysis

We discussed in Chapter 3 the issue of depth of analysis and its link with the structure of the data. Generally, an extended, unstructured and free-flowing narration allows for the most fine-tuned and sophisticated types of analysis that can capture structural features of speech patterns and psycho-linguistic processes of meaning making. To capture these in text form, you will require a very detailed transcript that will pick up on non-verbal cues, hesitations, emotional aspects of utterances and self-corrections. However, if your analysis does not go as deep and you focus more on the transcript's content, you may be more interested in preserving the interactions between the interviewer and the interviewee, or simply the general tone of the answers (for example, relative emphasis or amount of elaboration). This link between transcript preparation and analysis is a type of data reduction. Your decision to exclude things from the transcript means that they will be excluded from the analysis, so the decision needs to be justified.

Teamwork

Transcripts are prepared and formatted to facilitate the analytical work. Standard formatting, with fixed-line and page numbering, easy-to-read line spacing and font sizing, and easy-to-print or display formats, is essential for work within research teams when navigating to specific text sections. It enhances efficiency and constitutes excellent practice. The rules are not as strict for individual analysis. It is important to keep text formatting comfortable for any readers and easy for indexing, with enough space for possible notes and annotations, highlights and links.

Software coding

Another consideration in the preparation of the transcript is the possibility of using it for analysis with data management software, such as NVivo or Atlas.ti. In this case, it will be crucial to keep the transcript formatting as simple as possible. All text formatting can be adjusted within the software.

Software packages are constantly improving, but they do not do well with objects, such as tables and in-text objects that overlay each other. Some documents will work well; others will require an enormous effort to sort out within the package.

In the more advanced parts of software analysis, it is also possible to automatically code some sections of the text that are distinguished within the text by using the Word option of Headings (see Silver and Lewins, 2014). Again, this requires more advanced skills but can be very useful with more structured interview data.

Transcription rules adapted from the autobiographical narrative interview method[1]

The transcript should reflect data management principles as well as the transposition of the linguistic record from audio recording to a written text.

Title and data identifiers

Each transcript should consist of the name of the interviewee or interviewees in the title as assigned by the research team. This should not be their real name but something representative of the generation and ethnic group of the interviewee.

---

[1]These instructions have been adapted from the training materials developed by Fritz Schütze for the Euroidentities project.

The transcript should identify the interviewer and the date of the interview.

In some transcripts, you can find full demographic notes, including age, location, relationships, ethnicity and so on. How you store this type of data about your interviewees will depend on your data management structure. Remember to create an anonymised version of the transcript to work on.

Representation of speech contribution

The transcript should indicate the interviewer (I:) and the narrator (N:) within the text, assigning each to a new line of text.

I: So, can you please tell me your life story?
N: Yeah, but where do I start?
I: Where do you think you should start?
N: Well, I guess ….

The representation of natural speech units

Narrative accounts, when flowing freely, can be lengthy. Their representation within the transcript and how to space them on the page is the transcriber's decision. For some sociolinguistic and discourse analysis, sentence-by-sentence analysis requires sentence-by-sentence spacing. For content analysis, inserting paragraph breaks at the natural ending to the narrative unit will make more sense.

Speech pauses

Speech pauses are a meaningful part of the analysis and should be included in the transcription. It is essential not only to note that the pause occurred but also to note the long moments of silence. General recommendations for transcripts are to use:

- … to indicate a short speech pause
- [pause] to indicate a medium speech pause
- ((9sec)) to indicate a longer break of about 9 seconds.

Furthermore, the autobiographical narrative interview method pays close attention to the pause-like speech patterns that fill in the silence and give the narrator opportunity to think and process the flow of narration. These patterns should also be noted in the linguistic form they are occurring, for example:

-eh-, -ehm-, -mmh-   shorter markers of speech planning activity

/eh/, /ehm/, /mmh/   longer markers of speech planning activity

I: You were left alone?

N: Initially, yes. That was /ehm/ it was rather, rather ((6sec)) complicated is the
     wrong word. /Mmh/ It was excruciating frankly.

Unintelligible and unclear elements

Although the recording quality of devices is constantly improving, there is
still a chance that some elements of the transcript will be challenging to
understand.

   When the meaning of a recording is difficult to understand with high accuracy, it should still be included in the transcript in brackets, indicating that this
part of the text may not be completely accurate but still relevant for understanding the text.

N   (I would like to say) that people here, I mean -mmh- they are not what I would
    consider

The unintelligible elements of the text should also be clearly indicated within the
text, indicating the length of the break (????) or (????????) or (?? 20sec ??).

Non-linguistic communication

Unintelligible breaks within a recording are often associated with other non-linguistic
activities that naturally occur within interview situations and should also be anno-
tated in the interview transcript. We suggest using double-bracket annotations that
explain the situational disruptions:

N: At that point, I have suggested to her that maybe she should do it but
         (she didn't)

((wife of the narrator overheard from the other room and came in to correct this
statement))

NWife: No, this is not how this went.

N: So how was it according to you?

NWife: You never said anything to me ((pointing the finger at her husband and
        laughing)) I had to figure it out all by myself.

Speech characteristics associated with emotions

Paraverbal speech characteristics such as expression of emotions and emphasis are a vital part of a structural analysis and should be indicated in the transcript to preserve them for analysis. However, these elements of speech are culturally specific: while in some languages, emphasis and expressiveness are part of everyday language, in others they are rare. Therefore, the decision about which emotional occurrences to highlight in the transcript should be made consciously by the transcriber and according to the sociocultural rules of the language it represents:

- In the case of <u>emphasis</u>, the corresponding expression should be underlined <u>once</u>; in the case of <u>strong emphasis</u>, the corresponding expression should be underlined <u>twice</u>.
- Expressions of emotion should be identified throughout the text within double brackets in the position they occur, for example ((crying)), ((happy)), ((resentful)).
- Changes in tone, pace and volume associated with changes of emotional state can also be indicated to highlight a shifting emotional state, for example ((added in a low voice)), ((very silent)), ((laughing till +)) .... ((+)).

Speech characteristics associated with interpretation

The changes in tone and volume and shifts in the narrator's emotional state can be accompanied by other forms of linguistic expression that may affect the simple interpretation of the text. The use of sarcasm or irony would be an instance where the text would convey certain information, but the tone would contradict it. In the transcript, we recommend triple brackets to indicate these types of interpretative speech indicators, for example (((cynically))), (((mysteriously))), (((angrily))), (((honestly))).

The three bracket indicators signify an interpretative understanding of the situation, whereas two bracket indicators refer to physical parts of the speech recordings.

Interruptions and overlap of speech contributions

Like every interaction, interview situations tend to have an account of overlapping speech between the interviewer and the narrator or other interruptions. However, these instances can get particularly difficult to mark in the transcript if they affect the narrative flow, when the narrator reacts to an interruption and breaks out of the story. Therefore, in the transcript, we recommend using a hashtag # as an indicator of overlapping speech:

N: At that point, I was no longer willing to do that for them # because I have changed
I: #But why?
N: I changed # I was not interested in that anymore; they did nothing for me. I worked very hard for them, and they did nothing to recognise that.

Self-interruptions and self-corrections

The autobiographical narrative interview method is particularly interested in the process of self-corrections and instances where the narrator needs to bring forward some additional information. This type of language construction is often associated with background construction. In the transcript, we recommend marking this type of linguistic form with double forward slash //.

N: We were going to this party with my friends, and -eh-// what I should probably tell you about is that I also had known this one boy from my neighbourhood that I had a crush on. And we sort of knew each other but not very well // and so we went to this party, and we had a good time and we ran into this boy.

Explanations and anonymisation marks

Throughout the transcription text, you will be making anonymisation changes to the names and places. Therefore, it is essential to develop a set of rules for anonymisation. It will allow you to identify where the changes have been introduced, for example changing names of places in square brackets.

N: At that point we were living in [Manchester] and I went to school there.

If your project data will be stored in a data archive, it is excellent practice to develop anonymisation markers to streamline your data management and data curation later on.

Further sources of transcription guidelines that include sociolinguistic notations can be found in most of the sociolinguistic and discourse analysis manuals and handbooks – for example, Schiffrin D. (1994) *Approaches to Discourse*. London: Blackwell Publishing.

APPENDIX 2

LIST OF THE STUDIES

Study example	Title	Discipline	Country
Chapter 4 Study 1	Pressure and guilt: War experiences of a young German soldier and their biographical implications F. Schütze (1992)	Sociology	Germany
Chapter 4 Study 2	Biography and memory: The generational experience of the Shoah survivors K. Kazmierska (2013)	Sociology Diaspora studies	Poland Israel
Chapter 4 Study 3	Guest, trader or explorer: Biographical perspectives on the experiences of cross-border mobility in Europe M. Eichsteller (2018a)	Sociology Migration studies	Europe
Chapter 5 Study 1	How do people change their lives? The role of the narrative interview and the biographical trajectory for social work and pastoral care in the United States Jindra and Jindra (2019)	Social work	USA
Chapter 5 Study 2	A narrative method of learning from innovative coastal projects: Biographies of the Sand Engine Bontje and Slinger (2017)	Environmental sciences Engineering	Netherlands
Chapter 5 Study 3	Biography and discourse: A biography and discourse analysis combining case study on women's involvement in National Socialism Pohn-Lauggas (2017)	Sociolinguistics Sociology History	Germany
Chapter 5 Study 4	Education, ethnicity and gender: Educational biographies of 'Roma and Sinti' women in Germany Reimer (2016)	Education Gender studies	Germany

(Continued)

Study example	Title	Discipline	Country
Chapter 6 Study 1	The life history interview method: Applications to intervention development Goldman et al. (2003)	Health studies Medical sciences	USA
Chapter 6 Study 2	QCA analysis of cosmopolitan practices in biographical narrative perspective Eichsteller (2013)	Sociology	UK
Chapter 7 Study 1	Boundaries and relationships in homelessness work Wengraf, T. (2004)	Social Work	UK
Chapter 7 Study 2	Narratives of belonging Tilley, E. (2020)	Sociology	UK
Chapter 7 Study 3	The evolution of European identities: Biographical approaches Miller, R. and Day, G. (2012)	Sociology	Europe
Chapter 8 Study 1	Local civil society: Place, time and boundaries Mann, R. et al. (2021)	Sociology Community studies	UK
Chapter 8 Study 2	An illness story: Autoethnography as feminist method – Sensitising the feminist 'I' Ettore, E. (2017)	Health studies Sociology	UK
Chapter 8 Study 3	Walking, sensing, belonging: Ethno-mimesis as performative practice O'Neill, M. and Hubbard, P. (2010)	Sociology	UK Ireland
Chapter 9 Study 1	Neighbourhood cohesion and mental wellbeing among older adults Elliott et al. (2014)	Community studies Medical studies	UK
Chapter 9 Study 2	Geo-narrative: Extending geographic information systems for narrative analysis in qualitative and mixed method research Kwan, M. P. and Ding, G. (2008)	Human geography	USA
Chapter 9 Study 3	Parallel realities: Exploring poverty dynamics using mixed methods in rural Bangladesh Davis, P. and Baulch, B. (2011)	International development	Bangladesh
Chapter 9 Study 4	There is more than one way: A study of mixed analytical methods in biographical narrative research Eichsteller, M. (2018b)	Sociology Comparative methods	UK

APPENDIX 3

ADDITIONAL RESOURCES TO SUPPORT YOUR RESEARCH

Chapter 4

Apitzsch, U. and Siouti, I. (2007) Biographical analysis as an interdisciplinary research perspective in the field of migration studies. Biographical Analysis as an Interdisciplinary Research. University of York, April.

Diamond, L. (2006) Careful what you ask for: Reconsidering feminist epistemology and autobiographical narrative in research on sexual identity development. *Journal of Women in Culture and Society*, 31(2): 471–491. https://doi.org/10.1086/491684

Miller, R. and Day, G. (2012) *The Evolution of European Identities: Biographical approaches* (Identities and Modernities in Europe). Basingstoke: Palgrave Macmillan.

Mizuno, S. (2006) Transformative experiences of a Turkish woman in Germany: A case-mediated approach toward an autobiographical narrative interview. *Historical Social Research/Historische Sozialforschung*, 90–106. https://doi.org/10.12759/hsr.31.2006.3.90-106

Mrozowicki, A. (2011) *Coping with Social Change: Life strategies of workers in Poland's new capitalism*. Leuven: Leuven University Press.

Svašek, M. and Domecka, M. (2013) The autobiographical narrative interview: A potential arena of emotional remembering, performance and reflection. In J. Skinner (ed.), *The interview: An ethnographic approach*. London: A&C Black, pp. 107–126. https://doi.org/10.4324/9781003087014-7

Treichel, B. and Schwelling, B. (2006) Extended processes of biographical suffering and the allusive expression of deceit in an autobiographical narrative interview with a female migrant worker in Germany. *Historical Social Research/Historische Sozialforschung*, 127–150. https://doi.org/10.12759/hsr.31.2006.3.127-150

Chapter 5

Aleyne, B. (2015) *Narrative Networks: Storied approaches in a digital age*. London: Sage.

Apitzsch, U. and Siouti, I. (2007) Biographical analysis as an interdisciplinary research perspective in the field of migration studies. Biographical Analysis as an Interdisciplinary Research. University of York, April.

Bamberg, M. (2012) Narrative practice and identity navigation. In J. A. Holstein and J. F. Gubrium (eds), *Varieties of Narrative Analysis*. London: Sage, pp. 99–124.

Gubrium, J. F. and Holstein, J. A. (2008) Narrative ethnography. In S. N. Hesse-Biber and P. Leavy (eds), *Handbook of Emerging Methods*. New York: The Guilford Press, pp. 45–58.

Lahire, B. (2019) Sociological biography and socialisation process: A dispositionalist-contextualist conception. *Contemporary Social Science*, 14(3–4): 379–393. doi: 10.1080/21582041.2017.1399213

Linde, C. (1993) *Life Stories: The creation of coherence*. Oxford: Oxford University Press.

Merrill, B. and West, L. (2009) *Using Biographical Methods in Social Research*. London: Sage.

Miller, R. L. (2000) *Researching Life Stories and Family Histories*. London: Sage.

Scheffrin, D. (1996) Narrative as a self-portrait: Sociolinguistic constructions of identity. *Language in Society*, 25: 167–203.

Chapter 6

Life-course reference materials

Caetano, A. and Nico, M. (2019) Forever young: Creative responses to challenging issues in biographical research. *Contemporary Social Science*, 14(3–4): 361–378. doi: 10.1080/21582041.2018.1510134

Use of CAQAS reference material

Silver, C. and Lewins, A. (2014) *Using Software in Qualitative Research: A step-by-step guide*. London: Sage.

QCA reference materials

Ragin, C. C. (2008) *Redesigning Social Inquiry: Fuzzy sets and beyond.* Chicago, IL: University of Chicago Press.

Rihoux, B. and Ragin, C. C. (2008) *Configurational Comparative Methods: Qualitative comparative analysis (QCA) and related techniques.* London: Sage.

fsQCA – open-source software can be accessed via www.socsci.uci.edu/~cragin/fsQCA/software.shtml

For in-depth methodological discussion on the merits of QCA, see:

- Lucas, S. R. and Szatrowski, A. (2014) Qualitative comparative analysis in critical perspective. *Sociological Methodology,* 44(1): 1–79. doi: 10.1177/0081175014532763
- Ragin, C. C. (2014) Comment. *Sociological Methodology,* 44(1): 80–94. doi: 10.1177/0081175014542081

BIBLIOGRAPHY

Abrams, L. (2010) *Oral History Theory*. London: Routledge.

Adam, B. (1995) *Timewatch: The social analysis of time*. Cambridge: Polity Press.

Alexievich, S. (2016) *Secondhand Time: The last of the Soviets*. New York: Random House.

Alleyne, B. (2015) *Narrative Networks: Storied approaches in a digital age*. London: Sage.

Amelina, A. and Faist, T. (2012) De-naturalizing the national in research methodologies: Key concepts of transnational studies in migration. *Ethnic and Racial Studies*, 35(10): 1707–1724. doi: 10.1080/01419870.2012.659273

Anderson, N. (1923) *The Hobo: The sociology of the homeless man*. Chicago, IL: University Of Chicago Press.

Ankiah-Gangadeen, A. and Samuel, M. A. (2014) Biography, policy and language teaching practices in a multilingual context: Early childhood classrooms in Mauritius. *South African Journal of Childhood Education*, 4(2): 57–72.

Apitzsch, U. and Inowlocki, L. (2000) Biographical analysis: A 'German' school? In P. Chamberlayne, J. Bornat and T. Wengraf (eds), *The Turn to Biographical Methods in Social Science: Comparative issues and examples*. London: Routledge, pp. 53–70.

Apitzsch, U. and Siouti, I. (2007) Biographical analysis as an interdisciplinary research perspective in the field of migration studies. Biographical Analysis as an Interdisciplinary Research. University of York, April.

Apitzsch, U., Inowlocki, L. and Kontos, M. (2008) The method of biographical policy evaluation. In U. Apitzsch and M. Kontos (eds), *Self-Employment Activities of Women and Minorities*. Wiesbaden: VS Verlag für Sozialwissenschaften, pp. 12–18.

Archer, M. S. (2007) *Making our Way through the World*. Cambridge: Cambridge University Press.

Archer, M. S. (2011) *The Reflexive Imperative in Late Modernity*. Cambridge: Cambridge University Press.

Atkinson, R. (1998) *The Life Story Interview*. London: Sage.

Baker, S. E. and Edwards, R. (2012) How many qualitative interviews is enough? Review Paper. Southampton: National Centre for Research Methods (NCRM).

Bamberg, M. (2006) Stories: Big or small. *Narrative Inquiry*, 16(1): 139–147. doi: 10.1075/ni.16.1.18bam

Bamberg, M. (2011) Who am I? Narration and its contribution to self and identity. *Theory & Psychology*, 21(1): 1–22. doi: 10.1177/0959354309355852

Bamberg, M. (2012) Narrative practice and identity navigation. In J. A. Holstein and J. F. Gubrium (eds), *Varieties of Narrative Analysis*. London: Sage, pp. 99–124.

Bamberg, M., De Fina, A. and Schiffrin, D. (2011) Discourse and identity construction. In A. De Fina, D. Schiffrin and M. Bamberg (eds), *Handbook of Identity Theory and Research*. Cambridge: Cambridge University Press, pp. 177–199.

Bartel, A., Delcroix, C. and Pape, E. (2020) Refugees and the Dublin Convention: A biographical evaluation of inner European borders. *Borders in Globalization Review*, 1(2): 40–52.

Bates, C. and Rhys-Taylor, A. (eds) (2017) *Walking through Social Research*. Abingdon and New York: Routledge.

Bazeley, P. (2018) *Integrating Analyses in Mixed Methods Research*. London: Sage.

Beck, U. (1992) *Risk Society*. London: Sage.

Becker, H. (1993) Theory: The necessary evil. In D. J. Flinders and G. E. Mills (eds), *Theory and Concepts in Qualitative Research: Perspectives from the field*. New York: Teachers College Press, pp. 218–229.

Bertaux, D. (ed.) (1981) *Biography and Society: The life history approach in the social sciences*. London: Sage.

Bertaux, D. and Bertaux-Wiame, I. (1981) Artisanal bakery in France: How it lives and why it survives. In F. Bechhofer and B. Elliott (eds), *The Petite Bourgeoisie: Comparative studies of an uneasy stratum*. London: Macmillan, pp. 155–181.

Bertaux, D., Thompson, P. and Rotkirch A. (eds) (2004) *On Living through Soviet Russia*. London: Routledge.

Blaikie, N. (1991) A critique of the use of triangulation in social research. *Quality & Quantity*, 25: 115–136.

Blaikie, N. and Priest, J. (2018) *Designing Social Research: The logic of anticipation*, 3rd edition. Cambridge: Polity.

Blythe, R. (1969) *Akenfield: Portrait of an English Village*. London: Edition Guild.

Bontje, L. E. and Slinger, J. H. (2017) A narrative method of learning from innovative coastal projects: Biographies of the Sand Engine. *Ocean & Coastal Management*, 142: 186–197.

Bourdieu, P. (1986) The forms of capital. In I. Szeman and T. Kaposy (eds), *Cultural Theory: An anthology*. New York: Wiley, pp. 81–93.

Bourdieu, P. (1990) *The Logic of Practice*. Stanford, CA: Stanford University Press.

Bradley, H. (2015) *Fractured Identities: Changing patterns of inequality*, 2nd edition. London: Polity.

Brannen, J. (2005) Mixed methods research: A discussion paper. NCRM Methods Review Papers, NCRM/005.

Breckner, R. (1998) The biographical-interpretive method: Principles and procedures. Social Strategies in Risk Societies, Sostris Working Paper 2: Case study materials – The Early Retired, pp. 91–104.

Breckner, R. (2010) *Sozialtheorie des Bildes. Zur Interpretativen Analyse von Bildern und Fotografien [Social theory of the picture: On interpretive analysis of pictures and photographs]*. Bielefeld, Germany: Transcript.

Breckner, R. and Rupp, S. (2002) Discovering biographies in changing social worlds. In P. Chamberlayne, M. Rustin and T. Wengraf (eds), *Biography and Social Exclusion in Europe: Experiences and life journeys*. Bristol: Policy Press, pp. 289–308.

Bulmer, M. (1984) *The Chicago School of Sociology: Institutionalization, diversity, and the rise of sociological research*. Chicago, IL: University of Chicago Press.

Caetano, A. and Nico, M. (2019) Forever young: Creative responses to challenging issues in biographical research. *Contemporary Social Science*, 14(3–4): 361–378. doi: 10.1080/21582041.2018.1510134

Cerwonka, A. and Maliki, L. (2007) *Improvising Theory: Process and temporality in ethnographic fieldwork*. Chicago, IL: University of Chicago Press.

Chamberlayne, P. and King, A. (2000) *Cultures of Care: Biographies of carers in Britain and the two Germanies*. Bristol: Policy Press.

Chamberlayne, P. and Rustin, M. (1999) *Social Strategies in Risk Societies: 'From biography to social policy'*. Final Report of the SOSTRIS project. Brussels: European Union CORDIS.

Chamberlayne, P., Bornat, J. and Apitzsch, U. (2004) *Biographical Methods and Professional Practice: An international perspective*. London: Policy Press.

Chamberlayne, P., Bornat, J. and Wengraf, T. (eds) (2000) *The Turn to Biographical Methods in the Social Sciences: Comparative issues and examples*. Abingdon: Routledge.

Chamberlayne, P., Rustin, M. and Wengraf, T. (2002) *Biography and Social Exclusion in Europe: Experiences and life journeys*. London: Policy Press.

Chang, H. (2008) *Autoethnography as Method*. Walnut Creek, CA: Left Coast Press.

Charmaz, K. (1983) The grounded theory method: An explication and interpretation. In R. M. Emerson (ed.), *Contemporary Field Research*. Boston, MA: Little Brown, pp. 109–126.

Charmaz, K. (2006) *Constructing Grounded Theory: A practical guide through qualitative analysis*. London: Sage.

Charmaz, K. (2014) *Constructing Grounded Theory*, 2nd edition. London: Sage.

Cipriani, R. (2017) *Diffused Religion: Beyond secularization*. London: Palgrave Macmillan.

Cohen, A. P. (1985) *The Symbolic Construction of Community*. London: Tavistock.

Cole, A. L. and Knowles, J. G. (1995) Extending boundaries: Narratives on exchange. *The Narrative Study of Lives*, 3: 205–251.

Collins, P. H. and Bilge, S. (2016) *Intersectionality*. Cambridge: Polity Press.

Connerton, P. (1989) *How Societies Remember*. Cambridge: Cambridge University Press.

Corbin, J. M. and Strauss, A. (1990) Grounded theory research: Procedures, canons, and evaluative criteria. *Qualitative Sociology*, 13(1): 3–21. doi: 10.1007/BF00988593

Cote, J. E. (1996) Sociological perspectives on identity formation: The culture-identity link and identity capital. *Journal of Adolescence*, 19(5): 417–428. www.ncbi.nlm.nih.gov/pubmed/9245295

Creswell, J. W. and Plano Clark, V. L. (2017) *Designing and Conducting Mixed Methods Research*, 3rd edition. London: Sage.

Dannefer, D. (2003) Towards a global geography of the life course. In J. T. Mortimer and M. J. Shanahan (eds), *Handbook of the Life Course*. New York: Kluwer Academic/Plenum Publishers, pp. 647–659.

Davie, G. (2015) *Religion in Britain Since 1945: Believing without belonging*, 2nd edition. Chichester: Wiley-Blackwell.

Davis, H., Dallimore, D., Mann, R. and Eichsteller, M. (2021) Religion and local civil society: Participation and change in a post-industrial village. *Journal of Contemporary Religion*, 36(2): 287–309. https://doi.org/10.1080/13537903.2021.1936967; https://research.bangor.ac.uk/portal/files/39401791/13537903.2021.pdf

Davis, H., Day, G., Eichsteller, M. and Baker, S. (2017) Language in autobiographical narratives: Motivation, capital and transnational imaginations. *Language, Discourse & Society*, 5(1): 53–70.

Davis, J. (1992) Tense in ethnography: Some practical considerations. In J. Okely and H. Callaway (eds), *Anthropology and Autobiography*. London: Routledge, pp. 205–220.

Davis, P. and Baulch, B. (2011) Parallel realities: Exploring poverty dynamics using mixed methods in rural Bangladesh. *Journal of Development Studies*, 47(1): 118–142. doi: 10.1080/00220388.2010.492860

Day, A. (2013) *Believing in Belonging: Belief and social identity in the modern world*. Oxford: Oxford University Press.

Day, G. (2006) *Community and Everyday Life*. Abingdon: Routledge.

De Fina, A. de, Schiffrin, D. and Bamberg, M. (2006) *Discourse and Identity*. Cambridge: Cambridge University Press.

De Vaus, D. (2001) *Research Design in Social Research*. London: Sage.

Delamont, S. (2009) The only honest thing: Autoethnography, reflexivity and small crises in fieldwork. *Ethnography and Education*, 4(1): 51–63.

DeMeur, G., Rihoux, B. and Yamasaki, S. (2008) Addressing the critiques of QCA. In B. Rihoux and C. C. Ragin (eds), *Configurational Comparative Methods: Qualitative comparative analysis (QCA) and related techniques*. London: Sage, pp. 147–165.

Domecka, M., Eichsteller, M., Karakusheva, S., Musella, P., Ojamäe, L., Perone, E., … Waniek, K. (2012) Method in practice: Autobiographical narrative interviews in search of European phenomena. In G. Day and R. Miller (eds), *The Evolution of European Identities*. London: Palgrave Macmillan, pp. 21–45.

Eichsteller, M. J. (2013) 'Becoming a citizen of the world': Sociological study of biographical narratives of new cosmopolitans. PhD thesis, Bangor University. Available at: http://ethos.bl.uk/OrderDetails.do?uin=uk.bl.ethos.664616

Eichsteller, M. (2018a) Guest, trader or explorer: Biographical perspectives on the experiences of cross-border mobility in Europe. *Ethnic and Racial Studies*, 41(5): 977–995. https://doi.org/10.1080/01419870.2017.1315152

Eichsteller, M. (2018b) There is more than one way: A study of mixed analytical methods in biographical narrative research. *Contemporary Social Science: Journal of the Academy of Social Sciences*, 14(65): 1–16. doi: 10.1080/21582041.2017.1417626

Elliott, J., Gale, C. R., Parsons, S., Kuh, D. and HALCyon Study Team (2014) Neighbourhood cohesion and mental wellbeing among older adults: A mixed methods approach. *Social Science and Medicine*, 107: 44–51. doi: 10.1016/j.socscimed.2014.02.027

Ellis, C., Adams, T. and Bochner, A. (2010) Autoethnography: An overview. *Forum Qualitative Sozialforschung/Forum: Qualitative Social Research*, 12(1), Art. 10.

Erel, U. and Lutz, H. (2012) Gender and transnationalism. *European Journal of Women's Studies*, 19(4): 409–412. doi: 10.1177/1350506812461466

Ettore, E. (2017) *Autoethnography as Feminist Method: Sensitising the feminist 'I'*. Abingdon: Routledge.

Evans, G. R. (1956) *Ask the Fellows Who Cut the Hay*. London: Faber & Faber.

Fine, G. A. (ed.) (1995) *A Second Chicago School*. Chicago, IL: University of Chicago Press.

Flick, U. (ed.) (2018) *Designing Qualitative Research*, 2nd edition. London: Sage.

Froggett, L. and Chamberlayne, P. (2004) Narratives of social enterprise from biography to practice and policy critique. *Qualitative Social Work*, 3(1): 61–77.

Froggett, L., Chamberlayne, P., Buckner, S. and Wengraf, T. (2005) Report on the Bromley by Bow Healthy Living Centre's work with older people. University of Central Lancashire. Whole report available at: www.uclan.ac.uk/facs/health/socialwork/bromleybybow/publications.htm

Gabb, J. (2009) Researching family relationships: A qualitative mixed methods approach. *Methodological Innovations Online*, 4(2): 37–52.

Garfinkel, H. (1967) *Studies in Ethnomethodology*. Englewood Cliffs, NJ: Prentice Hall.

Gell, A. (1992) *The Anthropology of Time: Cultural constructions of temporal maps and images*. Oxford: Berg.

Gelsthorpe, L. (2007) The Jack-Roller: Telling a story? *Theoretical Criminology*, 11(4): 515–542.

Gerring, J. (2017) *Case Study Research: Principles and practices*, 2nd edition. Cambridge: Cambridge University Press.

Giddens, A. (1991) *Modernity and Self-identity*. Cambridge: Polity.

Glaser, B. G. and Strauss, A. L. (1967) *The Discovery of Grounded Theory: Strategies for qualitative research.* Chicago, IL: Aldine.

Glick Schiller, N. (2007) Beyond the nation state and its units of analysis: Towards a new research agenda for migration studies. In Concepts and Methods in Migration Research, Conference Reader, Bielefeld University.

Gobo, G. (2008a) *Doing Ethnography.* London: Sage.

Gobo, G. (2008b) Sampling, representativeness and generalizability. In C. Seale, G. Gobo, J. F. Gubrium and D. Silverman (eds), *Qualitative Research Practice.* London: Sage, pp. 435–456.

Goffman, E. (1990) *The Presentation of Self in Everyday Life.* London: Penguin.

Golczyńska-Grondas, A. (ed.) (2008) *European Studies on Inequalities and Social Cohesion,* 1/2 and 3/4. Lodz: Łódź University Press. www.profit.uni.lodz.pl/pub/dok/6ca34cbaf07ece58cbd1b4f24371c8c8/European_Studies_2008_vol_1.pdf

Goldman, R., Hunt, M. K., Allen, J. D., Hauser, S., Emmons, K., Maeda, M. and Sorensen, G. (2003) The life history interview method: Applications to intervention development. *Health Education and Behavior,* 30(5): 564–581. doi: 10.1177/1090198103254393

Gorard, S. (2013) *Research Design: Creating robust approaches for the social sciences.* London: Sage.

Greene, J. C. (2008) Is mixed methods social inquiry a distinctive methodology? *Journal of Mixed Methods Research,* 2(1): 7–22.

Gubrium, J. F. (2005) Introduction: Narrative environments and social problems. *Social Problems,* 52(4): 525–528.

Gubrium, J. F. and Holstein, J. A. (1995) Biographical work and new ethnography. In R. Josselson and A. Lieblich (eds), *Interpreting Experience: The narrative study of lives,* Vol. 3. London: Sage, pp. 45–58.

Gubrium, J. F. and Holstein, J. A. (2008) Narrative ethnography. In S. N. Hesse-Biber and P. Leavy (eds), *Handbook of Emerging Methods.* New York: The Guilford Press, pp. 45–58.

Gubrium, J. F. and Holstein, J. A. (2009) *Analyzing Narrative Reality.* London: Sage.

Hamilton, P. (1974) *Knowledge and Social Structure: An introduction to the classical argument in the sociology of knowledge.* London: Routledge.

Harding, S. (ed.) (2004) *The Feminist Standpoint Theory Reader.* London: Routledge.

Harrison, B. (ed.) (2008) *Life Story Research,* Vol. I. London: Sage.

Hollway, W. and Jefferson, T. (2000) *Doing Qualitative Research Differently: Free association, narrative and the interview method.* London: Sage.

Holman Jones, S., Adams, T. and Ellis, C. (eds) (2013) *Handbook of Autoethnography.* Abingdon: Routledge.

Holstein, J. A. and Gubrium, J. F. (2011a) The constructionist analytics of interpretive practice. In N. K. Denzin and Y. S. Lincoln (eds), *The SAGE Handbook of Qualitative Research,* 4th edition. London: Sage, pp. 341–358.

Holstein, J. A. and Gubrium, J. F. (2011b) *Varieties of Narrative Analysis*. London: Sage.

Hughes, E. (1971) *The Sociological Eye: Selected papers*. New Brunswick, NJ: Transaction Books.

Jindra, I. W. and Jindra, M. (2019) How do people change their lives? The role of the narrative interview and the biographical trajectory for social work and pastoral care in the United States. *Pastoral Psychology*, 68(2): 195–208. https://doi.org/10.1007/s11089-018-0857-6

Johnson, R. B. and Onwuegbuzie, A. J. (2004) Mixed methods research: A research paradigm whose time has come. *Educational Researcher*, 33(7): 14–26.

Johnson, R. B. and Turner, L. A. (2003) Data collection strategies in mixed methods research. In A. Tashakkori and C. Teddlie (eds), *Handbook of Mixed Methods in Social and Behavioral Research*. Thousand Oaks, CA: Sage, pp. 297–319.

Johnson, R. B., Onwuegbuzie, A. J. and Turner, L. A. (2007) Toward a definition of mixed methods research. *Journal of Mixed Methods Research*, 1(2): 112–133.

Kallmeyer, W. and Schütze, F. (1976) Konversationanalyse. *Studium Linguistik*, 1: 1–28.

Kazmierska, K. (2013) *Biography and Memory: The generational experience of the Shoah survivors*. Brighton: Academic Studies Press.

Kelle, U. (2008) Computer-assisted qualitative data analysis. In C. Seale, G. Gobo and J. F. Gubrium (eds), *Qualitative Research Practice*. London: Sage, pp. 443–459.

Khanenko-Friesen, N. and Grinchenko, G. (2015) *Reclaiming the Personal: Oral history in post-socialist Europe*. Toronto, ON: University of Toronto Press.

Kohli, M. (1981) Biography: Account, text, method. In D. Bertaux (ed.), *Biography and Society: The life history approach in the social sciences*. London: Sage, pp. 61–75.

Kohli, M. (2005) Biography: Account, text, method. In R. L. Miller (ed.), *Biographical Research Methods*, Vol. III. London: Sage, pp. 59–79.

Kosnick, K., Nowicka, M. and Rovisco, M. (2009) Cosmopolitan capital or multicultural community? Reflections on the production and management of differential mobilities in Germany's capital city. In M. Nowicka and M. Rovisco (eds), *Cosmopolitanism in Practice*. Aldershot: Ashgate, pp. 161–180.

Kwan, M. P. and Ding, G. (2008) Geo-narrative: Extending geographic information systems for narrative analysis in qualitative and mixed-method research. *Professional Geographer*, 60(4): 443–465. doi: 10.1080/00330120802211752

Lazarsfeld, P. F. and Rosenberg, M. (1955) *The Language of Social Research: A reader in the methodology of the social sciences*. Glencoe, NY: Free Press.

Lewis, O. (1961) *The Children of Sanchez: Autobiography of a Mexican family*. New York: Random House.

Linde, C. (1993) *Life Stories: The creation of coherence*. Oxford: Oxford University Press.

Linde, C. (2001) 'Narrative and social tacit knowledge', *Journal of Knowledge Management*, 5(2): 160–170.

Linde, C. (2009) *Working the Past, Narrative and Institutional Memory*. Oxford: Oxford University Press.

Lyotard, J-F. (1984) *The Postmodern Condition: A report on knowledge* (trans. G. Bennington and B. Massumi). Minneapolis, MN: University of Minnesota Press.

Mann, R., Dallimore, D., Davis, H., Day, G. and Eichsteller, M. (2021) *Local Civil Society: Place, time and boundaries*. Bristol: Policy Press.

McAdams, D. P. (2008) *The Life Story Interview*. The Foley Center for the Study of Lives, Evanston, IL: Northwestern University.

McAdams, D. P. (2010) Personal narratives and the life story. In O. P. John, R. W. Robins and L. A. Pervin (eds), *Handbook of Personality: Theory and research*, 3rd edition. New York: The Guilford Press, pp. 242–262.

McAdams, D. P. (2012) Exploring psychological themes through life-narrative accounts. In J. A. Holstein and J. F. Gubrium (eds), *Varieties of Narrative Analysis*. London: Sage, pp. 15–32.

Mead, G. H. (1934) *Mind, Self and Society*. Chicago, IL: University of Chicago Press.

Merrill, B. and West, L. (2009) *Using Biographical Methods in Social Research*. London: Sage.

Mertens, D. M. and Hesse-Biber, S. (2012) Triangulation and mixed methods research: Provocative positions. *Journal of Mixed Methods Research*, 6(2): 75–79.

Miller, R. and Day, G. (eds) (2012) *The Evolution of European Identities: Biographical approaches*. Basingstoke: Palgrave Macmillan.

Mitscherlich, A. and Mitscherlich, M. (1977) *The Inability to Mourn: Principles of collective behaviour*. Munich: Piper Verlag.

Nico, M. L. (2016) Bringing life 'back into life course research': Using the life grid as a research instrument for qualitative data collection and analysis. *Quality and Quantity*, 50(5): 2107–2120. doi: 10.1007/s11135-015-0253-6

Nilsen, A. and Brannen, J. (2010) The use of mixed methods in biographical research. In A. Tashakkori and C. Teddlie (eds), *SAGE Handbook of Mixed Methods in Social and Behavioral Research*. London: Sage, pp. 677–696. Available at: www.researchgate.net/publication/317539635

Nowicka, M. and Cieslik, A. (2014) Beyond methodological nationalism in insider research with migrants. *Migration Studies*, 2(1): 1–15. doi: 10.1093/migration/mnt024

O'Neill, M. (2008) Transnational refugees: The transformative role of art? *Forum: Qualitative Sozialforschung/Social Research*, 9(2), Art. 59, www.qualitative-research.net/index.php/fqs/article/view/403/874

O'Neill, M. and Hubbard, P. (2010) Walking, sensing, belonging: Ethno-mimesis as performative practice. *Visual Studies*, 25(1): 46–58.

O'Neill, M. and Roberts, B. (2020) *Walking Methods: Research on the move*. Abingdon and New York: Routledge.

O'Neill, M. and Stenning, P. (2013) Walking biographies and innovations in visual and participatory methods: Community, politics and resistance in downtown east side Vancouver. In C. Heinz and G. Hornung (eds), *The Medialization of Auto/biographies: Different forms and their communicative contexts*. Hamburg: UVH, pp. 215–246.

O'Neill, M., Roberts, B. and Sparkes, A. (eds) (2015) *Advances in Biographical Methods: Creative applications*. Abingdon and New York: Routledge.

O'Reilly, K. (2005) *Ethnographic Methods*. London: Routledge.

Oakley, A. (1974) *Housewife*. London: Allen Lane.

Plano Clark, V. and Ivankova, N. V. (2016) *Mixed Methods Research: A guide to the field*. London: Sage.

Platt, J. (1992) Cases of cases … of cases. In C. C. Ragin and H. S. Becker (eds), *What Is a Case? Exploring the foundations of social inquiry*. Cambridge: Cambridge University Press, pp. 21–52.

Plummer, K. (1983) *Documents of Life: An introduction to the problems and literature of a humanistic method*. London: Allen & Unwin.

Plummer, K. (2002) *Telling Sexual Stories: Power, change and social worlds*. London: Routledge.

Pohn-Lauggas, M. (2017) Biography and discourse: A biography and discourse analysis combining case study on women's involvement in National Socialism. *Current Sociology*, 65(7): 1094–1111.

Pollert, A. (1981) *Girls, Wives, Factory Lives*. London: Macmillan.

Polletta, F. (2012) Analyzing popular beliefs about storytelling. In J. A. Holstein and J. F. Gubrium (eds), *Varieties of Narrative Analysis*. London: Sage, pp. 229–250.

Polletta, F., Chen, P. C. B., Gardner, B. G. and Motes, A. (2011) The sociology of storytelling. *Annual Review of Sociology*, 37(1): 109–130. doi: 10.1146/annurev-soc-081309-150106

Portelli, A. (1981) The peculiarities of oral history. *History Workshop Journal*, 12(1): 96–107.

Ragin, C. C. (2008) *Redesigning Social Inquiry: Fuzzy sets and beyond*. Chicago, IL: University of Chicago Press.

Reimer (2016) Education, ethnicity and gender: Educational biographies of 'Roma and Sinti' women in Germany. *European Journal of Social Work*, 19(3–4): 556–569.

Riemann, G. (2003) A joint project against the backdrop of a research tradition: An introduction to 'doing biographical research'. *Forum Qualitative Sozialforschung/ Forum: Qualitative Social Research*, 4(3), Art. 18. http://nbn-resolving.de/ urn:nbn:de:0114-fqs0303185

Rihoux, B. and Ragin, C. C. (2008) *Configurational Comparative Methods: Qualitative comparative analysis (QCA) and related techniques*. London: Sage.

Rosenthal, G. (ed.) (1998) *The Holocaust in Three Generations: Families of survivors and perpetrators of the Nazi regime*. London: Cassell.

Rosenthal, G. (2008) Biographical research. In C. Seale, G. Gobo, J. F. Gubrium and D. Silverman (eds), *Qualitative Research Practice*. London: Sage, pp. 48–64.

Rosenthal, G. and Bar-On, D. (1992) A biographical case study of a victimizer's daughter's strategy: Pseudo-identification with the victims of the Holocaust. *Journal of Narrative and Life History*, 2(2): 105–127.

Roulston, K. (2011) Interview 'problems' as topics for analysis. *Applied Linguistics*, 32(1): 77–94. https://doi.org/10.1093/APPLIN/AMQ036

Rowbotham, S. and McCrindle, J. (eds) (1977) *Dutiful Daughters: Women talk about their lives*. London: Allen Lane.

Ryen, A. (2008) Ethical issues. In C. Seale, G. Gobo, J. F. Gubrium and D. Silverman (eds), *Qualitative Research Practice*. London: Sage, pp. 218–235.

Schiffrin D. (1994) *Approaches to Discourse*. London: Blackwell Publishing.

Schiffrin, D. (1996) Narrative as self-portrait: Sociolinguistic constructions of identity. *Language in Society*, 25(2): 167–203.

Schiffrin, D., Tannen, D. and Hamilton, H. E. (2008) *The Handbook of Discourse Analysis*. London: Wiley Blackwell.

Schubring, A., Mayer, J. and Thiel, A. (2019) Drawing careers: The value of a biographical mapping method in qualitative health research. *International Journal of Qualitative Methods*, 18. doi: 10.1177/1609406918809303

Schütz, A. (1972) *Collected Papers I: The Problem of Social Reality*, Vol. 1 (Phaenomenologica). (M. A. Natanson and H. L. van Breda, eds). Dordrecht: Martinus Nijhoff.

Schütze, F. (1983) Biographical research and the narrative interview. *Neue Praxis*, 3: 283–293.

Schütze, F. (1992) Pressure and guilt: War experiences of a young German soldier and their biographical implications (Part 1). *International Sociology*, 7(2): 187–208.

Schütze F. (2003) Hülya's migration to Germany as self-sacrifice undergone and suffered in love for her parents, and her later biographical individualisation: Biographical problems and biographical work of marginalisation and individualisation of a young Turkish woman in Germany. *Historical Social Research*, 31(3), 107–126.

Schütze, F. (2008) Biography analysis on the empirical base of the autobiographical narratives: How to analyse autobiographical narrative interviews, Part I and II (Biographical Counselling in Rehabilitative Vocational Training), www.biographicalcounselling.com/download/B2.1.pdf and www.biographicalcounselling.com/download/B2.2.pdf

Shaffer, P. (2013) *Q-Squared: Combining qualitative and quantitative approaches in poverty analysis*. Oxford: Oxford University Press.

Shaw, C. R. (1996 [1930]) *The Jack Roller: A delinquent boy's own story*. Chicago, IL: University of Chicago Press.

Sheridan, D. (1996) 'Damned anecdotes and dangerous confabulations': Mass-observation as life history. Mass Observation Occasional Paper No. 7, www.massobs.org.uk/images/occasional_papers/no7_sheridan.pdf

Silver, C. and Lewins, A. (2014) *Using Software in Qualitative Research: A step-by-step guide*, 2nd edition. London: Sage.

Small, M. L. (2011) How to conduct a mixed methods study: Recent trends in a rapidly growing literature. *Annual Review of Sociology*, 37(1): 57–86. doi: 10.1146/annurev.soc.012809.102657

Spanò, A. and Domecka, M. (2015) Going beyond standard categories and routine thinking: Understanding the crisis through the lens of biography. Paper presented at the 12th Conference of the European Sociological Association: Differences, Inequalities and Sociological Imagination. Prague, 25–28 August, pp. 1–21.

Stanley, S. (2010) To the letter: Thomas and Znaniecki's *The Polish Peasant* and writing a life, sociologically. *Life Writing*, 7(2): 139–151.

Stock, I. and Fröhlich, J. J. (2021) Migrants' social positioning strategies in transnational social spaces. *Social Inclusion*, 9(1): 91–103. doi: 10.17645/SI.V9I1.3584

Strauss, A. (1995) Identity, biography, history and symbolic representations. *Social Psychology Quarterly*, 58(1): 4–12.

Strauss, A. and Corbin, J. (1990) *Basics of Qualitative Research*. London: Sage.

Sutherland, E. H. (1988 [1937]) *The Professional Thief*. Chicago, IL: University of Chicago Press.

Svašek, M. and Domecka, M. (2013) The autobiographical narrative interview: A potential arena of emotional remembering, performance and reflection. In J. Skinner (ed.), *The interview: An ethnographic approach*. London: A&C Black, pp. 107–126. https://doi.org/10.4324/9781003087014-7

Szczepanik, R. and Siebert, S. (2016) The triple bind of narration: Fritz Schütze's biographical interview in prison research and beyond. *Sociology*, 50(2): 285–300. https://doi.org/10.1177/0038038515570145

Szerszynski, B. and Urry, J. (2006) Visuality, mobility and the cosmopolitan: Inhabiting the world from afar. *British Journal of Sociology*, 57(1): 113–131. doi: 10.1111/j.1468-4446.2006.00096.x

Tashakkori, A. and Teddlie, C. (eds) (2010) *Mixed Methods in Social and Behavioral Research*, 2nd edition. London: Sage.

Teddlie, C. and Tashakkori, A. (2006) A general typology of research designs featuring mixed methods. *Research in the Schools*, 13(1): 12–28.

Teddlie, C. and Tashakkori, A. (2009) *Foundations of Mixed Methods Research: Integrating quantitative and qualitative approaches in the social and behavioral sciences*. London: Sage.

ten Have, P. (2007) *Doing Conversation Analysis: A practical guide*, 2nd edition. London: Sage.

Thomas, W. I. and Znaniecki, F. (1919) *The Polish Peasant in Europe and America,* Vol. III (Life-record of an immigrant). Boston, MA: The Gorham Press.

Thomas, W. I. and Znaniecki, F. (1958) *The Polish Peasant in Europe and America,* Vols I and II. New York: Dover Publications.

Thompson, P. (1978) *The Voice of the Past* (4th revised edition, 2017). Oxford: Oxford University Press.

Thompson, P. (2004) Pioneering the life story method. *International Journal of Social Research Methodology,* 7(1): 81–84.

Tilley, E. (2020) Narratives of belonging: Experiences of learning and using Welsh of adult 'new speakers' in north-west Wales. PhD thesis, Bangor University, Bangor, North Wales.

Turk, J. and Mrozowicki, A. (eds) (2013) *Realist Biography and European Policy: An innovative approach to European policy studies.* Leuven: Leuven University Press.

Wengraf, T. (2000) Uncovering the general from within the particular: From contingencies to typologies in the understanding of cases. In P. Chamberlayne, J. Bornat and T. Wengraf (eds), *The Turn to Biographical Methods in Social Science: Comparative issues and examples.* London: Routledge, pp. 140–164.

Wengraf, T. (2001) *Qualitative Research Interviewing: Biographic narrative and semi-structured methods.* London: Sage.

Wengraf, T. (2004) Boundaries and relationships in homelessness work: Lola, an agency manager. *Forum: Qualitative Social Research,* 5(1). https://doi.org/10.17169/fqs-5.1.658

Wengraf, T. (2010) Interviewing for life-histories, lived situations and ongoing personal experiencing: The biographic-narrative-interpretative method (BNIM) [24.09.2010; version 10.09a]. Guide to BNIM Interviewing and Interpretation, available from tom@tomwengraf.com

Wright Mills, C. (1959) *The Sociological Imagination.* New York: Oxford University Press.

Yuval-Davis, N. (2011) *The Politics of Belonging: Intersectional contestations.* London: Sage.

Zerubavel, E. (2003) *Time Maps: Collective memory and the social shape of the past.* Chicago, IL: University of Chicago Press.

INDEX

abduction, 113
Abrams, L., 18
action scheme, 20, 59, 60–61;
    see also institutional action scheme, 60
active listening, 48, 56; *see also* interview
Adam, B., 149
age, 10, 16, 69–70, 107, 115, 133, 171–72
    see also life–course research
agency, 11, 33–34, 49, 56, 88, 109, 128,
    186–87;
    and structure, 12, 88, 128, 186–87
alcohol, 45,
    alcoholism, 64, 78
Alleyne, B., 184
Ankiah-Gangadeen, A. and Samuel, M., 162
anonymity, 41–42, 48; *see* ethics
anthropology, 4, 15, 67, 174; *see also*
    cultural anthropology
Apitzsch, U., 20, 53, 162
Archer, M., 187
argumentation, 20–22, 48–49, 51–52, 117
Atlas.ti software, 6, 74–75, 104, 112–18,
    124, 190
Atkinson, R., 30
attribution theory, 33
autobiographical narrative interview method,
    analytical structure, 59
    coda 33, 57–59, 62
    preamble, 33, 57–58, 59, 62, 65
    therapeutic value of, 71, 78
autobiography, definition, 24
autoethnography, 151–55
    definition, 24

background construction, 32, 65–66
Baker, S. and Edwards, R., 133
Bartel, A. et al., 163
Bates, C. and Ryhs–Taylor, A., 156
Bazeley, P., 147
Beck, U., 135
Becker, H., 15, 127
Bertaux, D. 17
Bertaux-Wiame, I., 17
BNIM (Biographical Narrative Interpretative
    Method), 21–23, 78, 100, 136–37, 159
biographical data,
    control over, 74, 104–9

depth of 35–37, 118–19, 189
distinction between life as lived and
    life as told, 19, 21–22, 78
temporality in, 149
units of 26–27
biographical work, 25, 27, 34, 69, 132
    conscious and unconscious, 59
biographical policy evaluation
    method, 161
biography, definition 10, 24
    and ethnography, 147–50
Bourdieu, P., 148, 186
Brannen, J., 166–8, 179
    Nilsen, A. and, 166, 173
Breckner, R., 79, 80
Brexit, 26

Caetano, A. and Nico, M., 105, 108
capital theory, 186
CAQDAS (computer-assisted qualitative data
    analysis software), 112–16, 112–13,
    116–17
case study, 129–34, 185
    cross-case comparison, 131–2
    cross-national comparison, 134–6
    cumulative, 133–4
    shadow cases, 130
    definition, 129–30
Cerwonka, A. and Maliki, L., 148
Chamberlayne, P., 21, 23, 78–79, 100, 135
Chang, H., 154
Charmaz, K., 117, 131, 133
Chicago School, 14–16, 76, 157
    Second Chicago School, 15
Cipriani, R., 150
coda, 33, 58–59, 62
coding, 104, 111–12, 190
    and data analysis, 112
    example of, 114
    saturation, 133
coherence, 32, 83, 113, 117
cohort studies, 173
Cole, A. and Knowles, J., 131
community studies, in UK 15
Corbin, J., 38
    Strauss, A. and, 111
compatibility thesis, 167, 178–9

computer-based analysis, 104, 111–21, 190
  critique of, 6, 111, 117
confidentiality, 41–42, 48; *see also* ethics
consent form, 42; *see also* ethics
Connerton, P., 149
cosmopolitan, 4, 121–3,186
Creswell, J. and Plano Clark, V., 144, 146
criminology, 5, 67–68, 130, 186; *see also*
  prison research
critical realism, 187
cultural anthropology, 4, 6, 154, 174

Dannefer, D., 109
data reduction, 105, 108, 166, 189
Davie, G., 150
Davis, H., et al., 150
Davis, J., 148
Davis, P. and Baulch, B., 176–7
Day, A., 150
deduction, 113, 118, 167
Delamont, S., 155
DeMeur, G.,
  Rihoux, B., Ragin, C. and, 123
development studies, 4, 105, 176–77
  and poverty trajectories, 105–107
discourse analysis, 35, 97–98, 191
Domecka, M., 65, 132, 187
domestic violence, 76, 81–82, 170–71
Dublin Convention, 162–3

education,
  studies of, 67, 80, 83, 131–2,
    154, 160
  trajectories, 61, 99
  vocational, 161
Eichsteller, M., 70, 121–3, 177–8
Elliott, J. at al., 171–2
Ellis, C., Adams, T., and
  Bochner, A., 152
emotion, 13, 20, 79, 160, 184, 189
  see also sentiment analysis
environment, 96–97
epiphany, 154
epistemology, 126–7, 170; *see also* way
  of knowing
ethics, 40–43;
  codes 41;
  anonymity 42–43
  informed consent, 41–42
ethnicity, 16, 20, 92, 99, 186–87
ethnography, 15, 143–44, 147–50,
  177–78
ethnomethodology, 20, 39
ethno-mimesis, 157
ethnosocial approach, 17
Ettore, E., 153–4

Euroidentities project, 3, 4, 21, 26, 54, 55,
  82, 89, 131, 134–5, 139–40, 190
  and European mental space, 21

family, 65–66, 83–85, 159–60
  and intimate relationships, 83–85
feminism, 18–19, 126
  feminist research, 151–55
  feminist standpoint theory 18
France, 163
  artisanal bakeries study, 17
  sociology in, 2, 53

Gabb, J., 159–60
Gell, A., 148
GDPR (EU General Data Protection
    Regulation), 42
gender, 16–18, 20, 25, 39, 43, 84–85, 99,
    113–15, 133, 150, 152–54, 160, 171,
    186–87
generalisation, 14, 16, 20–21, 37, 66–67,
    94, 120, 130, 166, 168–69
geotags, 184
Germany, 3, 26;
  and life under National Socialism, 20,
    23, 97–98
  German School of autobiographical
    narrative research, 20, 53
Gerring, J. 129, 130
Giddens, A., 135
GIS (geographic information
    system), 174
Glaser, B. and Strauss, A., 21
Gobo, G,. 39, 148
Goffman, E., 15, 88
Goldman, R. et al., 109–10
Golczyńska-Grondas, A., 161
Greene, J., 143
grounded theory, 21, 131, 133, 139
Gubrium, J.,
  Holstein, J. and, 24–26, 32, 35, 39, 46,
    76–77, 82, 85, 87, 89, 91, 93, 100

Harding, S., 18
Harrison, B., 16
health studies, 6, 67, 100, 105, 154, 160,
    171–72
hermeneutic case reconstruction,
    definition 79
history, 20–22, 34–35, 49, 67, 74, 100,
    120, 128, 160, 166,185
Hollway, W.
  Jefferson, T. and, 117
Holman Jones, S., Adams, T., and
    Ellis, C., 152
Holocaust, 69, 130

www.ingramcontent.com/pod-product-compliance
Lightning Source LLC
Chambersburg PA
CBHW080556030426
42336CB00019B/3216